The Providence and Rhode Island Cookbook

NARRAGANSETT

The Providence and Rhode Island Cookbook

Big Recipes from the Smallest State

LINDA BEAULIEU

INSIDERS' GUIDE®

GUILFORD, CONNECTICUT
AN IMPRINT OF THE GLOBE PEQUOT PRESS

INSIDERS' GUIDE®

Photographs by Al Malpa
Text design by Nancy Freeborn

Library of Congress Cataloging-in-Publication Data
Beaulieu, Linda.
    The Providence and Rhode Island cookbook / Linda Beaulieu.
        p. cm.
    ISBN 0-7627-3137-0
    1. Cookery, American—New England style. 2. Cookery—Rhode Island—Providence. I. Title.

TX715.2.N48B43 2005
641.59745—dc22   2005049199

Manufactured in the United States of America
First Edition/First Printing

Contents

TONY'S COLONIAL, FEDERAL HILL

Acknowledgments

I would like to thank my family, my friends, and the fine people of Rhode Island who have shared their recipes, stories, and cooking expertise with me over many years. All that information certainly helped me write this book about the unique food of Rhode Island and its capital city, Providence.

For years, my sister-in-law, June Giardino, has been providing me with precious family recipes. More recently, my cousin, Anne Pasquino, offered me a treasure trove of how our Italian grandmother taught her children to cook.

My friends, many of whom are successful cookbook authors, chefs, and extraordinary home cooks, have generously shared their recipes with me: Nancy Verde Barr, Nancy Carr Starziano, Mary Ann Esposito, Wayne Gibson, Don Hysko, Normand Leclair, Donna Lee, Martha Murphy, Maureen Pothier and Paul Inveen, Cindy Salvato, Nancy Sandbach, Frank Terranova, Mary Vadenais Dexter, Phoebe and Walter Zuromski, and the late Jean Hewitt.

Along the way in the writing of this book, I met many Rhode Islanders who also were willing to give me their recipes: Antonio DePetrillo, Walter and Norman Elwell, Eileen Fochler, Alan Gelfuso, Guiliano Hazan, Linda Kane, and Phillipe and Jorge, columnists for the *Providence Phoenix*.

My appreciation also goes to:

- Organizations that contributed recipes to this book: Autocrat Coffee Company, Blount Seafood, Nick, Ron and Pete at Cardi's Furniture, Chariho Rotary Club, Diamond Hill Vineyards, Glocester Heritage Society, Kenyon's Corn Meal Company, Little Compton Grange, Narragansett Indian Tribe, Oaklawn Grange, Ocean State Chocolates, Society for the Propagation of the Jonnycake Tradition in Rhode Island, South Kingstown Lions Club, Rhode Island Division of Agriculture, Saugy Inc.; and hotels, inns, and restaurants that did the same: Aaron Smith Farm, Bullock's,

Custy's, Hotel Manisses, Nathaniel Porter Inn, Richards' Bed & Breakfast, Rocky Point Chowder House, and Stagecoach Inn.

- Restaurant chefs and business owners that make Providence and the state of Rhode Island such a delicious dining destination: Johanne Killeen and George Germon of Al Forno, Bob Antignano of Angelo's Civita Farnese, Walter Potenza and Carmela Natale of Aquaviva, Carol Connolly of the Catering Collaborative, Alberto Lopez of Costantino's Ristorante, Captain Stu Tucker of Duffy's Tavern, Jean-Claude Bourlier and Chris Jessop of the General Stanton Inn, Iva Reynhart of Jigger's Diner, David Baccari of Johnny B's Diner, Bob LaMoia of LaMoia Restaurant & Tapas Bar, Gianfranco Campanella and Michele Calise of Mediterraneo, Mike Lepizzera of Mike's Kitchen, Nick Demou of the Modern Diner, Bruce Tillinghast of New Rivers, Derek Wagner of Nicks on Broadway, Paul Shire and Anthony Salemme of Oak, Louie Umberto of Palmieri's Bakery, Bob Burke of Pot au Feu, Mike Degnan of Providence Oyster Bar and Prime, Ralph Conte of Raphael Bar-Risto, David Drake of Spike's Junkyard Dogs, Susan DeAngelus of Twin Oaks, Salvatore Cefaliello, Cosimo Dellatore and Louie Forti of Venda Ravioli, and John Elkhay of XO Steakhouse, Ten Prime Steak & Sushi, and Big Fish.

- All the chefs of the Newport Harbor Corporation (Blackstone Catering, Castle Hill Inn & Resort, The Mooring, and 22 Bowen's Wine Bar & Grille) who provided recipes: Chris Ferris, Gary Jefferds, Brian Mansfield, Joe Melanson, Matthew Petersen, and Casey Riley.

My deepest appreciation goes to The Globe Pequot Press staff, who believed the time had come for a cookbook about Rhode Island and its capital city of Providence; to David Emblidge, acquisitions editor, who offered me the assignment; to Elizabeth Taylor, managing editor, who coordinated the entire project; to Cary Hull, who painstakingly worked with me on the final manuscript; to Al Malpa, who took all the photographs; and to the entire GPP team that made this book a reality.

Special thanks go to Phil Kukielski, managing editor (features) at the *Providence Journal*, who recommended me for this project.

I would like to especially thank Rhode Island Governor Don Carcieri and his wife Susan, Providence Mayor David N. Cicilline, former mayor Vincent "Buddy" Cianci, Chief Justice Frank J. Williams, and Federal Hill historian Joseph Muratore for their support in the writing of this book.

Very special thanks are extended to a small circle of restaurant owners who are also my dear friends: Sylvia Moubayed of CAV, Gianfranco Marrocco of Mediterraneo, Caffe Dolce Vita, Geppetto's Pizzeria, and Hotel Dolce Villa; and Alan Costantino of Venda Ravioli and Costantino's Ristorante.

The biggest "thank you" of all is reserved for my husband Brian who endured my working on this book nearly every day for the past two years. I'm sure little Beau, our cocker spaniel, kept him company.

Some recipes were adapted for home cooks, and those who contributed recipes are not responsible for any inadvertent errors or omissions.

PROVIDENCE SKYLINE

Introduction

Rhode Island may be the smallest state in the Union, but it's a giant when it comes to good food. Rhode Islanders are obsessed with restaurants and recipes. Almost always a conversation in Little Rhody will somehow find its way over to the topic of food—where to eat or what to cook.

And we're not talking ordinary food. Rhode Island has a unique food subculture concentrated in a very small area. Where else can you eat johnny-cakes and stuffies (baked stuffed clams), while drinking an Awful Awful (a very thick milk shake) or a coffee cabinet (a thick milk shake flavored with coffee syrup)? This diminutive state is famous for its New York System wieners (also known as "gaggers"), Del's Frozen Lemonade, and Dynamites (a hot sandwich made with a highly seasoned ground meat mixture). We like to put sweetened coffee syrup in our milk, and we like to eat pizza for breakfast, cold and often without any cheese! With a population of barely 1 million people (mostly between the ages of 25 and 54), Rhode Island has a surprising number of local dishes, food traditions, and culinary terms that are unique to the state—and none of them has ever strayed into the other New England states. Many recipes are closely guarded secrets, handed down from generation to generation.

Rhode Island, aptly called the Ocean State, is inextricably tied to the sea and its bounty. In the summer the beaches are packed with thousands of sunbathers and swimmers, all working up appetites for steamers (steamed clams), clam cakes, and lobster any way they can get it. No self-respecting Rhode Islander can dine on these delicacies without a cup of chowder on the side. And there are so many chowder recipes, an entire cookbook could be devoted to that single dish.

So what makes Rhode Island so special? Maybe it's all because of "divine" Providence, the ever-improving state capital. In recent years Providence has undergone an urban renewal most cities would envy, thanks to the controversial former mayor, Vincent "Buddy" Cianci, who was eventually sent to prison on a racketeering charge. Hundreds of millions of dollars were invested in Providence's very successful facelift, which included the diversion of rivers to provide such features as a four-acre park with Venetian-style bridges and gondolas that glide along a waterway through the heart of the city. On scheduled nights from spring through fall, the Providence River is magically ablaze with WaterFire, a dazzling visual arts performance that attracts thousands of people.

Once dirty, neglected, and virtually deserted at night, Providence used to be a city that people drove through, mostly on their way to New York City or Cape Cod. The streets of Providence are now alive with people drawn in by the arts, sporting events, and great restaurants. Providence has become a culinary mecca, rivaling Boston to the north and New York to the south. In fact, the entire state is a contemporary dining destination with hundreds of acclaimed restaurants—neighborhood haunts with devout regular customers, creaky colonial taverns serving old Yankee classics, fine-dining establishments, boisterous sports bars and pubs, Italian-American restaurants with their predictable red-sauce dishes, trendy cafes, and a growing number of ethnic restaurants featuring the foods of Africa, Asia, and Latin America.

Some people attribute Rhode Islanders' fascination with food to our ethnic mix, giving a reverential bow to the large Italian population and its inherent love of food, wine, and the good life. Others credit our wonderful homegrown produce—including some remarkable vineyards—and our native seafood. Still others say credit must be given to Johnson & Wales University, the largest culinary school in the world, based in Providence. Today many of the best chefs in Rhode Island hold degrees from Johnson & Wales. In fact, there are more chefs with college degrees in Providence than anywhere else in the nation.

How has Rhode Island managed to retain its vibrant food subculture, especially when the rest of America seems overrun with homogenized restau-

WATERFIRE

rant chains? Some observers suggest that native Rhode Islanders are provincial or simply devoted to family and close friends, keeping their unique culture close to their hearts. Indeed, even though the state of Rhode Island is the same size as some major U S. cities, many residents of Woonsocket in the north or Westerly in the south rarely venture into the capital city of Providence. For them, it's just too far away. Whatever the reasons, people who have moved to Rhode Island in recent years find these quirky values very appealing and quickly become proud of their new home state.

I am one of those people. I was born in Rhode Island but lived over the line in nearby Massachusetts for many years before making the move to the Ocean State. My heritage reflects that of many Rhode Islanders. My father, Daniel Giardino, was born in Italy; my mother, Mathilda Billiet, was of French and Belgian descent. They both came to this country in the early 1900s. As soon as they were old enough, they left school to work in the textile mills. They met at a dance on New Year's Eve as the Great Depression was coming to an end. They were married in 1935 and went to see a Boston Red Sox baseball game on their honeymoon. They eventually had a boy and a girl. Food was the centerpiece of their humble home life, a fusion of two very different cultures. I can vividly recall my Uncle Mike making ravioli from scratch in his kitchen and growing grapes out back so he could make wine, and my *Memere* serving wonderful crepes and steak au poivre.

My mother learned to cook Italian from her mother-in-law, and as a result almost all my childhood memories of food have an Italian accent. When I think of my late mother, I always picture her standing at the stove on Sunday mornings, with the smell of cooked onions in the air, making her "gravy" (like many Italian Americans in Rhode Island, we never called it tomato sauce). Even at Thanksgiving, that most American of holidays, we ate mostly Italian food. There was always macaroni or lasagna or stuffed shells, *porcetta*. . . and then came the turkey, followed by the salad. Yes, we ate macaroni, not *pasta*, as it is now called. And we always had our salad at the end of our meal, not the beginning.

Every May my father planted seventy-two tomato plants in our backyard. We had so many ripe tomatoes, he would sell them at a stand in front of our house—the most perfect tomatoes on earth for twenty-five cents a pound. To this day every May, I too plant a tomato garden—though much smaller—the way my father taught me.

I went from being a Giardino (the Italian word for garden) to a Beaulieu (the French word for beautiful place) when I married a guy from Maine with French-Canadian and Irish roots. Brian proposed to me in the kitchen. I think it was the aroma of a pot roast cooking in the oven that made him pop the question. We now live in Lincoln in the northern part of Rhode Island, and we are fortunate enough to have a summer home in Narragansett, not far from the beach where I played as a child. Our little beach house has an outdoor kitchen with a wood-burning grill. At either home, we entertain often. Many of our friends are chefs and restaurant owners. We are truly blessed to be Rhode Islanders.

This book explores the food of Rhode Island, especially in and around Providence, and tries to explain why it is so good, whether it's in someone's home or in a restaurant. Some of the recipes in this book were provided by talented chefs. Many were collected over many years from friends, and other recipes were handed down to me by family members. I hope you'll find it delicious reading.

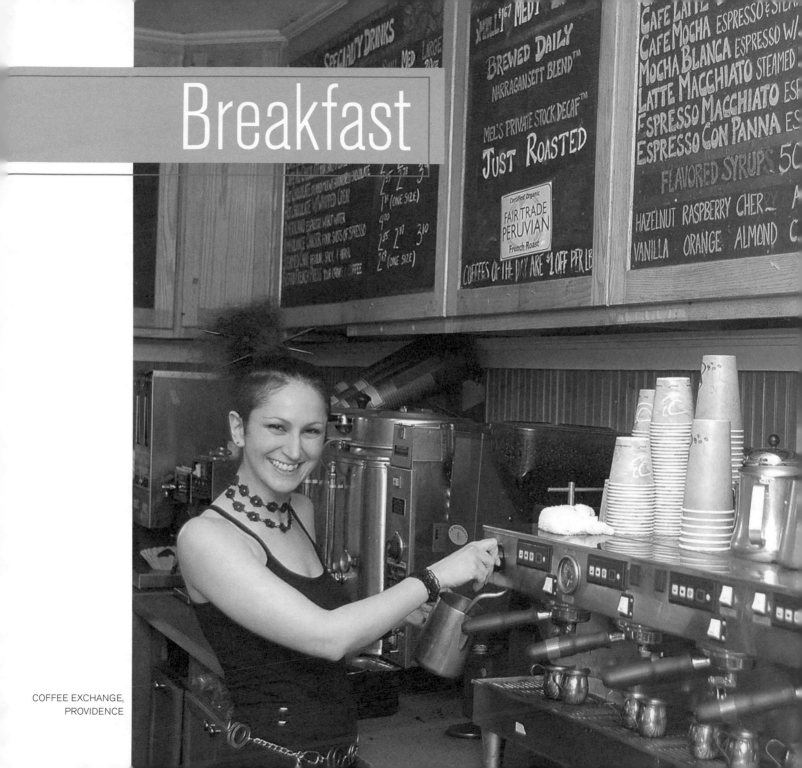

Breakfast

COFFEE EXCHANGE,
PROVIDENCE

Sportsman's Breakfast Sandwich

The Sportsman's Breakfast Sandwich is one with zing, quite popular with the sport fishermen of South County who rise before dawn to head out into Block Island Sound for a day at sea. The anchovy is what wakes them up. It may be omitted, but no self-respecting angler would ever admit to doing that.

---

1 English muffin

3 slices Swiss cheese

1 slice ham or Canadian bacon

1 anchovy

1 slice tomato

2 slices pineapple, fresh or canned

Preheat oven to 450 degrees.

Split the English muffin into 2 halves. On one half, place a slice of cheese, the ham or Canadian bacon, the anchovy, the tomato, and a second slice of cheese. On the other half of the muffin, place the remaining slice of cheese and the pineapple slices.

Combine the muffin halves to form a sandwich. Place the sandwich on a baking sheet. Bake for 5 minutes or until the cheese is melted and the sandwich is hot. Serve immediately.

MAKES 1 SANDWICH.

Pear and Almond Pancakes

The Modern Diner in the old mill town of Pawtucket (the Indian word for "the place by the waterfall") is a classic. The cream-colored Sterling Streamliner was built in 1940 and is one of only a handful of diners listed on the National Register of Historic Places. The art deco–style diner has a high arched ceiling, chrome stools at a long counter, and wooden booths worn with age. Like other traditional diners, the Modern is thriving, and it's not unusual to wait in line for breakfast, especially on weekends. Over the past century, the diner has survived wars, the Great Depression, and most recently the onslaught of fast-food restaurants and corporate chains. Diners offer down-home charm, friendly service, reasonable prices, and special menu items you rarely see at the chains, like these pancakes for which the Modern Diner is famous. Note that preparation starts the day before you plan to serve them.

---

5 Bartlett pears

10 ounces light maple syrup

1/2 cup sugar

1 box buttermilk pancake mix

Vanilla extract, to taste (about 1 teaspoon)

1 small package slivered almonds

10 ounces fig filling

Whipped butter, as needed

Confectioners' sugar, as needed

Peel and core the pears. Chop into 1/2-inch cubes. In a bowl, blend together half of the light maple syrup with half the sugar. Coat the pieces of pear in the maple mixture. Refrigerate overnight.

Prepare enough pancake mix for 4 servings, according to the package directions. Add the remaining sugar and the vanilla (be careful not to overdo the vanilla—too much can ruin any dish). Start making the pancakes on a hot griddle. Immediately add the pears and the slivered almonds to each pancake. Flip gently when bubbles appear on the top of each pancake.

In a saucepan, heat the remaining 5 ounces of maple syrup with the fig filling. Pour the mixture over the pancakes. Serve with whipped butter and confectioners' sugar.

MAKES 4 SERVINGS.

Tiramisu Pancakes with Espresso Ricotta Cream

Leave it to Chef David Baccari to give an Italian twist to his pancakes at Johnny B's Diner in the busy city of Cranston. There's been a diner at that location under one name or another since 1912, but it's unlikely any previous chef made tiramisu pancakes. Those in the know sit at the old enamel table in the dining room, where people leave anonymous notes in the table's two drawers. The notes are almost as interesting as the food.

1½ cups all-purpose flour

1½ tablespoons sugar

1 teaspoon salt

1½ teaspoons baking powder

1 teaspoon baking soda

3 tablespoons instant coffee granules

8 tablespoons confectioners' sugar, divided

2 large eggs, beaten

2 cups buttermilk

¼ cup melted butter, cooled

1 pound whole milk ricotta cheese

2 tablespoons instant powdered espresso

Whole coffee beans and powdered sugar, as needed for garnish

Into a large mixing bowl, sift the flour, sugar, salt, baking powder, baking soda, and instant coffee plus 4 tablespoons of the confectioners' sugar. Add the beaten eggs, buttermilk, and melted butter. Blend with a wire whisk until mixture is smooth. Set aside.

In a blender or food processor, blend the ricotta cheese, powdered espresso, and remaining 4 tablespoons of powdered sugar until well combined. Set aside in the refrigerator.

Spray a griddle or large frying pan with low-fat cooking spray. Bring it to medium-high heat. Pour approximately ¼ cup of pancake batter onto the hot griddle. Cook until the underside of the pancake is golden brown. Using a spatula, flip the pancake over and cook for another minute, or until golden brown on both sides. Remove the pancake to a warm serving platter. Pour and cook again to use all of the batter. This recipe makes approximately 18 pancakes.

To serve, place pancakes on warm plates. Top with a dollop of the espresso ricotta cream. Garnish with whole coffee beans. Sprinkle with powdered sugar.

MAKES 4 TO 6 SERVINGS.

Quiche with Chorizo, Spinach, and Cheddar

One of the specialties at Jigger's Diner in stylish East Greenwich is a quiche with Portuguese flavors. The key ingredient is chorizo, a highly seasoned pork sausage flavored with garlic, chili powder, and other spices. Jigger's has been around since 1928 in one fashion or another. The current diner was built in 1950 and restored in 1992 with bits and pieces of diners from other parts of the country. Jigger's is also well-known for its gingerbread pancakes served with homemade applesauce.

2½ cups flour

½ teaspoon salt

1 cup (2 sticks) cold butter, cut into small pieces

5 tablespoons very cold water

2 tablespoons olive oil

½ cup chopped onions

1 cup sliced mushrooms

10 ounces fresh spinach

1½ cups chopped chorizo

4 eggs

1 cup heavy cream

2 cups shredded cheddar cheese

Preheat oven to 350 degrees.

In a food processor or with a mixer, combine the flour, salt, and butter. Pulse until it resembles a coarse meal. Add the cold water. Pulse until the mixture just comes together. Turn out onto a floured work surface. Bring the dough together into a ball. Wrap in plastic wrap. Chill for at least 30 minutes.

Roll out the dough to fit a 9-inch pie plate, trimming the excess dough. Set aside.

In a large frying pan, heat the olive oil. Sauté the onions, mushrooms, spinach, and chorizo. (*Note:* The casing on the chorizo should be removed and the sausage crumbled before cooking.)

In a small bowl, whisk together the eggs and cream. Remove the frying pan from the heat. Stir in the egg mixture. Add the cheese and mix well. Pour this mixture into the prepared pie plate. Bake for 45 minutes.

MAKES 6 SERVINGS.

Best French Toast Ever

My good friend Phoebe Zuromski comes from a Portuguese family, and she taught me how to make "the best French toast ever" by using Portuguese sweet bread. It's so sweet, you don't need any vanilla extract or sugar in this recipe. Big round loaves of the soft yellow bread are available at Rhode Island's Portuguese bakeries and large supermarkets. If you go early to a bakery, the bread you purchase is still warm from the oven. Or you can make your own with the recipe in the Breads & Pizzas chapter in this book.

1 round loaf Portuguese sweet bread

4 tablespoons butter, divided

3 eggs

1 cup milk

Pure Rhode Island maple syrup, as needed

1 pound linguica (Portuguese sausage), cut into ¼-inch slices and fried

Cut the sweet bread into 8 equally thick slices. Place a large frying pan or griddle over medium-high heat. Add 2 tablespoons of the butter to the pan.

In a bowl, combine the eggs and milk. Beat well. Pour into a shallow glass dish. Dip the bread slices into the egg-milk mixture, making sure that both sides are well coated. Allow any excess to drip off the bread back into the dish.

Place the bread slices into the hot buttered frying pan or on the griddle. After 1 to 2 minutes, check the underside of the bread. When it is golden brown, flip the bread over and cook for another 2 minutes. Transfer the French toast to a heated platter. Cover with foil to keep warm. Repeat these steps, adding a tablespoon of butter as needed to the frying pan or griddle, until all the slices of bread have been dipped and toasted.

Serve the French toast with pure Rhode Island maple syrup, preferably warmed or at least at room temperature. On the side, serve fried linguica. (Linguica is a Portuguese sausage, slim in size with a strong garlic flavor, that can be found in Latin American markets and many supermarkets.)

MAKES 4 SERVINGS.

Eggs Benedict Newport-Style

Eggs Benedict is a classic breakfast and brunch dish that rises to a new level with the addition of lobster. Upscale restaurants in Newport offer this version, and many home cooks have added it to their recipe repertoire.

HOLLANDAISE SAUCE

3 egg yolks

2 tablespoons fresh lemon juice

¼ teaspoon white pepper

½ cup (1 stick) butter, melted

4 English muffins, split, toasted, and buttered

4 slices Canadian bacon or baked ham, warmed

8 poached eggs

1 boiled or steamed lobster, approximately 1 pound

Steamed asparagus or ripe tomato slices, for garnish (optional)

First make the Hollandaise Sauce. In a blender or food processor, combine the egg yolks, lemon juice, and white pepper. Blend for 1 minute. With the machine still running, gradually pour in the hot melted butter. Continue blending for 2 to 3 minutes, or until the sauce thickens.

Place 2 English muffin halves on each plate. Top each muffin half with a slice of Canadian bacon or ham, a poached egg, and some of the sauce. Garnish each plate with the meat from a lobster claw or a section of the tail. If desired, you may also garnish with steamed asparagus or tomato slices. Serve immediately.

MAKES 4 SERVINGS.

Saving the Franklin Spa

A few years ago, when word got out that the Franklin Spa in Newport was closing, one loyal fan took it upon himself to save the neighborhood eatery, where breakfast is served daily until mid-afternoon seven days a week. Maybe it was the really good coffee and huge omelets that mobilized Rocky Botelho, who couldn't imagine his mornings without a stop at the spa. He ended up purchasing the Spring Street restaurant, which now has even more loyal fans, including many locals and summer tourists. Located near St. Mary's Church, where John F. Kennedy married Jacqueline Bouvier, the Franklin Spa is known for its original creation, the Portuguese Sailor, a grilled breakfast sandwich consisting of a chorizo patty and eggs between two slices of Portuguese sweet bread.

Federal Hill Frittata

An Italian frittata is a combination of eggs, cheese, and other ingredients, often leftovers, such as onions, mushrooms, peppers, and tomatoes, fried until lightly browned and served warm for breakfast, or at room temperature as part of an antipasto. Rhode Islanders prefer to bake their frittatas and often add bits of meat. This classic version is the way a frittata is prepared at the many restaurants on Federal Hill, the Little Italy of Providence. It's an excellent dish to serve at a brunch.

1 dozen eggs, beaten

1 pound ricotta cheese

1 pound mozzarella, cut into small pieces

Salt and freshly ground black pepper, to taste

Leftover chopped onions, mushrooms, peppers, and tomatoes (about 1 cup)

¼ pound cooked Italian sausage, crumbled (optional)

½ stick pepperoni, cut into small pieces (optional)

¼ pound prosciutto, cut into small pieces (optional)

Preheat oven to 350 degrees.

In a large bowl, combine all the ingredients. Mix well. Pour mixture into a greased 9-inch-square glass baking dish. Bake for 45 minutes, or until edges are golden brown. Serve warm.

MAKES 6 SERVINGS.

Why Is It Named Federal Hill?

Federal Hill, the neighborhood in and around Atwells Avenue and Broadway in Providence, is the city's Little Italy. More than 100,000 Italian immigrants came to Rhode Island in the late 1800s and early 1900s, mostly from southern Italy, and many settled in Federal Hill. The name "Federal Hill" comes from the old Federal-style white houses that were built there for the Civil War militia.

A large concrete arch soaring high over Atwells Avenue was constructed in 1978 to serve as the entrance to the bustling neighborhood. At the center of the arch is the large Italian pinecone that produces the pignoli, or pine nut, the Italian symbol for hospitality and so prevalent in Italian cooking.

Ham and Cheese Strata

A strata is a wonderful dish to serve at brunch because all the work is done ahead of time. Italian families in Rhode Island make a ham and cheese strata, which is very much like a savory French toast casserole. A strata can also be made with sausage, bacon, chopped onions, and sliced mushroom—whatever you have on hand. And in the summer, for a non-Italian take on this Italian classic, a strata can also be made with small tender zucchini from the garden, plum tomatoes, Brie cheese, and sourdough bread, with finely chopped onions and freshly snipped dill as seasonings. Stratas became popular during World War I and the Depression because they were frugal and filling.

---

16 bread slices, crusts removed

1 pound ham, sliced

1 pound provolone cheese, sliced

1 pound cheddar cheese, sliced

6 eggs

3 cups milk

Salt, freshly ground black pepper, or garlic powder, to taste (optional)

In a large greased baking dish, 2 to 3 inches deep, lay 8 slices of bread to cover the bottom. Layer half of the ham and cheese slices on top of the bread. Repeat these steps, layering the remaining 8 slices of bread, then the ham, and ending with the cheese.

In a bowl, combine the eggs and milk. Beat well. Pour the egg-milk mixture over the layers of bread, ham, and cheese. Season to taste, if desired. Refrigerate overnight. Remove the pan from the refrigerator 1 hour before cooking.

Preheat oven to 375 degrees.

Bake for 1 hour, or until golden brown and bubbly. It's best to let the strata stand for 10 minutes after it comes out of the oven before serving. Cut into squares.

MAKES 8 SERVINGS.

Thin and Thick Johnnycakes

Native Rhode Islanders who live in Newport County make thin johnnycakes, while across Narragansett Bay in South County, residents prefer their johnnycakes on the thick side. Either type can be enjoyed at breakfast, lunch, and dinner. These diminutive flapjacks are delicious at breakfast drizzled with maple syrup and served with bacon or sausage and applesauce. They also can be eaten plain or topped with a sprinkling of sugar, or even with butter and salt as a savory accompaniment to pot roast or creamed codfish at lunch or dinner. Using a cast-iron skillet or griddle greased with corn oil, bacon fat, or lard is the best way to make johnnycakes, but a nonstick electric pan can also be used.

THIN JOHNNYCAKES FROM NEWPORT COUNTY

2 cups Rhode Island stone-ground whitecap cornmeal

½ teaspoon salt

¾ cup cold water

1½ cups milk

Combine cornmeal, salt, and water. Add milk, stirring to remove lumps. Batter will be on the thin side. Into a well-oiled frying pan over medium heat, pour enough batter to make a 3-inch johnnycake. Fry for 2 minutes, or until the edges of the johnnycake turn brown. Flip each johnnycake over to cook for 1 more minute on the other side.

MAKES 6 TO 8 SERVINGS.

THICK JOHNNYCAKES FROM SOUTH COUNTY

2 cups Rhode Island stone-ground
    whitecap cornmeal

2 teaspoons sugar

1 teaspoon salt

2 cups boiling water

¼ to ½ cup milk or cream

In a bowl, combine the cornmeal, sugar, and salt. Slowly add the boiling water, stirring thoroughly to completely moisten. Allow to stand a few minutes, as mixture will thicken. Add just enough milk or cream to turn the mixture into the consistency of soft mashed potatoes.

Into a hot, greased frying pan or griddle, drop enough batter by the spoonful to make a johnnycake 2 to 3 inches across and ½ inch thick. Fry for 6 minutes on each side, or until the inside is cooked and a golden crunchy crust is formed. Turn over each johnnycake only once for perfect results.

MAKES 4 TO 6 SERVINGS.

Johnnycakes (or is it Jonnycakes?)

No matter how you spell it, johnnycakes made with Rhode Island stone-ground whitecap cornmeal are a breakfast staple throughout the state. These unleavened cornmeal pancakes date back to the 1600s, when the Narragansett Indians showed the colonists how to make them. Today many of Rhode Island's restaurants offer johnnycakes on their menus. One of my favorite renditions is at the Commons Lunch on the Commons in Little Compton in easternmost Rhode Island. This small-town cafe—which was rebuilt after being destroyed in a fire—serves thin johnnycakes, piled two or three high on the plate. The edges are lacy, and the surface is just barely crisp.

Grandmother's Hash

Hash is very popular in Rhode Island, whether you make the old family recipe for hash at home or you try the hash at a local diner. Roughly translated, hash means "nothing goes out with the trash." It dates back to a time when many families had to stretch food or "make do." Hash can be made with leftover ham, corned beef, roast beef, and even any kind of white fish added to leftover mashed potatoes, then fried in butter or bacon fat—preferably in an old cast-iron skillet. The word *hash* comes from the old French word *hacher,* meaning "to chop." Down in South County, many home cooks make Grandmother's Hash, featuring ground-up meat from quahogs (thick-shelled clams) that are formed into 3-inch patties at least an inch thick. For a traditional Rhode Island meal, put a poached egg on top of each serving.

---

5 pounds quahogs (or 1 cup
  canned chopped clams, drained)

1 small onion, peeled and chopped

2 tablespoons butter

¼ cup clam broth or juice

1 egg, beaten

2 cups cooked mashed potato

Salt and pepper, to taste

2 tablespoons oil

6 poached eggs (optional)

Precook the quahogs by steaming them open in water in a large pot over medium-high heat. Remove the cooked clam meat and chop. Drain. Measure 1 cup cooked quahogs.

In a large frying pan, sauté the chopped onion in some of the butter until golden; do not let the onion brown. Add the chopped quahogs and broth and simmer until the clams are tender. Set aside to cool.

Add the beaten egg to the mashed potatoes. Then add the cooled chopped clam and onion mixture. Mix well. Taste and add salt and pepper as desired. Form into 6 cakes.

In a heavy frying pan or on a griddle, fry the cakes in the remaining butter and the oil until browned on both sides.

MAKES 6 SERVINGS.

May Breakfast Strudel

Strudel is a rolled pastry filled with nuts, streusel, fruit, or cheese. It is usually served as a dessert with coffee. Strudel was brought to the United States by German immigrants. Rhode Islanders of German descent created this May Breakfast Strudel, which is required eating at many May breakfasts in the Wakefield area down in South County near the seashore.

1 (3-ounce) package cream cheese

4 tablespoons butter

2 cups Bisquick mix

⅓ cup milk

¾ cup preserves, any flavor, your choice

1 cup confectioners' sugar

1 tablespoon milk

½ teaspoon vanilla

In a large bowl, cut the cream cheese and butter into the Bisquick until crumbly. Blend in milk. Turn dough onto floured work surface. Knead 8 to 10 times. On a sheet of waxed paper, roll out the dough into a 12x8-inch rectangle. Turn the rectangle of dough onto a lightly greased baking sheet. Remove waxed paper.

Preheat oven to 425 degrees.

Make 2½-inch cuts at 1-inch intervals on the long sides of the dough. Spread the preserves down the center of the dough. Fold dough strips over preserves. Bake for 12 to 15 minutes.

In a bowl, combine confectioners' sugar, milk, and vanilla to make an icing. Drizzle the icing over the strudel as soon as it comes out of the oven.

MAKES 8 SERVINGS.

Sugar Shacks

When we go to brunch at someone's home in Rhode Island, instead of flowers or that usual bottle of wine, we bring a bottle of 100 percent pure maple syrup, produced straight from Rhode Island sugar maples. At last count, there were five sugarhouses in Rhode Island turning sap into richly flavored, amber-colored maple syrup: Charlie's Sugar House in Coventry, Robert Harmon in Greene, Kingston Syrup in Kingston, Forge River Farms in North Kingstown and Spring Hill Sugar House in Richmond.

Bed-and-Breakfast Broiled Tomatoes

Broiled tomatoes, which are British in origin, are a regular item on the communal tables of bed-and-breakfast establishments throughout Rhode Island. They add a splash of color to any breakfast plate and are the perfect accompaniment to any egg dish. They also can be served at lunch or dinner. In late August and through September, when we have more tomatoes than we can handle, broiled tomatoes come to mind. Try different grated cheeses and even a sprinkling of oregano on these tomatoes.

4 or 5 fresh tomatoes, large and ripe

Olive oil, as needed

Salt and freshly ground black pepper, to taste

1/2 cup grated Parmesan cheese

1/4 cup minced fresh parsley

1 garlic clove, crushed, or 2 tablespoons snipped fresh chives

4 tablespoons butter, softened

1/2 cup bread crumbs (optional)

Preheat oven broiler.

Wash the tomatoes under cold running water. Cut the tomatoes in half or into 1/2-inch-thick slices, discarding the ends. Place the tomato halves cut side up in a baking dish or on a broiler pan. Brush the tomatoes with olive oil. Season with salt and pepper.

In a bowl, combine the Parmesan cheese, parsley, garlic, butter, and bread crumbs. Place an equal amount of the mixture on top of each tomato half. Place under the oven broiler for 3 to 5 minutes, or until the cheese is golden brown and bubbly. Serve immediately.

MAKES 4 SERVINGS.

Brunch at a Tiny Diner

Paris has its cafes, Dublin has its pubs, and Italy has the trattoria. In the United States it's the diner that gives us comfort and sustenance, especially first thing in the morning. Nicks on Broadway in Providence is a tiny diner with only eight seats at the counter and a smattering of tables. Chef-owner Derek Wagner keeps the place packed with his creative cuisine, and on Sundays, he offers a BYOB brunch with regular customers bringing in their own champagne to make mimosas.

Cranberry-Apple Muffins

The Rhode Island Greening apple is the official state fruit and the perfect crisp apple to use when making these moist muffins. Greening apples are grown throughout the state, but especially in the town of Smithfield in the rural northwest corner of Rhode Island, an area known as Apple Valley. Many roadside orchards allow you to pick your own if you like. Yellow-green in color, the Rhode Island Greening retains its sharp taste when cooked. In fact, it seems to intensify. Other apples, such as Cortland, Delicious, and Rome Beauty can be substituted.

½ cup whole cranberry sauce, canned or freshly made

½ teaspoon grated orange peel

1½ cups flour

½ cup sugar

1 teaspoon cinnamon

½ teaspoon baking soda

¼ teaspoon baking powder

¼ teaspoon salt

1 large egg

⅓ cup milk

½ cup oil

1 cup finely chopped, cored, and peeled Rhode Island Greening apples

Preheat oven to 350 degrees.

In a bowl, combine the cranberry sauce and orange peel. Set aside.

In another bowl, sift together the flour, sugar, cinnamon, baking soda, baking powder, and salt.

In a third large bowl, beat the egg with the milk and oil. Stir in the apples. Add the flour mixture. Combine well.

Spoon the batter into greased muffin cups. Make a well in the center of each muffin and spoon in a teaspoon of the cranberry–orange peel mixture. Bake for 14 to 20 minutes. Serve warm.

MAKES 12 MUFFINS.

Frittole (Italian Doughnuts)

The Italian *frittole* are really fritters with the characteristic raisins and grated orange or lemon peel often found in Italian baked foods.

---

2 cups flour

2 teaspoons baking powder

1/8 teaspoon salt

2 eggs

1 cup milk

1/2 cup raisins

1 teaspoon vanilla

Grated peel from 1/2 orange or
    lemon

Oil, as needed for frying

Sugar, as needed for sprinkling

In a large bowl, combine the flour, baking powder, and salt. Mix well. Add the eggs, milk, raisins, vanilla, and grated peel, and beat until smooth. Drop by rounded tablespoonfuls into hot oil and fry until golden brown, approximately 3 minutes. Drain on paper towels. While still warm, sprinkle with sugar. Serve immediately.

MAKES APPROXIMATELY 20 SMALL DOUGHNUTS.

"Dollars to Doughnuts"

First-time visitors to Rhode Island are often struck by the number of doughnut shops they find in their travels. In some parts of the state, there seems to be one on every corner. One of the best places for old-fashioned doughnuts is Allie's Donuts, a sprawling roadhouse in North Kingstown, where those in the know make a detour from the highway for the hot coffee and warm doughnuts, served in no-nonsense cardboard-box trays. The variety of Allie's big and sweet doughnuts is vast. It's not unusual for regular customers to buy a dozen for the office and another two or three to eat in the car on their way to work.

Here and there in Rhode Island, independent doughnut shops do a thriving business. Given a choice, Rhode Islanders seem to prefer the local handmade doughnuts over the more commercially produced fare of Dunkin' Donuts and Krispy Kreme. In fact, Rhode Island is generally known as a tough market for the big chain restaurants that thrive elsewhere in the United States. What is it about Rhode Island doughnuts that makes them preferable to other store-bought doughnuts? Perhaps it's their irregular shape, their crunchier surface, their warm and moist interior. The big-name doughnut stores do well enough in these parts, but I'm willing to bet "dollars to doughnuts" that the plain Rhode Island doughnut—like those made at Allie's—is the doughnut of choice.

French Doughnuts

These French doughnuts are baked in muffin cups rather than deep-fried and then rolled in what the French are known for—butter.

5 tablespoons butter

½ cup sugar

1 egg, beaten

1½ cups all-purpose flour

1 teaspoon salt

1 teaspoon nutmeg

½ cup milk

6 tablespoons butter, melted

¾ cup sugar

2 teaspoons cinnamon

Preheat oven to 350 degrees. Grease muffin cups.

In a bowl, cream the 5 tablespoons of butter and the ½ cup sugar. Add the beaten egg. Mix well. Combine the flour, salt, and nutmeg. Add milk to the butter-sugar mixture alternately with the dry ingredients. Fill greased muffin cups half full. Bake for 20 to 25 minutes.

Remove the pan from the oven. While still hot, roll the doughnuts in the melted butter and then in the combined mixture of ¾ cup sugar and cinnamon.

MAKES 12 DOUGHNUTS.

Mother of May Breakfasts

A true rite of spring, May breakfasts are held throughout the state every year, sponsored by volunteer fire departments, civic organizations, veterans' posts, the local grange, and churches. A "real" May breakfast should take place on May Day, the first of May, but often these fund-raisers are held on the first Saturday in the month to guarantee a great turnout. Some celebrate on May 4, Rhode Island's Independence Day. The more unusual May breakfast sites are the Quonset Air Museum in North Kingstown and the Norman Bird Sanctuary in Middletown. Each year the governor of the state hosts a May breakfast honoring Rhode Islanders who are 100 years old and older.

The mother of May breakfasts is the one at Oaklawn Community Baptist Church in Cranston. It's the biggest—nearly 1,000 guests last year—and the longest running, since 1867. The shopping list goes something like this: 180 dozen eggs, 120 pounds of cornmeal, and 233 pounds of ham. The all-you-can-eat menu includes scrambled eggs, ham, cornbread, clam cakes, apple pie, coffee, and juice, and it's all served by church members dressed in old-fashioned colonial attire.

Block Island Doughnuts

Block Island doughnuts are just old-fashioned Americana, fried to a light golden brown and then coated with cinnamon and sugar—guaranteed to melt in your mouth. Years back on Block Island, these doughnuts were usually made in a black cast-iron kettle, the kind that is used in fireplace cooking, suspended from a crane.

2 eggs

1 cup sugar

1 teaspoon vanilla

½ teaspoon nutmeg

2½ cups flour

1 teaspoon baking powder

½ teaspoon baking soda

1 cup buttermilk

3 tablespoons melted shortening

Oil, as needed for frying

Cinnamon (optional)

Confectioners' sugar (optional)

In a bowl, beat the eggs until light and fluffy. Add the sugar, vanilla, and nutmeg.

In another bowl, sift together the flour, baking powder, and baking soda. Add to egg mixture alternately with the buttermilk and melted shortening. The dough should be as soft as possible.

Move the dough onto a clean work surface. Add a little more flour only if needed to keep dough from sticking to the work surface. Roll out the dough to a desired thickness. Cut out the doughnuts and drop them into a deep pan of hot oil over medium-high heat. As soon as the doughnuts rise to the top, turn them over in the hot oil. Turn them again to brown on both sides.

Drain the doughnuts on paper towels. If desired, shake one doughnut at a time in a paper bag containing a mixture of cinnamon and confectioners' sugar.

MAKES 18 TO 24 DOUGHNUTS.

A Block Island Christmas

Picturesque Block Island is located about 12 miles off the coast of Rhode Island. Ferries out of Point Judith and Newport transport people to and from the tranquil island. In the summer, the population swells to more than 15,000, but in the off-season Block Island—with only 850 year-round residents—seems almost deserted. No ferry service is available on Christmas Day, but New England Airlines offers a free morning flight for those who might not otherwise be able to come to or leave the island to be with their families for the holiday. Everything is closed on Christmas Day, but the Block Island Depot is open with free doughnuts from 9:00 A.M. until noon.

Lunch

VENDA RAVIOLI,
FEDERAL HILL

Chowders & Soups

Rhode Island Quahog Chowder (in a Clear Broth)

Rhode Islanders whose forebears were early settlers in the state would never put anything but quahogs into a chowder. (If you are unable to obtain quahogs at the seafood market, you can purchase cans of chopped clams in major supermarkets—but we can't guarantee the chowder will be quite as good.) This old Yankee recipe has been handed down from generation to generation. It makes a zesty, clear-broth chowder.

16 cups (1 gallon) clam juice (available in bottles and cans in major supermarkets)

¼ pound salt pork, chopped

½ cup diced onions

8 pounds all-purpose potatoes, peeled and diced in ½-inch pieces

1 tablespoon white pepper

1 tablespoon Worcestershire sauce

2 cups chopped, cooked quahogs

In a large stockpot, heat the clam juice just to simmer, then cover and set aside.

In a frying pan, fry the salt pork. When the fat is cooked out, remove the salt pork and set aside. Sauté the onions in the fat until they are translucent. Do not allow the onions to brown.

Put the stockpot back on the heat. Add the onions to the clam juice and bring to a simmer. Add the potatoes and simmer until tender. Add the fried salt pork, pepper, and Worcestershire sauce. Add the chopped quahogs; heat through and serve.

MAKES 20 SERVINGS.

A Quahog Is a Clam

The official state shellfish in Rhode Island is the quahog, pronounced "KO-hog." To make it a bit more confusing, the word is sometimes spelled quahaug. It is one of four main types of hard-shelled clams (not to be confused with soft-shelled clams or "steamers"). The quahog is the clam that is always chopped or minced for use in making chowders, clam cakes, and stuffed clams.

Fresh Quahog Chowder for 25

Champlin's in Point Judith has been around since 1932. On the street level is the retail market where whole fish are displayed on beds of crushed ice and live lobsters are held in huge tanks of water. Above the market is Champlin's Restaurant, where you can eat your steamers and stuffies "in the rough" on the wooden deck overlooking Galilee Harbor. When you place your order, you have a choice of clear, red, or white clam chowder. The addition of cream is what turns a clear chowder into a white chowder.

4 cups cooked and shucked
   quahogs

8 cups diced peeled potatoes

4 cups water, drained from cooking
   the potatoes

½ pound salt pork, cubed

3 cups chopped onions

4 cups clam juice

3 cups light cream

1 teaspoon pepper

½ teaspoon thyme

Chop the quahog meat into pieces.

In a large stockpot, cook the potatoes in boiling water. Drain, saving 4 cups of the cooking liquid.

In a large (at least 4-quart) stockpot, fry the salt pork until crisp. Remove salt pork and set aside to use as garnish. Add the onions to the rendered fat in the stockpot, and cook until translucent. Add the reserved cooking liquid, the clam juice and the quahogs; bring to a simmer. Add the cooked potatoes.

In a separate saucepan, heat the cream (do not boil), then add it to the chowder. Season to taste with pepper and thyme. Top each serving with crisp fried pork.

MAKES 25 SERVINGS.

A Quahog Question

If you plan to steam open your own quahogs, and you need 2 cups chopped meat, you should ask the clerk at the fish market how many pounds of quahogs you will need to end up with 2 cups. It all depends on the size of the quahogs.

Rocky Point–Style Chowder

From 1847 to the 1990s, Rocky Point was a popular attraction in Warwick, south of Providence. Jutting out on Warwick Neck, surrounded by water, this amusement park drew thousands of people to its famous shore dinner hall where boiled lobsters were served with all the fixings—chowder, steamed clams, clam cakes, corn on the cob—and for dessert, juicy watermelon. The Rocky Point amusement park and its shore dinner hall are but a memory these days, but the chowder lives on at the Rocky Point Chowder House, a fast-food establishment near the state airport in Warwick.

½ pound ground or finely diced
   salt pork

1 pound onions, cut in medium dice

1 gallon clam juice

1 pound potatoes, diced

Salt and pepper, to taste

1 tablespoon paprika

2 cups canned tomato puree

Water, as needed

6 cups chopped, cooked quahogs

Pilot crackers, crumbled

In a large stockpot, heat the salt pork until the fat melts. Add the onions, and cook over low heat until very soft. Add the clam juice, potatoes, salt, pepper, paprika, tomato puree, and a little water. Simmer until the potatoes are soft and then add the chopped quahogs. Heat and taste for seasoning. Add more water, if needed. Serve with Pilot crackers (the bland, sturdy wafers that used to be called hardtack).

MAKES 16 SERVINGS.

Rhode Island Red Seafood Chowder for a Crowd

A good Rhode Island seafood chowder, like this one, will have plenty of local fish on which to feast. As the title says, it makes enough to feed a large group of people.

---

8 pounds potatoes, peeled and diced

1 pound small shrimp, shelled and deveined

1 pound monkfish, cut into bite-size pieces

1 pound tuna, cut into bite-size pieces

2 tablespoons butter

½ cup onions

1 cup chopped celery

¼ pound salt pork

½ pound mussels (in shells)

¼ pound scallops

1 pound clams or quahogs (in shells)

1 cup chopped tomatoes

1 gallon (16 cups) fish broth

1 (32-ounce) can Mott's Clamato juice

1 tablespoon white pepper

1 tablespoon Worcestershire sauce

Freshly ground black pepper, to taste

In a large stockpot, cook the potatoes in boiling water. When they are tender, drain.

In a large saucepan, sauté the shrimp, monkfish, and tuna in the butter. In another pan, sauté the onions and celery with the salt pork.

Combine all ingredients, including the cooked potatoes, in the large stockpot. Bring to a boil, then lower heat to a simmer until the clams and mussels open. Season to taste with black pepper and serve immediately.

MAKES 20 SERVINGS.

Just Steam Them Open

Whenever a recipe calls for something like 2 cups chopped quahogs, they are always already cooked. The quahogs in their clam shells are usually steamed open, either by the home cook or by the fish market or a major manufacturer, to remove the meat from the shells. This "cooks" the clams. This can be done in a large stockpot on top of the stove with an inch or two of water (or beer), or it can also be done in the oven. This is by far the easiest way to get the meat out of the clam shell. Shucking the uncooked quahog shells would take forever and is not an easy task.

Narragansett Bay Seafood Chowder

You can prepare this seafood chowder ahead of time, but wait to stir in the cream until just before serving. When both the cream and the broth are thoroughly heated, the chowder is ready to serve.

1 medium-size onion, chopped
(about 1 cup)

1 tablespoon butter

2 cups fish broth (or 1 cup clam
juice and 1 cup water)

2 cups peeled and diced potatoes

¾ cup lobster meat or shelled,
deveined shrimp

¾ cup bay scallops or cut-up sea
scallops

½ pound haddock, cod, or flounder
fillets

1 bay leaf

1 sprig fresh thyme, or 1 teaspoon
dried thyme

2 cups light cream or half-and-half

Salt and freshly ground pepper, to
taste

Chopped fresh parsley, for garnish

Paprika, for garnish

In a large stockpot, sauté the onion in the butter over medium-low heat until the onion is tender. Add the fish broth and potatoes. Bring to a boil, then reduce heat. Simmer until the potatoes are tender, about 10 to 12 minutes, adding more water if needed to cover the potatoes.

Cut the seafood and fish into bite-size chunks. Add to the stockpot with the bay leaft and thyme. Heat just enough to cook the seafood, about 2 minutes. Stir in the cream. Season to taste with salt and pepper. Remove the bay leaf and thyme sprig.

Ladle into soup bowls. Sprinkle with fresh parsley and dust with paprika.

MAKES 6 SERVINGS.

If You Like It Nice and Thick . . .

Rhode Island cooks rarely thicken their chowders. However, if you wish to do so, there are a couple of methods.

If you like a creamy, thick chowder, use a fork to stir 4 tablespoons flour into 1/2 cup water to make what is called a "slurry." Gradually add the slurry to the chowder as it cooks; stir until it is as thick as you desire.

You can instead blend 3 tablespoons of softened butter with 3 tablespoons of flour and add this mixture gradually into your simmering chowder. Stir constantly over very low heat until the chowder thickens slightly.

In Rhode Island, we serve Pilot crackers, common crackers, or oyster crackers with our chowders. They can be added whole or crushed into each bowl of chowder, if desired, which results in a thicker—and somewhat lumpy—chowder.

Creamy Fish Chowder

The Bluepoint Oyster Bar and Restaurant in Providence no longer exists, but its recipes still float around Rhode Island like fishing boats on the bay. Former owners Maureen Pothier and Paul Inveen are quite the team—she's a chef and he's a wine expert. Their fans are hoping the husband-and-wife team will someday soon open another restaurant. When it was open, the Bluepoint was frequented by Jackie Kennedy Onassis and her son, John F. Kennedy Jr., while "John John" was a student at nearby Brown University. The restaurant's fish chowder was one of their favorites.

---

2 tablespoons chopped fresh herbs of your choice, such as dill, tarragon, summer savory, or thyme

¼ pound bacon, diced small

1 cup diced onions

3 cups diced red-skinned potatoes, scrubbed, not peeled

4 cups fish broth or clam juice

1 cup heavy cream

1½ cups milk

3 pounds codfish (or other flaky whitefish), cut into 2-inch pieces

Salt, to taste

50 grinds of fresh black pepper from peppermill (approximately ¾ teaspoon)

3 tablespoons chopped fresh chives for garnish

If the herbs are still on their stems, strip them off the stems and chop the leaves. Set aside.

In a heavy-bottomed large saucepan or stockpot over low to medium heat, brown the bacon. Add the onions and sauté until translucent. Add the potatoes and cook until tender; stir often to avoid sticking and to ensure even cooking. Add fish broth or clam juice, and simmer for a few minutes.

About 15 minutes before serving, add the cream, milk, and fish pieces to the hot broth; heat through to scalding but do not boil. Stir gently so as not to break up the fish too much. Add salt, pepper, and the chopped herbs to taste. Garnish each serving of chowder with a sprinkle of the chopped chives.

MAKES ABOUT 8 SERVINGS.

Lobster Chowder

When purchasing lobsters, always check to see that their shells are hard. This is a sign that the meat inside the lobster is firm. Lobsters routinely shed their soft shells, a process known as molting. The meat inside a soft-shell lobster can be a bit mushy, which could be a problem when making any kind of lobster dish, especially a lobster chowder.

---

2 live lobsters, each 1½ pounds

¼ pound salt pork, cut into ½-inch dice

2 medium onions, chopped medium-fine

4 medium potatoes, peeled, cut in ½-inch dice (about 3 cups)

4 cups whole milk, at room temperature

2 tablespoons butter, at room temperature

¼ teaspoon freshly ground black pepper

Salt, to taste

Place the live lobsters in a large stockpot, and cover them generously with lightly salted boiling water. Cook over high heat until the water returns to a boil. Reduce heat and simmer about 10 minutes. Remove the lobsters and allow them to cool. Boil the remaining liquid in the pot, uncovered, until it is reduced to about 2 cups. Strain the liquid and set aside.

With a very sharp knife, split the lobsters in half lengthwise along their backs. Remove the meat, including the roe (eggs), if any, and the tomalley (liver). Crack the claws and remove the meat. Cut all the lobster meat into 1-inch chunks.

In a heavy saucepan, cook the salt pork pieces over moderate heat until crisp and golden. Remove the pieces and set them aside on a paper towel. Add the chopped onions to the rendered fat in the saucepan, and cook them slowly until they are tender. Add the potatoes, the strained lobster liquid, and additional water, if needed, to cover the potatoes by 1 inch.

Simmer, covered, about 20 minutes or until the potatoes are just tender. Add the lobster meat, roe, and tomalley. Heat for 5 minutes, then add the milk and butter. Warm until the mixture begins to steam, but do not allow it to boil or it will curdle. Add salt pork pieces, if desired. Season with pepper, and if needed, with salt to taste. Serve immediately.

MAKES 8 TO 10 SERVINGS.

Chowder in the Ocean State

Traditionally, chowder is a seafood soup made in a large stockpot. There is much debate on the origin of the word—from the French *chaudiere* or from the old Cornwall word *jowter* for fish peddler. Men on fishing boats were probably the first to make a chowder when they threw part of their daily catch into a large pot to make an onboard meal for the crew. The chowder was thick because fresh water was always in short supply on ships and could be used only sparingly for broth.

The first New England chowders came to a simmer in the early 1730s, with fish, usually, as the main ingredient. In the 1800s clam chowder became popular. By the end of that century, various regions of New England had developed distinct kinds of chowder, but generally they were all

creamy white soups flavored with fish (cod, haddock, whiting, flounder, hake, or halibut) or clams.

Rhode Islanders are pretty divided when it comes to chowder. Folks down in South County insist that a true Rhode Island chowder has a clear broth chock-full of chopped clams and small, tender chunks of potato. In and around the capital city of Providence and to the north, tomatoes have been added to the basic chowder recipe—perhaps because of the influx of Italian and Portuguese immigrants. Rhode Island is the only New England state to serve a red chowder, but it should not be confused with New York's Manhattan clam chowder, which became popular in the 1930s. Rhode Island's red chowder is decidedly creamier than that of Manhattan.

The search for the best chowder is a perennial effort in Rhode Island, with the accolades going to recipes that contain lots of well-washed succulent clams and just the right amount of potatoes, not too many, not too few, and, yes, they absolutely must be cooked to a perfectly tender state. Old-timers insist the best chowders were made by their mothers on big, black, cast-iron stoves. Some cooks claim the secret ingredient is a can of ready-made potato soup, or even a tablespoon of sugar, resulting in chowders so thick, your spoon will stand upright in the center of the bowl. Chowder lovers do agree on one thing—don't skimp on the clams. And for really good chowder, allow it to sit overnight in the refrigerator. Reheat it gently the next day for that old-fashioned flavor.

Scallop Chowder

The Mooring Restaurant in Newport is famous for its scallop chowder, which draws rave reviews from the many tourists who visit this city by the sea. It must be the touch of white wine and fresh dill. Located on Sayer's Wharf, the Mooring offers a front-row seat to the display of million-dollar yachts and equally chic celebrities who often stop at the bar for a drink or two during the high season of summer.

ROUX

½ cup (1 stick) unsalted butter

3 cups diced onions

1 tablespoon minced fresh parsley

1 teaspoon dill weed

1 cup flour

STOCK

10 cups clam juice

¼ cup white wine

2 bay leaves

1 pound bay scallops

2 cups half-and-half

1 cup cooked sweet native corn,
    at room temperature

Start by making the roux. In a large stockpot, melt the butter. Add the onions and sauté until transparent. Add half the parsley and dill weed. Cook for 1 minute. Add the flour. Blend well and cook for 2 minutes. Set the roux aside.

Next make the broth. In a separate stockpot, combine the clam juice, wine, and bay leaves. Bring to a boil. Reduce by about a third, or until you have about 2 quarts of liquid left in the pot.

Slowly add the broth to the roux. Whisk thoroughly to eliminate lumps. Bring to a boil over medium-high heat, stirring occasionally. Reduce heat to low. Add the scallops and half-and-half. Simmer for 5 minutes, or until the scallops are tender.

Place 2 teaspoons of corn in each warm soup bowl. Top off with the chowder. Garnish with remaining parsley and dill weed.

MAKES 10 SERVINGS.

Little Compton Corn Chowder

When you cross the bridge from Aquidneck Island to the mainland town of Tiverton on the eastern side of Narragansett Bay, head south on Route 77 through gracious Little Compton. On a perfect summer day, this is as good as it gets in Rhode Island. That's the Sakonnet River to the west, and when you come to Sakonnet Point, you are looking out at magnificent Rhode Island Sound. Along the way you pass Sakonnet Vineyards, where award-winning wines are made, and colorful produce stands, where the finest native fruits and vegetables are displayed in quaint bushel baskets from summer on into the fall. With local potatoes and fresh ears of sweet corn, you can make this corn chowder, or "chowdah" as they say in Rhode Island.

---

6 ears fresh sweet corn

4 bacon slices, diced

1 white onion, chopped fine

2 potatoes, peeled and cubed

1 cup water

1 quart milk

1 quart heavy cream

Salt and freshly ground black
    pepper, to taste

Using a heavy sharp knife, cut the kernels from each ear of corn. Place the kernels in a bowl. Set aside.

In a large saucepan or stockpot, cook the bacon over medium heat until crisp. Remove the bacon from the pan and set it aside. In the pan with the bacon drippings, cook the onion over medium heat until tender. Add the potatoes and water. Bring to a simmer and cook for 15 to 20 minutes, or until the potatoes are tender.

Add the corn, milk, and cream to the pan. Season to taste. Continue to cook until heated through, stirring occasionally. Serve in heated soup bowls. Garnish each bowl with a sprinkling of crumbled bacon.

MAKES 4 SERVINGS.

Native Oyster Bisque

Chef Gary Jefferds, of 22 Bowen's Wine Bar & Grille on Bowen's Wharf in Newport, recommends using Sakonnet oysters when making this bisque. We respect such local enthusiasm, but really any oyster can be used if it's fresh. Sakonnet is that long leg of Rhode Island facing the eastern part of Narragansett Bay with its back running along the Massachusetts border. With fertile green farmland rolling down to the sea, tranquil Sakonnet Vineyards makes its home here. Often described as "God's country," the Sakonnet area is quiet, even during the summer months; it just might be Rhode Island's best-kept secret.

---

2 sticks plus 4 tablespoons butter

1 cup diced Spanish onion

1 teaspoon minced garlic

½ gallon shucked Sakonnet (or any native) oysters, with their juice

2 quarts clam broth

1 quart heavy cream

2 tablespoons salt

1 teaspoon white pepper

1 cup flour

Chopped fresh chives for garnish (optional)

In a large saucepan, melt 4 tablespoons of butter over medium heat. Add the onions and garlic, and stir for 1 minute.

Separate the oysters from their juice by straining them in a colander over a bowl. Add the oysters to the pan. Set the juice aside.

Cook the oysters in the melted butter for 4 to 5 minutes, then transfer the oysters to a dish and set aside. Add the oyster juice and clam broth to the saucepan and raise the heat to high. Once it starts to simmer, add the heavy cream, salt, and pepper.

In a small sauté pan, melt the rest of the butter over medium heat. Add the flour to the melted butter a little at a time, keeping it over medium heat and stirring constantly. The mixture should look like wet sand and will thicken the bisque.

Add the flour mixture a little at a time to the large saucepan, stirring with a whisk after each addition. Cook for 5 minutes. Strain through cheesecloth or a fine metal strainer into a soup tureen or serving bowl. Add the oysters back in and serve immediately, garnished with chopped chives, if desired.

MAKES 10 SERVINGS.

Italian Wedding Soup

Hardly a wedding, Italian or otherwise, takes place in Rhode Island without the Italian Wedding Soup served as a first course at the reception. In Italian homes the soup is made in various ways, depending on what part of Italy the family comes from. This is the way my father's family made it in Lanciano, Italy—a walled medieval city near the Adriatic Sea, west of Rome.

2 heads escarole, rinsed clean and chopped

1 pound lean ground beef

4 eggs, divided

1 cup bread crumbs

2 tablespoons dried basil

1 teaspoon dried parsley flakes

1 teaspoon onion powder

$1\frac{1}{2}$ cups grated Parmesan cheese, plus additional cheese for sprinkling

8 cups chicken broth

$\frac{1}{2}$ cup finely chopped carrots

In a large pot of boiling salted water, cook the escarole until it wilts, about 10 to 15 minutes. Drain the cooked greens in a colander. Allow the escarole to cool. Squeeze out all excess liquid through a strainer.

In a large bowl, combine the ground beef, 1 egg, bread crumbs, basil, parsley flakes, onion powder, and $\frac{1}{2}$ cup of the grated Parmesan cheese. Using your hands, mix well. Form small meatballs, no more than $\frac{3}{4}$ inch in diameter.

In a separate stockpot over medium-high heat, bring the chicken broth to a boil. Add the chopped carrots. Reduce to a simmer. Drop the small meatballs into the broth. When the meatballs rise to the top, they are cooked. At that time, add the escarole to the broth.

In a separate bowl, combine the remaining 3 eggs with the remaining cup of Parmesan cheese. Mix well. Pour this mixture into the soup, stirring constantly. Simmer for 10 minutes. Serve in heated soup bowls, along with additional grated Parmesan cheese.

MAKES 8 SERVINGS.

Stracciatella (Egg and Cheese Soup)

The last time Elvis Presley appeared in concert in Providence, shortly before his death, the king of rock 'n' roll dined at Camille's. Elvis went into the kitchen and told chef Walter Potenza that he wasn't feeling well. The chef prepared this classic Italian soup for the man from Memphis. Elvis went on stage that night at the Civic Center and gave an electrifying performance. Could the soup have been magical? Today Potenza is the chef-owner of his own restaurant—Aquaviva, located on Federal Hill in Providence.

1 quart cold clear chicken broth

2 eggs, beaten

2 tablespoons grated Parmesan cheese

2 tablespoons farina or semolina, or 2 to 3 tablespoons flour

Salt, white pepper, and nutmeg, to taste

Set aside ½ cup of cold chicken broth. Bring the rest of the chicken broth to a slow boil in a large pot.

In a bowl, combine the eggs, cheese, farina (or flour), and seasonings. Add the cold chicken broth. Mix well. Pour the cold mixture into the boiling soup, stirring constantly. Bring the soup to a full boil, then turn off heat. Adjust seasoning and serve immediately.

MAKES 6 SERVINGS.

French Fish Soup

Chez Pascal, a very fine French restaurant on the fashionable East Side of Providence, made fish soup famous with this wonderful broth, loaded with garlic and saffron and served with Gruyère cheese and croutons. Fans of this soup can't seem to ever get enough of it. Here is a version for you to try. It includes herbes de Provence, a mix of dried herbs often associated with cooking in the south of France. The blend usually includes basil, fennel seed, lavender, marjoram, rosemary, sage, summer savory, and thyme. It can be found packaged in small clay crocks in gourmet food shops.

---

1 pound fish, your choice, cut into
    bite-size pieces

1 cup white wine

½ cup lemon juice

3 carrots, diced

4 celery stalks, diced

2 onions, diced

1 whole garlic head, chopped

4 tablespoons butter

2 quarts fish broth

4 potatoes, peeled and diced

4 ripe tomatoes, chopped

2 tablespoons herbes de Provence

Salt and white pepper, to taste

½ cup cream

½ cup chopped fresh parsley

Marinate the fish in a mixture of the wine and lemon juice for at least 2 hours, preferably overnight in the refrigerator.

In a frying pan, sauté the carrots, celery, onions, and garlic in the butter until tender. Remove the fish from the marinade. Set the fish aside. Add the marinade to the frying pan. Simmer until it is reduced by half. Add the fish broth, potatoes, tomatoes, and herbes de Provence. Simmer until the potatoes are almost cooked, about 10 minutes. Add the fish and cook for another 10 minutes, or just until the fish is cooked through. Season to taste. Just before serving, stir in the cream and garnish with the parsley.

MAKES 4 SERVINGS.

Caldo Verde Tradicional (Traditional Portuguese Kale Soup)

From start to finish, kale soup takes at least 3 hours to make, but it's definitely worth the effort. Kale has a mild, cabbagelike flavor and is full of vitamins and minerals. During summer and early fall, fresh kale, which is available at local produce stands, may be used instead of frozen kale. You'll need one head for this soup. The fresh kale should be rinsed well and chopped into bite-size pieces before being added to the soup. The Portuguese sausage called linguica, made from pork and flavored with a great deal of garlic, is another key ingredient. This soup is even more flavorful if made a day ahead of time and reheated.

---

1 soup bone, marrow bone, or beef shank bone

1 pound lean beef (sirloin tips or chuck meat)

1 large onion, chopped

1 tablespoon dried celery flakes

1/2 teaspoon salt

1/8 teaspoon freshly ground black pepper

1 pound linguica

1 (10-ounce) package frozen chopped kale, thawed

1 (19-ounce) can red kidney beans, rinsed and drained

1 (19-ounce) can chick peas, rinsed and drained

3 tablespoons tubettini macaroni

3 medium-size potatoes, peeled and cubed

2 beef bouillon cubes (optional)

Place soup bone, beef, onion, celery flakes, salt, and pepper in a large Dutch oven or stockpot. Add enough water to cover the meat by 1 inch. Bring to a boil, reduce heat, and simmer for 1 hour.

Cut the linguica into bite-size pieces and place them in a large saucepan. Cover with water. Bring to a boil, reduce heat, and simmer for 30 minutes. Drain off water. Add the linguica to the soup mixture. Simmer 1 hour.

Add the kale, red kidney beans, and chick peas. Bring to a boil, reduce heat, and simmer 30 minutes. Add the uncooked macaroni and potatoes. Bring to a boil, reduce heat, and simmer for 30 minutes.

Season to taste. If desired, you may add 2 beef bouillon cubes at this time, but if you do, omit the salt. If the soup is too thick, add water.

MAKES 8 SERVINGS.

Salads & Sandwiches

The Classic Rhode Island Salad

For decades the classic Rhode Island salad has been served in restaurants of all kinds, from diners to cafes, from family restaurants to fine-dining establishments. Home cooks found this to be an easy dish to replicate. In recent years the trend has been toward field greens and mesclun salad, garnished with everything from sun-dried tomatoes to chopped walnuts. But the classic Rhode Island salad continues to hang in there as a local favorite, whether you are dining in or out. And it thrives on iceberg lettuce.

1 head iceberg lettuce

1 ripe tomato, cut into wedges

1 cucumber, cut into slices

1 red or yellow onion, cut into
paper-thin slices

Black pitted olives, as needed

Pure olive oil, as needed

Red wine vinegar, as needed

Salt and freshly ground black
pepper, to taste

Using your hands, tear the iceberg lettuce into bite-size pieces and place in a large salad bowl. In a decorative fashion, place the tomato wedges, cucumber slices, onion slices, and black olives on top of the lettuce. Drizzle with a liberal amount of olive oil and vinegar. Season to taste with salt and a generous sprinkling of black pepper.

For the best flavor, allow the salad to sit at room temperature for about 1 hour before serving.

MAKES 8 SERVINGS.

Wedge Salad

Made famous by the well-respected Capital Grille national restaurant chain, which began in 1992 in Providence, the Wedge Salad has brought iceberg lettuce back onto the fine-dining scene and given it the respect it deserves. This is an easy salad to duplicate at home. The secret ingredient is the salad dressing. The bottled variety just won't do. *Note:* A nonhomogenized raw milk blue cheese such as Great Hill Blue from Great Hill Dairy in Marion, Massachusetts, is recommended.

---

1 head iceberg lettuce

**Blue Cheese Salad Dressing
(recipe follows)**

1 pound bacon, cooked until crisp

**1 large ripe tomato, cut into small
dice**

**Extra crumbled Roquefort or blue
cheese, as needed**

Cut the head of lettuce into 4 wedges of equal size. Cut the stem off each wedge. Place each wedge on a large salad plate. Drizzle with a generous amount of dressing. Sprinkle with plenty of crumbled pieces of crisp bacon, diced tomato, and a bit of extra crumbled blue cheese over the top.

BLUE CHEESE SALAD DRESSING

¾ cup mayonnaise

½ cup buttermilk

¼ cup crumbled blue cheese

½ teaspoon sugar

¼ teaspoon ground black pepper

¼ teaspoon garlic powder

⅛ teaspoon onion powder

⅛ teaspoon salt

In a bowl, combine all ingredients using a whisk or an electric mixer. Use as a salad dressing. Refrigerate any leftovers.

MAKES 4 SERVINGS.

Native Tomato Salad with Fresh Mozzarella

The secret to the best-tasting tomato salad is to use beautifully red, perfectly ripe, native tomatoes, which come tumbling out of Rhode Island gardens from July through September. The best tomatoes seem to be those grown along the seacoast, where the milder weather allows home gardeners to get their plants started early. Every spring there seems to be more and more varieties from which to choose. Early Girl (among the first to ripen) and Big Boy (a large, heavy tomato) are two of the most popular grown in Rhode Island. I recently planted Beefy Boy, Sun Sugar, and Whopper varieties down at my summer home in Narragansett with great results. Never, ever refrigerate tomatoes. That's the quickest way to make them lose their wonderful flavor. Fresh mozzarella, not the prepackaged kind, is available in Italian gourmet shops and in the international cheese sections of major supermarkets.

---

6 ripe tomatoes, cut into ¼-inch slices

2 scallions, thinly sliced on the diagonal

6 tablespoons extra-virgin olive oil

3 tablespoons balsamic vinegar

Salt and freshly ground black pepper, to taste

Fresh basil leaves, as needed

1 pound fresh mozzarella (optional)

Arrange the tomato slices on a large platter in a decorative pattern. In a bowl, combine the scallions, oil, vinegar, salt, and pepper. Mix well. Drizzle the dressing over the tomato slices.

Cut the fresh basil leaves into thin strips. Sprinkle the basil over the tomato slices.

If desired, alternate the tomato slices with ¼-inch slices of fresh mozzarella. The colors of the tomato, basil, and mozzarella are the colors of the Italian flag.

MAKES 4 SERVINGS.

Federal Hill Antipasto

Antipasto is Italian for "before the meal." It can be found in any Little Italy, from New York to San Francisco. But the Little Italy section of Providence—called Federal Hill—is considered one of the best in the nation, so it's only logical that this antipasto is one of the best. Atwells Avenue is the main street that runs through Federal Hill, and it is lined with dozens of Italian restaurants, all trying to outdo one another when it comes to authentic Italian food. This particular antipasto is a blend of the best those restaurants have to offer, representing various items from the regions of Italy, including many canned items that are ready to eat. Italian-American families in Rhode Island count stuffed mushrooms and preserved vegetables as their favorite antipasto items. An authentic antipasto is always artfully arranged and served at room temperature.

Prepare as large an antipasto as you wish. A small one serves two people; a large antipasto serves four to six; a very large antipasto serves up to twelve.

VENDA RAVIOLI, FEDERAL HILL

Lettuce, your choice

Thin strips of provolone cheese

Thin slices of salami, prosciutto, and pepperoni

A variety of olives, including cured black olives from Sicily and purple *gaeta* olives from Campania

Cherry tomatoes or tomato wedges

Marinated artichoke hearts

Italian tuna

Cannellini beans

Anchovies and sardines

A wedge of frittata (an Italian egg dish—see recipe on page 8)

Arancini (Sicilian rice balls—see recipe on page 163)

Hard-boiled eggs

Pickled onions

Pickled beets

Stuffed tomatoes and peppers

Slices of sweet and hot green peppers

Slices of roasted red peppers

Olive oil, as needed

Red wine vinegar, as needed

On a large platter, arrange a bed of lettuce. Arrange the rest of the ingredients on the lettuce. The various ingredients should be grouped attractively on the platter so that the antipasto is almost a miniature buffet from which you can choose what appeals to you the most. Drizzle with a good-quality olive oil and red wine vinegar.

Serve with crusty Italian bread for lunch or as a first course at dinner. Feel free to add or delete any ingredients to suit your taste.

Note: Olive oils and aged vinegars now have the status that was once given only to wines. Tastings are offered in gourmet shops, with experts explaining the difference between extra-virgin (the finest olive oil, having only 1 percent acid, ideal for drizzling on salads) to pure olive oil (recommended for use in cooking). Most of the olive oil in the United States is imported from Italy, Spain, and Greece.

MAKES 2 TO 12 SERVINGS, DEPENDING ON AMOUNTS USED.

The Real Deal

According to celebrity chef Mario Batali, Federal Hill in Providence is one of the very best Little Italy neighborhoods in the United States. "People speaking Italian on the streets and the piazza outside Venda Ravioli make Providence the real deal," he was quoted as saying in *Newsweek* magazine.

French-Style Tomato Salad

In late summer and early fall, when native tomatoes are at their peak, the French know best how to enhance their flavor—with a classic vinaigrette.

---

3 to 4 ripe tomatoes

1 teaspoon salt

¼ teaspoon brown mustard

⅛ teaspoon freshly ground black pepper

1 teaspoon chopped fresh parsley

1 teaspoon basil

1 teaspoon chopped onion

1 teaspoon minced hard-boiled egg (optional)

2 teaspoons red wine vinegar

2 to 3 teaspoons olive oil

Thinly slice the tomatoes, or cut them into wedges. Place the tomatoes in a large bowl.

In a separate bowl, combine the remaining ingredients. Mix well. Refrigerate the dressing for 1 hour before serving.

Pour chilled dressing over tomatoes.

MAKES 4 SERVINGS.

The Not-So-Terrible Tomato

Once summer arrives, so do the sweet, juicy tomatoes that are grown in Rhode Island. The rest of the year we have to depend on shipments from the southern and western parts of the nation. According to the Rhode Island Division of Agriculture, in colonial times it took a long time for tomatoes to catch on in Rhode Island because they were believed to be poisonous. One skeptical man stood on the steps of a courthouse and ate several tomatoes in full view of a crowd that had gathered to watch him die. When he didn't, the local undertaker lost a customer, and tomatoes began a steady climb as a popular and versatile food.

Kidney Bean Salad

Bowls of kidney bean salad are offered at many Rhode Island restaurants that have a colonial atmosphere or in quaint taverns where you can enjoy a cocktail or two. Spread on a firm cracker, this salad is positively addictive.

2 cans (16 ounces each) kidney beans, rinsed

½ cup sweet relish

½ cup mayonnaise

1 tablespoon sugar

2 tablespoons dry mustard

1 teaspoon salt

½ cup minced onions

½ teaspoon white pepper

3 large garlic cloves, minced

2 tablespoons chopped fresh parsley (optional)

Combine all ingredients in a serving bowl. This salad tastes even better if made a day ahead. Store in the refrigerator. Serve with firm crackers, such as Triscuits.

MAKES 8 SERVINGS.

Potato Salad, Italian-Style

Rhode Island is known for its potatoes—the leading crop in the state—grown mostly in the southeastern region, especially in the Tiverton–Little Compton area. Italians who immigrated to Rhode Island created this simple summer salad recipe. French immigrants did much the same, but they added cooked green beans to the mix. Either way, it's a refreshing change from the usual American potato salad that is laden with mayonnaise.

4 cups peeled potatoes, cut into bite-size chunks

½ cup chopped onions

½ cup olive oil

½ cup red wine vinegar

1 garlic clove, minced

Salt and freshly ground black pepper, to taste

½ pound cooked green beans (optional)

2 tablespoons minced fresh parsley

Parmesan cheese (optional)

In a stockpot of boiling water, cook the potatoes until tender. Drain and place the potatoes in a large bowl. While the potatoes are still warm, add the onions, olive oil, vinegar, and garlic. Season with salt and pepper. If desired, carefully mix in the green beans. Mix gently. Cover and set aside for at least 30 minutes to allow the flavors to marry. Just before serving, sprinkle in the minced parsley. Italian-American cooks also sprinkle a little Parmesan cheese on this salad just before serving.

MAKES 8 SERVINGS.

Dandelion Salad

Years ago the elders in Italian families were famous for making dandelion salads, but only with young and tender greens. Today this northern Italian dish is finding its way onto the menus of upscale restaurants. This is how my *nonna* made it. The dandelion greens that didn't make it to the salad bowl were used to make dandelion wine. See page 240 if you want to make dandelion wine.

1 pound young dandelion greens

3 tablespoons oil

1 tablespoon red wine vinegar

¼ teaspoon salt, more or less to taste

1 teaspoon freshly ground black pepper

2 hard-boiled eggs, chopped

1 garlic clove, minced

4 anchovy fillets, chopped

Remove the roots and tough stems from the dandelions. Wash the dandelion greens thoroughly. Drain on paper towels. When dry, place the greens in a large bowl.

In a small bowl, combine the remaining ingredients. Mix well, then pour over the greens. Toss and serve immediately.

MAKES 4 SERVINGS.

Farmers' Markets

Rhode Island farmers' markets are open one or two days a week, generally from May through October, in every region of the state, even on Block Island. One of the best is held every Saturday morning on the campus of the University of Rhode Island in the village of Kingston. There's always a good turnout, even when it rains. Depending on the season, there are plants, produce, artisan breads from a local bakery, kettle-cooked popcorn, and much more. As summer begins to fade, the market is ablaze with the colors of fall—orange pumpkins and yellowed corn stalks. Everyone seems sad to see the season come to an end.

Antonio's Snail Salad

Just about any fresh fish market in Rhode Island sells conch snails that have been cleaned and are ready to be cooked, or you can buy them precooked. Popular with the Italians and Portuguese, snail salad is easy to assemble, even when made from scratch, but this is one dish that needs to sit for a couple of days in the refrigerator for the best taste. Snail salad should be tender and pungent. This recipe from Antonio DePetrillo of Johnston is no exception to that rule. Tony is retired and loves to create recipes for his neighbors, friends, and relatives. He's such an avid cook, he has a Web site (www.pizzarecipes.com) with hundreds of recipes.

---

1 medium-size red onion, chopped

1 (6-ounce) can black olives, sliced

3 stalks celery, chopped

2 tablespoons dried parsley

½ teaspoon salt

½ tablespoon black pepper

½ cup olive oil

1 cup white vinegar

4 to 5 pounds cooked snails, sliced thin

Lettuce, as needed

In a large container combine the red onion, black olives, celery, parsley, salt, pepper, olive oil, and white vinegar. Cover and marinate overnight in the refrigerator.

Using a small plastic netting scrubber, scrub all the black off the snails, and rinse the snails often in cold water. Once all the blackened portions are removed, cut off the feelers and any excess parts. Slice the snails very thin either by hand or with a slicing machine, if you have one. Place the sliced snails in a container, cover, and refrigerate overnight.

Combine the sliced snails with the marinated mixture. Cover and store in the refrigerator for two days. Stir the mixture two to three times a day.

Just before serving, drain the marinated snail mixture with a slotted ladle or through a colander. Serve the snail salad cold on a bed of lettuce.

MAKES 12 SERVINGS.

Grilled Lobster Salad

Chef Wayne Gibson, who has left his culinary calling card at several top Rhode Island restaurants, uses lobsters freshly caught in Narragansett Bay when he makes this salad. Fresh lobsters are available in fish markets throughout the state, and they can be purchased right off the lobster boats that pull into Point Judith almost every afternoon, especially in the summer. The average American lobster, also sometimes referred to as the Maine lobster, weighs between 1 and 2 pounds. If you have your choice of lobsters, select a female—its wider body contains more of the highly desirable tail meat.

---

2 live lobsters, about 1¼ pounds each

Olive oil, as needed

Grated zest of ½ lemon

Chopped fresh parsley, as needed

Assorted salad greens, as needed

Tarragon Salad Dressing (recipe follows)

Add the live lobsters to a large stockpot of boiling water. Poach 2 to 3 minutes, remove from the stockpot, and split the lobsters in half lengthwise.

Brush the cut surface of each lobster half with olive oil. Place cut-side down on a hot grill for a few moments, then turn and sprinkle with lemon zest and fresh parsley. Grill until heated through, about 2 to 3 minutes, depending on the intensity of the grill.

Arrange the greens on 4 salad plates. Place grilled lobster half on top of salad greens. Drizzle with tarragon salad dressing (this is easy to do if you put the dressing in a squeeze-type plastic bottle usually used for mustard or ketchup).

TARRAGON SALAD DRESSING

4 eggs

2 teaspoons sugar

Juice from 2 lemons

2 tablespoons minced fresh tarragon

2 cups salad oil or olive oil

Salt and freshly ground black pepper, to taste

Whisk the eggs in a saucepan set over another saucepan of simmering water, or in a double boiler. Beat them just until hot but not scrambled, and then immediately remove the egg pan from heat. This procedure is intended to kill bacteria; raw eggs should not be used in salad dressings.

Transfer the eggs to a clean bowl. Whisk in the sugar, lemon juice, and tarragon. Whisk in the oil, adding a little at a time, until a stiff mixture forms. If too thick, whisk in a little cold water. Season to taste with salt and pepper. Any leftover dressing can be stored in the refrigerator up to one week.

MAKES 4 SERVINGS.

Spiedino di Gamberetti (Grilled Shrimp Salad)

One of the most popular menu items at Salvatore's Caffe inside Venda Ravioli, an Italian food emporium on Federal Hill, *Spiedino di Gamberetti* is a grilled shrimp salad, with the shrimp served atop mesclun greens dressed in a lemony vinaigrette. This salad was created by Chef Salvatore Cefaliello.

½ cup freshly squeezed lemon juice

1 cup extra-virgin olive oil

Salt and freshly ground black pepper, to taste

24 extra-large shrimp, peeled, with tails left on

Juice from 2 lemons

2 garlic cloves, minced

2 tablespoons chopped fresh parsley

Salt and freshly ground black pepper, to taste

Mesclun greens, enough for 4 servings

To make the lemon vinaigrette, combine in a glass bowl or large glass measuring cup the ½ cup lemon juice, olive oil, salt, and pepper to taste. Mix well. Set aside.

While you prepare the grill, marinate the shrimp in a glass bowl containing the juice from 2 lemons, the minced garlic, half of the chopped parsley, salt, and pepper to taste. Place the shrimp on the grill for just a few minutes, turning often until they are pink on both sides and cooked through. Transfer the shrimp from the grill to a plate.

Dress the mesclun greens in a large glass bowl with the lemon vinaigrette. Divide the greens equally on 4 salad plates. Place 6 grilled shrimp on top of the greens on each plate. Garnish each plate with the remaining chopped parsley.

MAKES 4 SERVINGS.

Venda Ravioli

Just say "Venda Ravioli" in Providence and people nod, almost with reverence. Considered one of the best Italian gourmet stores in all of New England, it's located at 275 Atwells Avenue, on Federal Hill, overlooking DePasquale Plaza, where Italian music fills the air amid your choice of sophisticated restaurants and casual cafes.

Venda Ravioli offers a real slice of life, Italian-style. This bright and busy store, open seven days a week, is filled to the brim with authentic Italian products. The colorful take-out counter offers large trays of prepared specialties, like stuffed artichokes, lasagna, meatballs, veal chops, frittata, *arancini* (Sicilian rice balls), chicken Marsala. A tempting array of cold Italian salads draws you farther into the shop, past a display of everything you will ever need for entertaining at home—espresso makers, linens, kitchen gadgets, handmade ceramic dishes, and more—all imported from Italy.

Within Venda Ravioli is an authentic Italian cafe, serving lunch only on a daily basis. The handwritten menu proposes exquisite delights—perfectly cooked asparagus wrapped with prosciutto and topped with shavings of the finest Parmigiano-Reggiano cheese; the freshest salads imaginable; and pasta dishes like Mama used to make. Watch the humble Chef Salvatore Cefaliello and his talented staff at work in their open kitchen. At the authentic espresso bar, customers savor cappuccino or perhaps some Italian chocolates, biscotti, or gelato (ice cream).

Beyond the appealing butcher's counter is a vast array of exotic imported olives, then aisles of Italian goodies, and a full wall of refrigerator cases holding more than thirty kinds of fresh and frozen pasta—Venda Ravioli's signature food. They've been making pasta in the old-world tradition for more than seventy years. Jumbo stuffed shells, manicotti, tricolored egg noodles, tortellini, tortelloni, agnolotti, angel hair, and lobster ravioli are just some of the offerings.

Just when you think it can't get any better, Venda Ravioli goes over the top with its international cheese counter, a cornucopia of more than 200 extraordinary cheeses. Sign up for the Cheese of the Month Club to enjoy in-store cooking demonstrations, recipes, and a discount on the featured cheeses.

When New York restaurant critic and cookbook author John Mariani last visited Venda Ravioli, he savored every moment and declared, "This is just like being in Italy."

Raspberry Vinaigrette

Every summer our Rhode Island backyards are lush with ripe raspberries, begging to be picked. This vinaigrette can be used as a salad dressing or as a marinade for chicken that is to be grilled.

RASPBERRY VINEGAR

1 cup fresh raspberries

2 cups white wine vinegar

VINAIGRETTE

2 cups homemade or canned
   chicken broth

1 cup raspberry vinegar

1/4 cup olive oil

2 tablespoons cornstarch

1 tablespoon water

2 tablespoons chopped fresh herbs,
   your choice

2 large garlic cloves, minced

1 to 2 teaspoons sugar, or to taste

To make the raspberry vinegar, gently rinse and drain the raspberries. Pour them into a large glass bottle. Add the white wine vinegar. Tightly cover the bottle and store it in a cool dark place for 2 weeks before using the vinegar.

To make the vinaigrette, combine the chicken broth, 1 cup of the raspberry vinegar, and olive oil in a small saucepan. Cook over medium-high heat for 2 to 3 minutes. Combine the cornstarch and water to make a slurry. Gradually whisk the slurry into the saucepan. Reduce heat to a simmer. Continue cooking for 5 minutes, stirring constantly. Remove from heat and allow to cool. Stir in the fresh herbs, garlic, and sugar. Cover and refrigerate.

MAKES 3 TO 4 CUPS.

Pesto Vinaigrette

When your basil plants are flourishing, make this vinaigrette. It's a terrific dressing for romaine lettuce. It also can be used to marinate chicken or pork.

½ cup olive oil

1 garlic clove

2 cups freshly picked basil leaves

2 tablespoons pignoli (pine nuts)

1 cup grated Parmesan cheese

Salt, to taste

¼ cup red wine vinegar

¼ cup water

In a food processor or blender, combine the olive oil and garlic. Puree until the garlic is minced. Add the fresh basil, pignoli, Parmesan cheese, and salt (in batches, if necessary). Puree until smooth. Transfer mixture to a glass container with a lid. Stir in the vinegar and water. Mix well. Cover and refrigerate.

MAKES 2 CUPS.

CEDAR EDGE FARM,
WYOMING

Pepper and Egg Sandwich

Ever since I was a little girl, I can remember pepper and egg sandwiches being made by my father in what was usually considered my mother's kitchen. For some reason she refused to make these particular sandwiches. Dad either had to go to his favorite diner or make it himself. This is how he made it.

¼ cup olive oil

1 medium-size onion, sliced

2 green peppers, cut into strips

2 garlic cloves, minced

Salt and freshly ground black pepper, to taste

4 eggs

¼ cup grated Parmesan cheese

4 slices Italian bread or 2 torpedo rolls

In a frying pan, heat the oil over medium heat. Add the sliced onions, peppers, garlic, salt, and pepper. Cook, stirring occasionally, until the peppers are tender, approximately 15 minutes.

In a small bowl, combine the eggs, Parmesan cheese, salt, and pepper. Beat until well mixed. Add the egg mixture to the peppers in the skillet. Cook, stirring occasionally, until the eggs are set. Serve on slices of fresh Italian bread or in a torpedo (grinder) roll.

MAKES 2 SANDWICHES.

Talking the Talk

The way many Rhode Islanders talk is about as unique as the food we eat here in the Ocean State. We like to drink *kaw-fee* milk when we eat our *grindahs,* or when we go out for *weeniz.* If we're in the mood for drinks, we take our *cah* to get to our favorite *bah.* We also like to go to *dinna* down by the *oh-shin* where we get *steemas* and *chowdah.* One of our favorite *sangwiches* is *sauce-each* and *peppiz,* which is always good to serve family and friends at *suppa* or when you have a *potty.* And *not for nuttin,* we always have a *wicket* good time.

The Classic Rhode Island Grinder

The classic Rhode Island grinder, which has even been dubbed "the Sinatra" in more than one local deli, features the finest Italian cold cuts dressed with olive oil and red wine vinegar. If the olive oil runs out of the sandwich and down your arm, you're holding a classic Rhode Island grinder.

1 soft torpedo roll, sliced in half lengthwise

Olive oil and red wine vinegar, as needed

1 small onion, sliced very thin

1 ripe tomato, sliced thin

Mixed greens, shredded

2 thin slices Italian ham, salami, and mortadella

2 thin slices provolone cheese

Brush the inside of the torpedo roll with a generous amount of olive oil and a drizzle of red wine vinegar. On one side of the roll, place a single layer of thin onions slices, then a layer of tomato slices. Add as much mixed greens as desired. Continue to place layers of Italian meats and cheese on the roll. Top the filled side of the torpedo roll with the other side of the roll. Press firmly together. Slice in half at an angle.

MAKES 1 SANDWICH.

Grinders and Subs

Sandwiches aren't just sandwiches in Rhode Island. They are sometimes called "grinders" or "subs" (short for submarine) and are often made on "torpedo" rolls, a small loaf of soft white bread that slightly resembles a torpedo. The rolls are split lengthwise and then filled with everything from sliced meats, cheeses, iceberg lettuce, tomatoes, onions, peppers, and pickles. Some of the most popular versions include a meatball grinder, stuffed with whole meatballs and tomato sauce, and a veal parmigiana sub, filled with a breaded veal cutlet that has been fried and topped with cheese and tomato sauce. In other parts of the country, these sandwiches are called heroes; perhaps because one must be a hero to eat such a sandwich. One can only wonder why in Philadelphia they are called hoagies, and in the deep South, they are known as po'boys.

Rhode Island Grinder Sauce

Spike's Junkyard Dogs is a Rhode Island original—a chain of casual restaurants selling award-winning hot dogs of every kind. We're talking 100 percent all-beef jumbo hot dogs served in a hot, soft, French roll, not those little wieners in fluffy white buns sold at New York Systems. The first Spike's, at 723 Thayer Street in Providence, in the College Hill area, has been around since 1994, serving hot dogs to many a starving student. Spike is a real-life English bulldog that has become a Rhode Island icon through his public appearances at the various Spike's, including other spots in Providence and the suburbs. Spike's signature hot dog—the Junkyard Dog—is topped with tomatoes, green onions, brown mustard, a pickle spear, and a hot pepper. If you can eat six—and keep them down—you're made a member of the Kennel Club, with your photo on the wall and your very own Spike's T-shirt. (The record, by the way, is seventeen.) Here is Spike's original recipe for the sauce they put on their Rhode Island Grinder Dog.

¼ **cup diced onion**

¼ **cup chopped dill pickles**

4 plum tomatoes, chopped

¼ **teaspoon salt**

½ **teaspoon freshly ground black pepper**

⅛ **teaspoon hot pepper flakes**

1 teaspoon garlic powder

1 teaspoon oregano

½ **cup salad oil**

2 tablespoons red wine vinegar

In a mixing bowl, combine the diced onion, chopped dill pickles, and chopped plum tomatoes. Add the remaining ingredients. Mix well, using a rubber spatula to scrape down the sides of the bowl. Refrigerate in a tightly sealed container.

MAKES ABOUT 3 CUPS.

The New York System

If you've never done so, find the courage to enter one of the many urban luncheonettes that have worked the New York System into their name. The quintessential choice is the Olneyville New York System restaurant in the grim Olneyville section of Providence, where 4-inch wieners cook slowly all day on a greasy griddle before being served in a pillowy soft, steamed roll of white bread. New York System restaurants are lunch-counter eateries, and they tend to be open very late at night. New York System wieners often come to mind when you are hit with "the late-night munchies."

The term *New York System* dates back to the early 1900s, when the wiener (also known as the wienie, weenie, weiner, hot dog, dog, frankfurter, frank, and red hot) became popular in New York, especially at Coney Island. This was America's first fast food, and it quickly spread north to the city of Providence and elsewhere. Strangely enough, the New York System can be found in all parts of Rhode Island but nowhere in New York.

The New York System is not only an establishment that sells wieners. It is also the way the wieners are ritualistically prepared and served. And it is not for the faint of heart. To begin with, the busy "griddle man" at any New York System restaurant seems to almost always be wearing a dirty apron. It's nearly impossible to be spotlessly clean when the orders start coming and the sauce starts flying.

Since these wieners are small, it's not unusual for someone to order more than one. (I once saw my brother eat a dozen!) With the order taken, the griddle man places the necessary number of rolls on the inside part of his outstretched arm. This is dubiously called "up the arm." With his free hand, he then quickly places a hot wiener in each roll, then ladles on the meat sauce, the true hallmark of the New York System wiener. The sauce resembles watered-down chili. If you want yours "all the way," the tender wieners are then topped with chili sauce, mustard, chopped raw onions, and celery salt.

For the full Rhode Island experience, you must wash down your wieners with a glass of ice-cold coffee milk or a coffee cabinet (see the Drinks section).

OLNEYVILLE NEW YORK SYSTEM

Rhode Island Wiener Sauce

This sauce, which is poured on top of the small wieners sold at New York Systems throughout Rhode Island, is sometimes referred to as the Coney Island Wiener Sauce because it originated in Coney Island. Do not confuse it with the Rhode Island Grinder Sauce. But both will wake up your taste buds.

½ pound ground beef

1 medium-size onion, chopped

1 (8-ounce) can tomato sauce

1 tablespoon chili powder

½ teaspoon Worcestershire sauce

Cinnamon, to taste

In a large frying pan, cook the ground beef and the onion until tender. Add the tomato sauce, chili powder, and Worcestershire sauce. Add cinnamon to taste. Keeps 3 to 5 days in refrigerator.

MAKES 5 CUPS.

SEAVIEW CAFE, MATUNUCK

Dinner

CHAMPLIN'S
SEAFOOD,
POINT JUDITH

Appetizers

Smoked Bluefish Pâté

Narragansett Bay is known for its ferocious bluefish, a great catch in sport fishing that has a strong flavor. Bluefish migrate in schools along the Atlantic coast, often attacking other schools of fish in a feeding frenzy. Bluefish does not freeze well, so it is usually available at fairly low prices in markets in the vicinity of where the fish have been landed. You can easily make a bluefish pâté by combining a pound of smoked bluefish with cream cheese, horseradish, and a little salt. The following recipe is more involved but worth the effort. It comes from Martha Murphy of Narragansett, whose husband was a commercial fisherman. Whenever they throw a summer cocktail party, you can be sure their guests are looking for the bluefish pâté to spread on crisp crackers.

1 tablespoon olive oil

1 tablespoon butter

¼ cup chopped onion

1 cup sliced mushrooms

2 peppercorns

1 whole clove

1 bay leaf

3 juniper berries, crushed (optional)

¼ cup brandy

½ pound smoked bluefish, skin removed

5 ounces goat cheese

2 tablespoons light cream

Crisp crackers

In a large, heavy skillet, heat the oil and butter over medium heat. Add the onions, mushrooms, peppercorns, cloves, bay leaf, and, if desired, juniper berries. Cook, stirring occasionally, until the onions are tender and have golden brown edges. Pour in the brandy and continue to cook until the liquid has reduced by half. Remove from the heat, and allow to cool. Remove and discard the bay leaf.

Place the mixture in the bowl of a food processor. Break apart the smoked bluefish into chunks, and add it to the mixture. Add the goat cheese in bits and the light cream. Pulse to blend completely, scraping down the sides of the bowl with a spatula. When the mixture is smooth, transfer it to a small serving bowl. Cover and refrigerate for at least 1 hour before serving. Serve with crisp crackers.

MAKES ABOUT 2 CUPS.

Paulie's Calamari

It just might be that Rhode Islanders consume more squid than any other state. Almost every restaurant offers squid on its menu, sometimes in more than one preparation. When the squid is cleaned, the tube-like body is sliced into rings. The most popular form of squid is called calamari—fried squid rings served usually with peperoncino, the Italian version of the chile pepper. This is one of the best calamari dishes in the entire state, from Paul Shire, chef-owner of Oak in Providence. Be careful not to overcook the squid, or it will become tough and rubbery.

SAUCE

1 tablespoon olive oil

1 to 2 teaspoons minced garlic

$1/4$ cup sliced peperoncino, or to taste

$1/8$ cup roasted red peppers

1 tablespoon sliced black olives

2 tablespoons fresh basil, cut into thin strips

1 cup white wine

1 cup clam juice

1 tablespoon butter

CALAMARI

1 cup all-purpose flour

$1/4$ cup cornmeal

1 teaspoon cayenne

Salt and freshly ground black pepper, to taste

4 cups fresh squid (tubes only), sliced into rings

2 cups vegetable oil

First make the sauce. In a frying pan, heat the olive oil, add the garlic, and fry until golden brown. Add the sliced peperoncino, roasted red peppers, black olives, and basil. Add the white wine and clam juice. Bring to a boil and reduce by more than half, about 20 to 30 minutes. Remove from the heat and add the butter. Keep warm until the calamari is done.

In a bowl, combine the flour, cornmeal, cayenne, salt, and pepper. Toss the squid rings in the flour mixture, coating well. Heat the 2 cups vegetable oil in a deep frying pan. Fry the squid rings in the oil for 3 to 4 minutes, or until golden brown and crispy. Remove the calamari from the oil, drain on paper towels, then place in a serving bowl, and toss with the sauce.

MAKES 4 SERVINGS.

Swordfish Dumplings with Cilantro Sauce

Chef Jean-Claude Bourlier, who cooked for the stars in Los Angeles for almost a quarter century and then went to the General Stanton Inn in Charlestown, developed this appetizer recipe to make use of the fresh swordfish caught in the waters off Block Island. The swordfish filling is enclosed in wonton skins, all-purpose wrappers used for all sorts of appetizers. Packages of paper-thin wonton skins are available in the Asian produce food section of major supermarkets.

12 ounces fresh swordfish, cubed
or cut into bite-size chunks

3 egg whites

2 cups chopped scallions

2 pounds spinach, steamed and
chopped

1 fresh ginger root

4 water chestnuts, chopped

3 ounces chopped shiitake mushrooms (to make ⅓ cup)

2 tablespoons rice wine vinegar

2 tablespoons soy sauce

1 teaspoon dry sherry

2 tablespoons cornstarch

48 wonton skins

Cilantro Sauce (recipe follows)

Combine the swordfish and egg whites by hand or in a food processor. Add the egg whites, scallions, spinach, ginger root, water chestnuts, mushrooms, rice wine vinegar, soy sauce, and sherry. Set aside.

Place 2 teaspoons of the filling in the center of each wonton skin. Moisten the edges with water and fold in half to form a dumpling. Be careful not to flatten the filling. Press the edges together, forming a half moon. Moisten each end and pinch the moistened ends together, making a little cap. Place on a sheet of waxed paper lightly dusted with cornstarch. Refrigerate until ready to cook.

In a stockpot, bring 4 quarts of water to a vigorous boil. Add the dumplings to the pot, giving a gentle stir. When the dumplings float to the surface (in about 3 minutes), gently lift the dumplings into a colander to drain. Transfer to a serving dish and baste lightly with the Cilantro Sauce.

CILANTRO SAUCE

½ cup peanut oil

½ cup rice wine vinegar

¼ cup soy sauce

½ teaspoon chili oil

2 egg whites

2 bunches cilantro

In a blender or food processor, combine all the ingredients until creamy. Set aside until needed. Do not refrigerate before use.

MAKES 48 DUMPLINGS.

Rhode Island: A Small Wonder

Rhode Island is the smallest state in the Union. How small is that? Statistically, it is only 1,214 square miles of land. In other words, it would take 200 states the size of Rhode Island to equal the size of Texas. There's even an old saying down south that Texas could wear Rhode Island as a watch fob.

As the crow flies from west to east, it's a mere 42 miles from the state's border with Connecticut to its border with Massachusetts, from the tip of Victorian Watch Hill to bucolic Little Compton. North to south, that same crow would fly a whopping 48 miles.

Every resident of the state lives either along the coastline or within a 30-mile car ride to the water, whether it's tranquil Narragansett Bay or the mighty Atlantic Ocean. Rhode Island may be small, but it has more than 400 miles of shoreline because of the way Narragansett Bay—with its thirty-eight islands—divides the state nearly in half.

The state population in the 2000 census was 1,048,319. Many cities in America have much higher populations. Providence is the largest city in the state with a population of approximately 173,000.

Rhode Island may be the smallest state in the Union, but its official name is a mouthful—State of Rhode Island and Providence Plantations.

Crab Cakes with Roasted Corn Salsa

Inexpensive fresh crabs are available year-round in Rhode Island. Crabmeat left over from a crab boil, similar to a New England clambake, can easily be turned into crab cakes. Chef Brian Mansfield at the Mooring Restaurant in Newport serves his crab cakes with a salsa made primarily with native sweet corn that's been roasted in the oven. If you find picking the meat from crabs to be too time consuming, you can purchase lump crabmeat at most fish markets. There are more than 4,400 species of crab, all edible. The rock crab listed for the following recipe is an East Coast variety that lives among rocks and in deep water. The recipe also calls for Old Bay Seasoning, the brand name for a unique herb and spice blend that's been an Atlantic coastline seafood staple since 1939. The seasoning contains a robust blend of celery salt, mustard, red pepper, bay leaves, cloves, allspice, ginger, mace, cardamom, cinnamon, and paprika.

---

2 pounds rock crabmeat

½ cup mayonnaise

2 whole eggs

½ tablespoon Old Bay Seasoning

1 teaspoon kosher salt

1 teaspoon freshly ground black pepper

1 teaspoon dry mustard

1 teaspoon freshly chopped parsley

Dry bread crumbs, as needed

Olive oil, as needed for frying

Roasted Native Corn Salsa (recipe follows)

Preheat oven to 350 degrees.

Lightly squeeze the crabmeat to remove excess moisture.

In a bowl, combine the mayonnaise, eggs, seasonings, and parsley. Whisk until blended. Fold in the crabmeat and combine thoroughly. Add the bread crumbs in small increments and combine just until the mixture is lightly bound together. (Too many bread crumbs will result in a doughy cake.) Portion into 3-ounce cakes.

In a frying pan, heat the olive oil. There should be just enough to coat the bottom of the pan. Sear the crab cakes on both sides to golden brown. Place the crab cakes in the oven for 5 minutes before serving. Serve with corn salsa.

ROASTED NATIVE CORN SALSA

12 ears fresh local sweet corn, shucked

¼ cup olive oil, or enough to coat the corn

½ tablespoon kosher salt

½ tablespoon freshly ground black pepper

½ cup diced red onion

½ cup diced red pepper

1 tablespoon chopped fresh parsley

¼ cup red wine vinegar

½ cup olive oil

Preheat oven to 350 degrees.

In a stockpot filled with boiling salted water, cook the corn on the cob until tender. Remove the corn from the water and allow it to cool. Shave off the kernels from the cob using a large chef's knife. Toss the corn in ¼ cup olive oil to coat, then season with kosher salt and pepper. Place the corn in an even layer on a baking sheet. Roast the corn in the oven until golden brown. Remove and allow to cool.

In a bowl, combine the roasted corn, onion, pepper, parsley, vinegar, and ½ cup olive oil. Serve with crab cakes. Makes 4 cups of salsa. You can refrigerate leftover salsa for up to 5 days.

MAKES 12 CRAB CAKES.

Rhode Island Corn

In Rhode Island from July through September, you can purchase fresh local corn that is classified as "sweet," "super sweet," and "ultra sweet." The traditional types of sweet corn lose sweetness and freshness quickly after being harvested. The sweeter varieties stay sweeter for longer periods of time. The local varieties include Silver Queen and Sweet Sue (sweet), Kandy Korn and Double Delight (super sweet), and Summer Sweet (ultra sweet).

Lobster and Corn Fritters

An upscale appetizer with down-home ingredients, these fritters have Rhode Island written all over them, from the yellow cornmeal to the native corn to the lobster caught in Narragansett Bay. Wayne Gibson created these fritters when he was the executive chef at the Castle Hill Inn & Resort in Newport.

1½ cups yellow cornmeal

2½ cups all-purpose flour

2 tablespoons baking powder

2 teaspoons kosher salt

1 teaspoon freshly ground black pepper

½ teaspoon cayenne pepper

4 eggs

1 cup milk

1 cup buttermilk

1 red pepper, cut into ¼-inch dice

1 chile poblano (or other mild green chile), cut into ¼-inch dice

2 sweet onions, cut into ¼-inch dice

1 bunch scallions, sliced fine

2 cups fresh native sweet corn kernels, blanched

3 tablespoons butter

2 cups diced lobster meat, well drained

Vegetable oil, as needed for frying

Combine the cornmeal, flour, baking powder, salt, black pepper, and cayenne pepper, and sift together into a large mixing bowl. In a separate bowl, whisk together the eggs, milk, and buttermilk. Add the liquid mixture to the dry mixture. Stir with a wooden spoon until well mixed, with no dry lumps.

In a large frying pan, sauté the red pepper, chile, onions, scallions, and corn kernels in the butter. Add these cooked vegetables and the diced lobster meat to the batter. Drop by the tablespoonful into a frying pan containing 2 inches of hot (350 degrees) oil. Fry until golden brown on the outside, light and fluffy inside. Drain on paper towels before serving.

MAKES 32 FRITTERS.

Swamp Yankee Quahog Fritters

Just what is a swamp Yankee? Some Rhode Islanders claim the term was first applied to Anglo-Saxon farmers in South County. Others maintain a swamp Yankee is one from poor origins, a person who lived in the woodland swamps and who became fiercely independent, stubborn, and generally unaware of what was going on in the outside world. But one thing for sure—swamp Yankees know how to cook. You can cut this recipe in half, or you can freeze half the batter for later use.

---

2 sleeves packaged butter-flavored crackers (such as Ritz), ground into crumbs

2 sleeves packaged saltine crackers, ground into crumbs

2 cups ground quahogs

$1/2$ cup chopped onion

1 tablespoon garlic powder

$1/4$ cup grated Parmesan cheese

$1/4$ cup dried parsley flakes

1 teaspoon dried oregano

2 eggs

2 cups clam juice

Combine all ingredients. Mix until the batter is smooth. Grease a frying pan with nonstick spray or cooking oil and heat. Drop 1 tablespoon of batter for each fritter into the pan, and cook on both sides until deep golden brown. Each fritter should be about $3/8$ inch thick.

MAKES ABOUT 50 FRITTERS.

Swamp Yankee Days

A festive, old-fashioned weekend of food, crafts, and music strictly for local folk—called "Swamp Yankee Days"—takes place every year in late June in the South County village of Ashaway, sponsored by the Chariho Rotary Club. *Chariho* sounds like a wonderful Native American word, but it really stands for three South County towns: Charlestown, Richmond, and Hopkinton. Ashaway is part of Hopkinton. Perennial entertainment includes the Old Fiddlers Club of Rhode Island and live country music from Skinny Mulligan and the RPM Band; an antique car show; and the cornmeal grinding exhibit. The Rotary Club provides all the food, with members cooking hot dogs, burgers, fries, clam chowder, and clam cakes. A right neighborly time.

Clams Casino

Clams Casino was "invented" by Julius Keller, the maître d' in the original Casino next to the seaside Towers in Narragansett. The Casino burned to the ground in 1905 and was rebuilt with a grand restaurant, but then burned again in 1956. Clams Casino is now a classic Rhode Island appetizer, appearing on almost every restaurant menu and at the same time a popular dish with home cooks who want to impress their guests. Clams Casino resemble the beloved stuffed quahog but are generally made with the smaller littleneck or cherrystone clam. Topping it with bacon is what makes it different. My Italian cousins who have cottages on Hog Island dig their own quahogs and make garlic-loaded batches of clams Casino as appetizers, followed by mounds of spaghetti with clam sauce, chicken cacciatore, and garlic bread.

---

12 cherrystone or littleneck clams

2 tablespoons butter

¼ cup minced onions

¼ cup minced green pepper

1 cup seasoned bread crumbs, or more if needed

¼ cup minced fresh flat-leaf parsley

Freshly ground black pepper, to taste

1 teaspoon anchovy paste (optional)

4 strips bacon, cut into 24 equal pieces

Rock salt, as needed

Lemon wedges, for garnish

Split open the clams over a bowl, being careful to save as much juice as possible. Remove the clam meat. Cut the clam meat in half. Return half of the clam meat to each half shell.

In a small saucepan, melt the butter. Add the onions and green pepper. Cook until tender. Add the reserved clam juice, bread crumbs, parsley, black pepper, and, if desired, anchovy paste to make a moist stuffing. Mix well. Set aside.

In a frying pan, cook the bacon for 1 to 2 minutes. Do not overcook.

Place a teaspoon of the stuffing on top of the raw clam in each half shell. Top with a piece of bacon. Set the clam shells on a bed of rock salt in a large shallow baking pan. Place the pan in the middle of the oven. Broil for 10 minutes, or until the bacon is crisp. Serve with lemon wedges on the side.

MAKES 24 APPETIZERS.

Red Rooster Tavern Clam Cakes

Until it closed a while back, the venerable Red Rooster Tavern in North Kingstown was known for satisfying generations of families with traditional New England fare. So it's not surprising that new owners plan to reopen this legendary restaurant. These clam cakes were one of the Red Rooster's most popular dishes. In Rhode Island clam cakes are almost always served alongside a bowl of clam chowder.

$2\frac{1}{2}$ cups flour

1 teaspoon sugar

$\frac{1}{2}$ teaspoon salt

4 teaspoons baking powder

3 eggs

$\frac{1}{2}$ cup milk

1 cup clam broth

2 cups chopped quahogs

Oil, as needed for deep-frying

In a large bowl, mix all the ingredients except the oil until smooth. In a deep fryer or heavy saucepan, heat the oil to 350 degrees. Pour the batter into the oil a tablespoonful at a time. Cook until each clam cake is golden on all sides. Drain on paper towels. Keep warm in a low oven until all the clam cakes are cooked.

MAKES 24 SERVINGS.

The Legendary Normand Leclair

Normand J. Leclair has been in the restaurant business in Rhode Island since 1952. He understands the typical Rhode Islander better than most restaurateurs. The founder and retired owner of the Red Rooster Tavern in North Kingstown, he has many stories to tell.

Like the time when Cornish game hens became the hot new dinner food in the United States. He put them on his menu but didn't sell a single bird. When he redid the menu and offered them as "roasted little chickens," he sold out.

Or the time the flamboyant pianist Liberace came in for dinner and asked where he could shop for antiques. Leclair gave him a list of local dealers. The next day all the shop owners called Leclair to thank him—Liberace had purchased everything the antiques stores had for sale. He was opening an antiques store in Las Vegas and needed to stock it.

Today Leclair is a prolific cookbook author and teaches cooking classes around the state.

Newport-Style Clam Cakes

From the other side of Narragansett Bay, Newport to be precise, comes this simple recipe for clam cakes. The recipe may be short and sweet, but the results are big and tasty.

1 cup minced quahogs

1 egg

$^3/_4$ cup flour

1 teaspoon baking powder

$^1/_2$ teaspoon salt

Freshly ground pepper, to taste

Vegetable oil, as needed for frying

Strain the quahogs. Add them to the rest of the ingredients to make a batter, and fry like pancakes.

MAKES 8 SERVINGS.

Steamers, Stuffies, and Clam Cakes

Here we go again with a culinary vocabulary like no other state in the Union. Steamers, stuffies, and clam cakes are definitely connected, yet very different from one another.

Steamers are clams that have been steamed open in a little water or beer. Most people use their fingers to remove the clams from their shells, dip them in melted butter, and eat them whole. The steamer consists of a tender, plump belly and a rubbery neck. Some people eat only the belly, biting off the neck and leaving it on their plates.

Stuffies is short for "stuffed clams," made from the larger (and chewier) quahog clams that have been steamed open and then refilled with a flavorful stuffing. The stuffing is a mixture of bread crumbs, seasonings and the "meat" found inside the clam, all ground together. You use a fork to eat a stuffie, and they are always served with lemon wedges and hot pepper sauce on the side.

Clam cakes aren't cakes at all but rather fritters, containing bits of chopped-up clams in a heavy batter. They are deep-fried and served with plenty of salt. You order clam cakes by the dozen, and they come to the table piping hot in a small basket, or in a paper bag if they are ordered "to go" from a seaside clam shack.

Stuffed Quahogs

The International Quahog Festival is held every August in Charlestown. Thousands of people find their way to this quiet seaside community to pay homage to the humble quahog. This hard-shelled clam is devoured in all manner of recipes—in chowders that have red, white, or clear broths; in clam cakes; in garlicky pasta dishes; and most important, in stuffed quahogs, also known as "stuffies." A contest is always held to determine who makes the best stuffed quahogs. Here is the winning recipe from the 1990 competition. The secret to making really good stuffies is to mince the onion and peppers very finely. For the hot pepper sauce, many Rhode Island cooks prefer to use Rhode Island Red, a product made locally by Chef Linda Kane. Her "sauce with an attitude" is popular because its sweet heat does not overpower the food it seasons.

8 quahogs

1 onion, finely chopped

1 green pepper, finely chopped

1 red bell pepper, finely chopped

3 tablespoons butter

1 clove garlic, crushed

1 cup fresh bread crumbs

¼ teaspoon dried oregano

About 4 teaspoons grated Romano
or Parmesan cheese

Additional butter, melted, as needed
for moistening

Clam juice, as needed for
moistening

Lemon wedges and hot pepper
sauce, as needed for seasoning

To facilitate the opening of the quahogs, place the well-scrubbed clams in a pan in a moderate (350-degree) oven and heat until they open. Discard any that do not open. When cool enough to handle, remove the quahogs from their shells. Pour the liquid left in each clamshell into a bowl. Set aside the clamshells and the clam juice. Poach the quahogs for 3 minutes in simmering water. Chop the quahogs into pieces.

In a large frying pan, sauté the onion and peppers in the butter until translucent. Add the garlic and cook over low heat another 1 to 2 minutes . Stir in the chopped quahogs, an equal amount of fresh bread crumbs, and the oregano. Add about $1/2$ teaspoon grated cheese per clam. Moisten with additional melted butter and/or clam juice.

Preheat oven to 375 degrees.

Separate the clamshells. Mound the stuffing into each clamshell half, and place them on a baking sheet. Bake in the oven until hot and slightly browned, approximately 20 minutes. Serve with lemon wedges and hot pepper sauce.

MAKES 16 STUFFIES.

June's Famous Stuffies

I've been eating baked stuffed quahogs all my life, and these are simply the best. They come from my sister-in-law, June Giardino. When June makes her famous stuffies, she has to make hundreds of them, and they still disappear in a matter of minutes.

10 pounds quahogs

1 extra-large yellow onion, chopped fine

2 tablespoons minced garlic

1 cup (2 sticks) butter, divided

1½ cups bread crumbs

Freshly ground black pepper, to taste

Paprika, as needed

Dried parsley flakes, as needed

Lemon wedges and hot pepper sauce, as needed

Rinse the quahogs in plenty of cold water several times to remove any sand. In a large stockpot, combine the quahogs with about 1 inch of water. Over high heat, cook the quahogs until all the shells have opened. Remove the open quahogs from the pot so they can cool. Discard any quahogs that do not open. Save the quahog broth in the pot.

In a large saucepan, cook the onion and garlic in ½ cup of the butter until tender.

Remove the meat from each quahog. Clean the quahog shells and set aside. (Some home cooks clean their quahog shells by running them through the dishwasher without any soap being used.)

Using an old-fashioned hand-cranked meat grinder (or a modern-day food processor), grind the quahog meat. In a large bowl, combine the ground quahog meat with the cooked onion and garlic and the bread crumbs. Season to taste with pepper.

Strain the quahog broth through cheesecloth. Add the strained broth to the quahog meat mixture. Mix well.

Preheat oven to 325 degrees.

Stuff the clean quahog shells with the quahog meat mixture. Sprinkle each stuffed quahog with a little paprika and parsley flakes. Add a small pat of butter (about 1 teaspoon) to the top of each stuffed quahog. Bake the stuffed quahogs on a baking sheet for 20 minutes. Serve immediately with lemon wedges and hot pepper sauce.

MAKES APPROXIMATELY 24 STUFFIES.

Clam Puffs

No one seems to know where this easy-to-make recipe originated. It's been around for years in my family and continues to be a favorite, especially in the northern part of the state in and around the city of Woonsocket, where many French-Canadian families still reside.

8 ounces cream cheese, at room temperature

1 egg, separated

1 cup minced quahogs, drained

Salt and freshly ground black pepper, to taste

9 slices white bread, crusts removed, cut into rounds

Combine the cream cheese with the yolk of the egg. Mix well. Add the quahogs, salt, and pepper. In a separate bowl, beat the egg white until stiff peaks form. Fold the egg white into the clam mixture. Spread the mixture on the bread rounds. Place under the oven broiler until puffed and lightly browned. Serve immediately.

MAKES 36 APPETIZERS.

Choosing and Cleaning Clams

It's wise to buy hard-shelled clams at fresh-fish markets, especially those located in fishing villages like Galilee. It doesn't get any fresher than that. In most locations you pick the clams yourself from huge plastic tubs set on crushed ice. This way you get exactly the size clams you prefer. In our family, we like them large—the bigger, the better. Others prefer the tiny "baby" clams that tend to be more tender. But in a pinch, you can also buy clams in any of the major supermarkets throughout the state, though you won't be able to hand-select them.

In either situation, make sure the clams you purchase are tightly closed. When you're ready to cook them, scrub them under cold running water to remove all sand and grit. A potato scrub brush is good for this task.

Baked Sakonnet Oysters with Champagne and Leeks

Chris Ferris, executive chef at 22 Bowen's Wine Bar & Grille in Newport, created this recipe to celebrate the good life. What better combination can there be but fresh oysters and champagne? Ferris likes to use oysters from the Sakonnet region of Rhode Island, the easternmost section of the state that looks over the broad Sakonnet River toward Newport. More than just a river, the Sakonnet is much like the East River between Manhattan and Long Island in New York, connecting two bigger bodies of ocean water.

---

12 Sakonnet oysters

1 bunch leeks

1/2 cup (1 stick) butter

1 cup champagne

1 cup heavy cream

1 cup butter cracker crumbs

Rinse the oysters in cold running water before opening them. Carefully open the oysters. If you find this step too difficult, have it done at the seafood market where you purchase the oysters. Place opened oysters on a baking pan. Set aside.

Preheat oven to 350 degrees.

Trim the leeks and cut into 1-inch strips, then soak them in cold water to let sand and dirt fall to the bottom. Heat the butter in a frying pan and add the leeks. Sauté on low heat until the leeks caramelize, about 8 to 10 minutes. Add the champagne and reduce to almost a syrup. Add the cream to the leeks, and allow the mixture to reduce and thicken.

Spoon the leek mixture over the oysters. Sprinkle the cracker crumbs over the oysters. Place the oysters in the oven for 10 minutes. Serve immediately.

MAKES 6 SERVINGS.

Mussel-Stuffed Mushrooms

Mussels are probably the most affordable shellfish you'll find in Rhode Island. Most mussels are now farm-raised, uniform in size and quality. Stuffed into mushroom caps, they make a fine appetizer that can be served warm or cold.

24 mussels

24 large white mushrooms

1 small onion, chopped

¼ cup mayonnaise

½ cup finely chopped celery

1 hard-boiled egg, chopped

Salt and freshly ground black
    pepper, to taste

Soak the mussels in cold water for 1 hour. Rinse the mussels under cold running water, scrubbing away any grit and removing any beards (the wiry threads that these animals secrete to anchor themselves to rocks and pilings). Place the mussels in a large pot with about 1 inch of water. Over high heat, steam the mussels until they open. Discard any that do not open. Allow the mussels to cool slightly. Remove the yellow-orange meat from inside each mussel shell. Set aside.

Preheat oven to 350 degrees.

Remove the stems from the mushrooms. Chop the stems into tiny pieces. Combine the chopped stems with the meat from the mussels and the remaining ingredients to make a moist stuffing mixture. Mix well. Stuff each mushroom cap. Place the caps on a lightly greased baking sheet. Bake for 10 minutes. Serve warm or cold.

MAKES 24 APPETIZERS.

French-Canadian Gorton

French Canadians in the Woonsocket area have been making this unusual appetizer for decades. Lard—yes, lard—is added to the meat mixture to make it more spreadable. It's usually served cold with Ritz or similar crackers. The recipe calls for Bell's Seasoning, a blend of seven spices that has been sold since 1867 and is available in most supermarkets.

---

2 to 3 pounds pork tenderloin or blade meat, cut into pieces

3 medium-size onions, chopped roughly

Salt and freshly ground black pepper, to taste

$\frac{1}{2}$ to 1 teaspoon Bell's Seasoning

$\frac{1}{4}$ to $\frac{1}{2}$ teaspoon ground cinnamon

$\frac{1}{8}$ teaspoon ground cloves

$\frac{1}{4}$ pound lard

Crackers

In a food processor or meat grinder, grind together the pork and onions. Season to taste with salt and pepper. Add the remaining ingredients except crackers. Cook the mixture slowly in a heavy saucepan over low heat for several hours until the onions are translucent and tender. Pour the mixture into several small plastic containers. Allow to cool. Cover and refrigerate.

When it's time to serve this appetizer, you can scoop it into a suitable serving dish surrounded by crackers.

MAKES 24 TO 32 SERVINGS.

French Canadians in Rhode Island

From the end of the Civil War to the early years of the twentieth century, Rhode Island had national respect, power, and recognition because its many manufacturers—from textile goods to jewelry and silverware—were at the forefront of the Industrial Revolution at that time. To keep up with demands, the state needed cheap labor and soon became a magnet for French-Canadian immigrants. They were known as "the Chinese of the East" because of their willingness to work long hours for little pay and because of their stubborn loyalty to the French language. At first, they were the second-most prominent ethnic group in the state (the Irish were first), but by 1910 the French Canadians outnumbered the Irish. Soon they were both outnumbered by Italian immigrants.

Gougères (Cheese Puffs)

A French-Canadian favorite, *gougères* are small balls of cheese-flavored puff pastry that can be eaten as is or filled with savory mixtures such as shrimp, crab, duck, or smoked salmon. Brushing the puff pastry with egg wash aids in browning.

1 cup water

¼ cup butter

½ teaspoon salt

¼ teaspoon pepper

Dash nutmeg

1 cup all-purpose flour

1 cup grated Gruyère cheese

4 whole eggs

1 egg white

1 egg yolk

Preheat oven to 400 degrees.

In a small saucepan, bring to a boil the water, butter, salt, pepper, and nutmeg. Add the flour and stir with a wooden spoon until it pulls away from the sides. Remove the saucepan from the heat and add half the cheese; then add the whole eggs and the egg white, blending until smooth.

Combine the remaining egg yolk with 1 tablespoon of water to make an egg wash.

Place about 1 tablespoon of the dough onto a greased baking sheet. Repeat until all the dough is used up. Brush each mound of dough with egg wash and sprinkle remaining cheese on top. Bake at 400 degrees for 15 minutes, then for 10 minutes at 300 degrees or until brown and somewhat dry.

If you plan to fill these puffs, remove them from the oven. Turn the oven off. With a small sharp knife, make a tiny slit in each puff. Place the puffs back in the oven for 10 minutes. Make sure the oven is turned off. Remove the puffs from the oven. Fill the puffs once they have cooled. These puffs can be made ahead and refrigerated or even frozen.

MAKES 36 APPETIZERS.

Mozzarella in Carrozza (Fried Mozzarella Sticks)

Long before they became popular in restaurants, fried mozzarella sticks were being served in Rhode Island homes as a way to use up leftover mozzarella. Some families cut the mozzarella into thin slices and make cheese sandwiches with day-old bread, which are then dipped in egg and flour and fried. Others prefer to make mozzarella "sticks." Either way, it's *delizioso*! *Note*: If you are unable to find freshly made mozzarella, you can substitute scamorza or mild provolone.

---

1 pound freshly made mozzarella, cut into sticks about 2 inches long and ½ inch thick

3 eggs, beaten

¼ cup all-purpose flour

⅔ cup seasoned bread crumbs

MARINARA SAUCE

1 small garlic clove, minced

4 tablespoons olive oil

1 (28-ounce) can tomatoes, cut up

¼ teaspoon salt

⅛ teaspoon freshly ground black pepper

¼ teaspoon dried basil

1 teaspoon dried oregano

¼ teaspoon sugar (optional)

Dip the mozzarella sticks in the beaten eggs, then in the flour, then in the eggs again, and finally in the bread crumbs. Place the sticks on a baking sheet lined with waxed paper. Refrigerate for 1 hour.

Make the marinara sauce. In a large heavy saucepan, sauté the minced garlic in 1 tablespoon of olive oil. Add the tomatoes and seasonings. Mix well. Simmer uncovered for 45 minutes, or until the sauce is thick.

In a large frying pan, heat the remaining 3 tablespoons of oil. Fry the cheese sticks until brown on all sides, turning once. This should take no more than 2 to 3 minutes. Drain on paper towels. Serve with the marinara sauce.

MAKES 6 SERVINGS.

Mushroom-Tomato Bruschetta

Simply put, bruschetta is toasted bread, often rubbed with fresh garlic and drizzled with high-quality olive oil. Years ago it was how Italian families would make use of stale bread. In recent years bruschetta has become a trendy appetizer, especially in restaurants. This particular bruschetta is excellent when made with perfectly ripe Roma tomatoes from the backyard garden.

---

2 cups fresh mushrooms, sliced

6 Roma or plum tomatoes, diced

2 garlic cloves, minced

3 tablespoons extra-virgin olive oil

$2\frac{1}{4}$ teaspoons balsamic vinegar

2 tablespoons chopped fresh basil

$\frac{1}{2}$ teaspoon salt

$\frac{1}{4}$ teaspoon pepper

8 slices Italian bread, about $\frac{1}{2}$ inch thick

2 whole garlic cloves

2 tablespoons grated Parmigiano-Reggiano cheese

In a dry, very hot frying pan, cook the sliced mushrooms quickly. Set aside.

In a medium bowl, combine the tomatoes with the minced garlic, olive oil, vinegar, basil, salt, and pepper. Mix well. Allow to sit at room temperature for at least 20 minutes to allow the flavors to blend. You may store this mixture in the refrigerator for up to 3 hours, but after that the tomatoes will become soft.

Toast the bread slices under a broiler until lightly brown on both sides. When cool enough to handle, rub each bread slice with the whole garlic cloves. Lay the bread slices on an ovenproof serving plate. Top the bread slices first with the tomato mixture, then with the mushrooms. Sprinkle a little of the cheese on top of each bread slice. Place the serving plate under a hot broiler until the cheese melts. Serve immediately.

MAKES 8 SERVINGS.

Fried Artichoke Hearts

Artichokes are a local favorite with Italian-American families, prepared in all sorts of ways—with wild mushrooms in a tarragon cream sauce or stuffed with Italian sausage. This is one of the most popular ways to serve artichoke hearts as an appetizer.

---

1 (14-ounce) can artichoke hearts, drained

Olive oil, as needed for deep-frying

¼ cup flour

Salt and freshly ground black pepper, to taste

1 teaspoon baking powder

1 egg, beaten

1 to 2 teaspoons grated Romano cheese, more or less to taste

Lettuce, as needed

Lemon wedges and chopped fresh parsley, for garnish

Pat dry the artichoke hearts with a paper towel. Cut each one in half.

In a deep frying pan, heat the oil. If using an electric skillet or frying machine, set it at 325 degrees.

In a bowl, combine the flour, salt, pepper, and baking powder. Mix well.

In another bowl, combine the beaten egg and grated cheese. Mix well.

Toss the artichoke hearts into the flour mixture, then dip into the egg-cheese mixture. Deep-fry the artichoke hearts for approximately 1 minute, or until golden brown on all sides. Serve on a lettuce-lined platter. Garnish with lemon wedges and chopped fresh parsley.

MAKES APPROXIMATELY 10 SERVINGS.

Zucchini Flowers

A real delicacy for Rhode Islanders with home gardens is the fried zucchini flower, something we learned about from the Italians. These flowers must be picked early in the morning and then carefully washed and dried. Gourmet cooks have been known to stuff their zucchini flowers with cheesy concoctions, but purists prefer this simple recipe.

2 eggs, beaten

1 cup water

2 cups all-purpose flour

2 heaping teaspoons baking powder

Salt and freshly ground black pepper, to taste

18 zucchini flowers, washed and dried

Vegetable oil, as needed for frying

Combine the beaten eggs, water, flour, baking powder, salt, and pepper. Mix until smooth and thick. Carefully dip each flower into the batter, making sure the entire flower is coated. Place 2 or 3 flowers at a time in a large skillet containing $1/2$ inch of hot oil. When golden brown on one side, turn once, and brown the other side. Drain on paper towels. Serve warm.

MAKES 18 APPETIZERS.

Pasta

Lobster Ravioli

The one pasta dish that best represents Providence is lobster ravioli, appearing on the menus of the very best restaurants as *ravioli con aragosta* and often duplicated by home cooks for dinner parties. Ideally it is made with fresh pasta and with the firm meat from fresh native lobsters caught in the cold waters of Narragansett Bay. There are many lobster ravioli recipes, but this one is particularly good. It is adapted from a recipe created by Italian cookbook author Mary Ann Esposito, who tapes her popular television cooking show *Ciao Italia* at the PBS station in Providence. Pink vodka sauce can be served with any kind of pasta, but it goes especially well with lobster ravioli.

2 cups cooked lobster meat

1 large egg, beaten

1 teaspoon fine sea salt

1 teaspoon white pepper

1/4 cup grated Parmigiano-Reggiano
   cheese

2 tablespoons finely minced fresh
   parsley

Fresh Pasta Dough (recipe follows)

Pink Vodka Sauce (recipe follows)

Using a knife or food processor, mince the lobster meat. In a large bowl, combine the minced lobster meat, egg, sea salt, pepper, cheese, and parsley. Mix well. Cover and refrigerate.

Roll the pasta dough through a pasta machine to the finest setting, or roll it out with a rolling pin on a floured surface as thin as possible. Cut into strips that are approximately 5 inches wide and 12 inches long.

If you have a ravioli form, place a strip of dough over the bottom half of the form, making sure the dough hangs over all the edges of the form by 1/2 inch. Place 1 teaspoon of filling in each compartment. Cover the filled strip of dough with another sheet of dough. With a rolling pin, roll over the form several times to seal the edges and separate each ravioli. Use the leftover pieces to make another strip of dough. Loosen the filled ravioli from the form. Place the filled ravioli on a clean towel or on a floured baking sheet.

If you prefer to cut your ravioli by hand, place your rolled-out strips of dough on a floured surface. Place teaspoons of filling 2 inches apart on the strip of dough. Cover with another strip of dough. Press down around each mound to seal the dough strips together. Using a sharp knife or pasta wheel, cut the ravioli in squares. You can also cut the ravioli in circles, using a large glass or a cookie cutter. Place the filled ravioli on a clean towel or on a floured baking sheet.

Bring a large stockpot of salted water to a rolling boil. Cook the ravioli in batches of 12 at a time. As soon as the ravioli float to the surface of the boiling water, they are done. Using a slotted spoon, remove the cooked ravioli from the water and drain them. Place the cooked ravioli in a large bowl. Serve with pink vodka sauce or the sauce of your choice.

This recipe makes at least 150 regular-size (1½ inches) ravioli. Cook as many as needed, and then freeze the rest. To freeze freshly made ravioli, place the ravioli in a single layer on a small baking sheet. Cover with plastic wrap or aluminum foil. Place in freezer and freeze. When the ravioli are frozen solid, place them in plastic bags marked with the date. Fresh ravioli can be kept frozen for up to 3 months. Do not thaw the ravioli before boiling.

NARRAGANSETT BAY LOBSTERS, POINT JUDITH

FRESH PASTA DOUGH

2 cups flour

3 eggs

1/4 cup cold water

Fresh pasta dough can be made traditionally by hand in a bowl or on a countertop, but it is easier and less tricky to make it in a food processor. It takes only a few minutes and tastes the same as handmade dough. Place the flour in a food processor. Add the eggs, 1 at a time, with the processor running constantly. Process for at least 15 additional seconds. Add the cold water gradually until the mixture forms into a ball.

Remove the ball of dough from the processor and place on a lightly floured surface. Knead until smooth. Allow the dough to rest, covered, for 30 minutes. Divide the dough into 4 equal portions. Keep the portions covered. One at a time, roll each portion through a pasta machine at the widest setting. Fold dough into thirds and roll through the pasta machine again and again, for a total of five times, always folding the dough into thirds.

Continue to roll the dough unfolded through the pasta machine, reducing the setting every time from the widest to the thinnest setting. Repeat this process with each portion of dough.

This dough can be cut into various pasta widths, from spaghetti to linguine, or left whole for ravioli. *Note:* Fresh pasta cooks much more quickly than dried pasta. In most recipes, fresh pasta is cooked in boiling water for 2 minutes or until al dente.

PINK VODKA SAUCE

3 ounces vodka

1 quart favorite marinara sauce

1/2 pint heavy cream

Carefully pour the vodka into a saucepan, and allow it to ignite from the flame on the burner or by striking a match to burn off the alcohol. This takes just about 1 minute.

To this reduction, add the marinara sauce and bring to a boil. Reduce heat, add the cream, and stir until silky smooth.

Add more cream or a splash of vodka for additional taste. Simmer and serve. The sauce will keep up to a week in the refrigerator or it can be frozen.

MAKES 4 SERVINGS.

Lobster and Asparagus Agnolotti

When celebrity chef Mario Batali came to Federal Hill in Providence to tape segments for his *Ciao America* TV show on the Food Channel, he was in search of authentic Italian food with a strong Rhode Island connection. He found just what he was looking for. An expert on Italian food and culture, Batali learned how to make this agnolotti dish from Salvatore Cefaliello, executive chef at Venda Ravioli. Chef Sal, as he is known to his many fans, makes this dish with fresh Rhode Island littleneck clams. Agnolotti are crescent-shaped or half-moon ravioli. Although this recipe is for one serving, it is easily doubled, tripled, etc. for more diners.

4 agnolotti filled with lobster and asparagus (available fresh or frozen at upscale Italian markets)

2 tablespoons olive oil

1 garlic clove, minced

1/2 teaspoon red pepper flakes

4 Rhode Island littleneck clams

3 large fresh shrimp, with heads still attached

1/2 cup white wine

1 small ripe tomato, diced

1 tablespoon chopped fresh Italian parsley

Salt and freshly ground black pepper, to taste

In a stockpot of boiling water, cook the agnolotti according to directions on the package.

In a large frying pan, heat the olive oil and add the minced garlic, being careful not to burn it. Add the red pepper flakes, clams, and shrimp, which cook quickly. Once the clams have opened and the shrimp have turned pink in color, add the white wine and diced tomatoes. Allow the wine to evaporate. Finally, add the chopped parsley.

Drain the agnolotti and place on a serving dish. Pour the sauce over the agnolotti. Serve with salt and pepper for individual seasoning.

MAKES 1 SERVING.

Right Off the Boats

Like many Rhode Islanders, we buy lobsters right off the boats in Galilee, a small fishing village in the town of Narragansett. The boats come into port every afternoon, and it's fun to go from boat to boat to see who has the best price. It's wise to get there by 3:00 P.M. before they are sold out. Live lobsters are also available in local seafood markets such as Champlin's in Galilee.

Buyer beware—always make certain you ask for hard-shelled lobsters. At certain times of the year, soft-shelled lobsters are mixed in with their hard-shelled cousins. They look the same, but often the meat inside these lobsters is soft and mushy—which can be greatly disappointing to lobster lovers.

NARRAGANSETT BAY LOBSTERS, POINT JUDITH

South County Seafood Lasagna

Fresh native flounder is the key ingredient in this seafood lasagna recipe that has been used by many South County cooks looking to feed a crowd. Chopped clams, tuna, and lobster are also swimming in the sauce that cooks the dry lasagna noodles. Fresh bay scallops and fresh chopped quahogs may also be used. This is a perfect recipe for cooks who hate to precook lasagna noodles. This recipe also may be altered according to individual taste. You can add Italian seasoning, dried tarragon, hot pepper flakes, or sliced pepperoni, if desired. To reheat leftovers in a conventional oven, cover the lasagna with aluminum foil so it won't dry out. Or place the leftovers in a casserole dish that has a cover.

1 (1-pound box) dry lasagna noodles (do not cook)

1 (15-ounce) can white clam sauce

1 (7-ounce) can tuna, packed in water, shredded

½ pound flounder (trimmed fillet pieces or scraps of flounder may be used)

2 cups chopped clams (fresh are recommended, but frozen or canned may be used)

2 cups grated mozzarella cheese

2 cups grated cheddar cheese

1 cup ricotta cheese

1 (15-ounce) can red clam sauce

2 cups clam juice, plus extra for moistening during baking

2 cups favorite spaghetti sauce

1 cup freshly grated Romano or Parmesan cheese

Preheat oven to 350 degrees.

Line the bottom of a greased 13x9-inch glass baking dish with a layer of uncooked lasagna noodles. Top with the white clam sauce, the shredded tuna with its water, the flounder pieces, and half (1 cup) of the chopped clams. Add another layer of uncooked lasagna noodles. Sprinkle with the grated mozzarella and cheddar cheeses, and dot with the ricotta cheese. Pour the red clam sauce over the cheese. Add another layer of uncooked lasagna noodles. Top with the rest of the clams. Pour the clam juice over the entire lasagna. Cover the top layer with spaghetti sauce. Sprinkle with the freshly grated Romano or Parmesan cheese.

Bake for about 1 hour. Add more clam juice if needed. The entire lasagna should be covered with liquids. Do not let this dish dry out while cooking.

Remove the lasagna from the oven. Allow to cool slightly before cutting the lasagna into 2-inch squares for serving.

MAKES 24 SERVINGS.

Penne Pasta a la Snug Harbor

Snug Harbor can be found in Wakefield, site of fishing tournaments from June through September. The directions to Snug Harbor are a delight. From Route 1, take the Snug Harbor exit onto Succotash Road, then bear left onto Gooseberry Road. If you go too far, you'll end up in Jerusalem, which is across the channel from Galilee. Located near a large salt-water marsh, Snug Harbor is a home to many charter fishing boat captains who lead anglers to nearby schools of striped bass, bluefish, and fluke, or head offshore in pursuit of shark, tuna, and cod. Local "party" boats offer the chance to catch sea bass, tautog, and more. This recipe comes from Alan Gelfuso, a Rhode Island attorney and avid sportsman who loves to cook. Fellow anglers who partake in Gelfuso's gourmet meals refer to him as "chef par excellence." Strangely enough, there's no seafood to be found in this recipe, but it's delicious nonetheless.

¼ cup finely chopped onions

½ celery stalk, minced

¼ cup olive oil

6 large garlic cloves, minced

¼ cup pignoli (pine nuts)

1 (28-ounce) can imported whole
   tomatoes, peeled

2 tablespoons chopped fresh
   parsley, plus a bit more for
   garnish if desired

6 fresh basil leaves, chopped

1 pound imported Italian penne
   pasta

½ to ¾ cup light cream

Freshly grated Parmesan cheese for
   sprinkling (optional)

In a large nonstick frying pan, sauté the onions and celery in the olive oil over medium heat until translucent. Add the garlic and continue to sauté until the mixture begins to brown. Add the pine nuts and brown slightly. Add the tomatoes, parsley, and basil. Bring to a boil. Lower the heat. Cover and simmer for 45 minutes.

In a large stockpot, cook the pasta in 6 quarts of boiling salted water until al dente. Drain.

Add the light cream to the sauce, more or less to taste. Do not allow the sauce to boil. Add the cooked pasta to the sauce in the saucepan. Toss over low heat. Garnish with additional chopped parsley, if desired. Serve in the saucepan along with freshly grated Parmesan cheese at the table.

MAKES 4 SERVINGS.

St. Joseph's Feast Day Pasta

St. Joseph's Day on March 19 is a big deal in Rhode Island. It is traditional for Italians, Italian Americans, and people who wish they were Italian to mark the day with the eating of *zeppoles*, fried puffs of dough, and *frittelle*, or rice fritters. If you are still hungry for dinner, you can try this pasta dish served in honor of San Giuseppe, the patron saint of the working man.

½ pound pasta (homemade is recommended)

¼ cup olive oil, or more if needed

1 large garlic clove, minced

1 tablespoon minced fresh parsley

½ cup coarse bread crumbs

¼ to ½ cup finely chopped walnuts or pignoli (pine nuts)

¼ cup grated Parmesan cheese

In a stockpot, cook the pasta in boiling salted water until al dente. Drain and set aside.

In a saucepan, heat the olive oil and cook the garlic until golden brown in color. Add the parsley, bread crumbs, and nuts. Simmer gently for 2 to 3 minutes. Add sauce to drained pasta. Sprinkle with Parmesan cheese. Serve immediately.

MAKES 2 SERVINGS.

A St. Joseph's Day Tradition

Zeppoles are the traditional sweet that Neapolitans have always made to celebrate the patron saint of the working man. The Pastry Gourmet, with six stores in the state, sells out by 8:00 A.M. on St. Joseph's Day because so many people bring boxes of *zeppoles* to work. At Zaccagnini's Pastry Shop in Cranston, Joe Zaccagnini has been making *zeppoles* since 1956. He figures he's made "about a million" *zeppoles* in that time. Joe won't reveal his recipe, but his fans say his *zeppoles* are filled with boiled cream flavored with rum extract. The biggest *zeppoles* can be found at Felicia's in East Greenwich, where the massive cream puffs come in five varieties—Italian or classic, as well as filled with whipped cream, cream that's flavored with coffee, and cream flavored with Bailey's Irish Cream.

For Adults Only Macaroni and Cheese

This is not your mother's mac and cheese. Served in the finest restaurants and at upscale dinner parties in private homes, this creamy concoction—with a variety of Italian, French, and Swiss cheeses—is definitely for adult taste buds. Even the old-fashioned elbow macaroni has been replaced with trendier penne pasta. Feel free to be creative when making this dish. This recipe is from Frank Terranova, a chef-instructor at Johnson & Wales University and host of the long-running cooking show called *Cooking with Class* on the local NBC station.

---

1 pound penne pasta

¼ cup butter

3 tablespoons flour

2 cups chicken broth

¼ cup sherry

2 cups milk

1 cup shredded Fontina cheese

½ cup Gruyère cheese

½ cup shredded Swiss cheese

½ teaspoon thyme

⅛ teaspoon nutmeg

Salt and cayenne pepper, to taste

¼ cup bread crumbs

¼ cup grated Parmesan cheese

In a stockpot, cook the pasta in salted boiling water until it is slightly under-cooked. Drain and set aside.

In a large frying pan, melt the butter. Stir in the flour and cook for 1 minute, stirring constantly. Add the chicken broth gradually, mixing well. Bring to a boil and cook for 2 minutes. Add the sherry and milk. Bring to a boil again. Remove from the heat and set aside.

To the frying pan, add the Fontina, Gruyère, and Swiss cheeses, stirring constantly until all the cheese has melted. Stir in the undercooked pasta. Season with thyme, nutmeg, salt, and cayenne pepper. Mix well.

Preheat oven to 375 degrees. Transfer the pasta into a 9x13-inch baking pan. Sprinkle bread crumbs and Parmesan cheese over the top. Bake for 30 minutes.

MAKES 8 SERVINGS.

Spaghetti alla Puttanesca

You'll find this racy dish on the menu at Mediterraneo Caffe on Federal Hill in Providence. Mediterraneo is considered the hottest, sexiest restaurant around and *the* place to see celebrities who come to the city. *Alla puttanesca* means "harlot style." Supposedly in Italy this was a sauce made quickly by enterprising ladies of the evening in between visits from clients. This zesty red sauce is a southern Italian dish that immigrants brought with them when they settled in the Providence area.

---

6 tablespoons olive oil

3 garlic cloves, sliced

1 red chile pepper, chopped

1 pound plum tomatoes, peeled

3 canned anchovy fillets

1 pound spaghetti

3 tablespoons capers

1/3 cup small pitted black olives (kalamata or *gaeta*)

Salt and freshly ground black pepper, to taste

1/2 bunch fresh Italian parsley, chopped

Freshly grated Parmesan cheese, as needed for sprinkling

In a large saucepan, heat the olive oil. Add the garlic and chile pepper, stirring constantly. Add the tomatoes and anchovies. Simmer for 15 minutes, uncovered.

In a large stockpot, bring 4 quarts of salted water to a boil. Cook the spaghetti until al dente.

Stir the capers and olives into the sauce. Season to taste with salt and pepper.

Drain the spaghetti and fold immediately into the sauce. Sprinkle with parsley. Serve with freshly grated Parmesan cheese, if desired.

MAKES 4 SERVINGS.

Linguine a la NIROPE

In Rhode Island everyone knows that NIROPE stands for Nick, Ron and Pete Cardi, local businesspeople who are famous for their charitable contributions. As the owners of the Cardi furniture store chain, they are familiar faces on local television, with clever commercials that are always topical and quite comical. The Cardi boys, as they are called, love good food. Here is one of their creations. It's basically a pasta primavera dish with the addition of seafood.

---

1 tablespoon chopped garlic

$1/4$ cup olive oil

1 pound large raw shrimp (15 to 20), peeled, tails removed, deveined

3 small zucchini, cut into $1/2$-inch slices

3 small summer squash, cut into $1/2$-inch slices

1 large red bell pepper, chopped

3 carrots, peeled, cut diagonally into thin slices

2 teaspoons garlic salt

Pepper, to taste

1 pound linguine

$1/4$ cup olive oil

In a large frying pan, sauté the garlic in the first $1/4$ cup olive oil over medium heat. Be careful not to burn the garlic or it will taste bitter. Add the shrimp. Sauté until the shrimp turn pink. Add the zucchini, squash, bell pepper, and carrots to the shrimp mixture. Cook, covered, for 3 to 5 minutes, or just until the vegetables are tender. Do not overcook. Season with garlic salt and pepper.

In a stockpot, bring 2 quarts of water to a boil. Add the linguine. Cook until al dente. Drain and rinse. Toss the cooked linguine with the second $1/4$ cup olive oil. Spoon the cooked shrimp and vegetable mixture over the top. Serve immediately.

MAKES 4 SERVINGS.

Pasta Providence

Variations of Pasta Providence have been surfacing in Rhode Island for several years now. The tomato sauce is optional. The marinade and white wine actually make enough sauce for the dish, but some folks like to add the tomato sauce for more traditional results.

---

1 (6-ounce) jar marinated artichoke hearts

1 cup sliced fresh mushrooms

1 tablespoon grated onion

1 garlic clove, minced

2 cups tomato sauce (optional)

1 cup dry white wine

1/4 cup sliced black olives

2 teaspoons dried basil

2 teaspoons dried oregano

1/2 teaspoon fennel seeds

1 teaspoon salt

1/4 teaspoon freshly ground black pepper

1 pound spaghetti (angel hair is recommended)

Freshly grated Parmesan cheese, to taste

Drain the artichoke hearts, reserving the marinade. Chop the artichoke hearts into bite-size pieces.

In a large frying pan, heat the marinade until it begins to bubble. Add the mushrooms, onion, and garlic. Sauté for 5 minutes. Add the chopped artichoke hearts, tomato sauce (if desired), wine, black olives, basil, oregano, fennel seeds, salt, and pepper. Simmer for 20 minutes.

Cook the spaghetti according to package directions. Drain. Place the cooked spaghetti in a large serving bowl. Pour the sauce over the spaghetti. Sprinkle with Parmesan cheese. Have additional Parmesan cheese on the table to suit individual tastes. Serve immediately.

MAKES 4 SERVINGS.

Baked Ziti with Sweet and Hot Italian Sausages

The best way to make any recipe calling for Italian sausage is with the sweet and hot sausages from Graziano's Sausage Company in North Providence. Some of the finest chefs in Rhode Island consider Graziano sausages to be the best in the state.

1 pound pasta (your choice—
   mostaccioli is recommended)

1 tablespoon olive oil

1 pound sweet Italian sausage

1 pound hot Italian sausage

4 garlic cloves, minced

4 cups tomato sauce

1/2 cup sliced mushrooms (optional)

1/2 cup dry red wine

1 teaspoon chopped fresh
   rosemary

1 tablespoon chopped fresh basil

1 1/2 cups ricotta cheese

1 cup freshly grated Parmesan
   cheese

In a stockpot, cook the pasta in salted boiling water until it just begins to soften. Do not cook completely. It will finish cooking when it bakes in the oven. Drain the pasta and set aside.

In a large saucepan, heat the olive oil. Add the sausages. If desired, the sausage casings can be removed, but this is not required. Cook the sausages until they are evenly browned. Remove the sausages from the pan and slice them thinly.

Add the garlic to the pan and cook over medium heat just until the garlic begins to become golden in color. Add the tomato sauce to the pan, as well as the sliced sausage, mushrooms, wine, and fresh rosemary and basil. Mix well. Bring to a simmer. Cover and simmer for 15 to 20 minutes, stirring occasionally.

Preheat oven to 350 degrees.

In a 13x9-inch greased baking dish, alternate layers of the half-cooked pasta, the tomato sauce-sausage mixture, and ricotta cheese until all the ingredients are used. Sprinkle the grated Parmesan cheese over the top of the dish. Bake for 20 to 25 minutes or until the sauce is bubbly and the top is golden brown. Remove the baking dish from the oven. Allow to stand for 10 minutes before serving.

MAKES 4 SERVINGS.

Padre's Pasta

The Italian-speaking Catholics of Woonsocket attended services regularly in the basement of St. Charles Church, a predominantly French parish, until 1928, when the Italians finally built their own church— St. Anthony's Church, named after St. Anthony of Padua, Italy. Father Joseph Santurri, who served as pastor of St. Anthony's Church from 1970 to 1985, was known for this simple pasta creation. It became a favorite of his parishioners and continues to this day to be a familiar dish in northern Rhode Island. Father Santurri always recommended that it be served with salad, followed by fruit compote for dessert.

½ pound spaghetti

2 (2-ounce) cans anchovies

2 garlic cloves, minced

¾ cup tomato juice

1 tablespoon minced fresh parsley

Freshly grated Romano cheese,
    to taste

Cook the spaghetti according to the package directions.

Drain the oil from the anchovies into a hot frying pan. Add the garlic and fry lightly, being careful not to burn the garlic. Add the anchovies, tomato juice, and parsley. Bring to a boil and simmer for 5 minutes, or until the anchovies fall apart.

Drain the spaghetti. Place the spaghetti in a large bowl. Pour the sauce over the spaghetti. Sprinkle with grated Romano cheese. Serve immediately.

MAKES 2 SERVINGS.

Graziano Gourmet Foods

It's easy to miss Graziano Gourmet Foods when you drive down Charles Street in North Providence. The nondescript brick building at 787 Charles almost looks abandoned, but nothing could be further from the truth. Step into one of the smallest shops in the city and you have a world of Italian imports at your fingertips.

It all began in 1960 when Graziano Broccoli left Italy on a boat to America with only $17 in his pocket. He also carried with him what five generations of Broccoli butchers had given him—the art of sausage making, hot or sweet, without preservatives or additives, and with little fat. For years Broccoli worked as a butcher for other businesses, saving his money in order to open his own store, which he did in 1976. Today, in addition to the sausage, the store is known for Graziano's own line of San Marzano tomatoes, canned in Naples, as well as the best products Italy has to offer—all made with the best ingredients.

Seafood Pasta Alfredo with Narragansett Bay Scallops

Back in the 1970s the Rhode Island restaurant scene was pretty dismal by today's standards. A big night out meant going to a certain steak house out near the state airport in Warwick for a slab of prime rib served with a baked potato wrapped in aluminum foil and a small wooden bowl filled with iceberg lettuce, a tomato wedge, a slice of cucumber, and one black olive. But then something began to happen at restaurants, especially in the capital city. Steak houses such as Winkler's in downtown Providence started serving new and exciting dishes, such as this one—Seafood Pasta Alfredo. I remember the first time I had this particular dish at Winkler's. It was unlike anything else I had ever had. And that was just the beginning of an exciting food revolution. Winkler's is long gone, but it certainly helped pave the way for dozens of new upscale restaurants.

1 tablespoon butter

½ cup chopped scallions

¼ cup sliced fresh mushrooms

½ cup Narragansett Bay scallops

½ cup baby shrimp

½ cup cooked lobster

2½ cups heavy cream

1 egg yolk

½ cup white wine

¼ cup grated Parmesan cheese

Salt and freshly ground black
pepper, to taste

½ pound egg or spinach fettuccine

Chopped fresh parsley, for garnish

Parmesan cheese, as needed for
sprinkling

In a large frying pan, melt the butter over medium-high heat. Add the scallions and mushrooms. Sauté until tender, about 5 minutes, stirring constantly. Add the scallops, shrimp, and lobster and sauté for 1 minute. Reduce heat. Add the cream and egg yolk, stirring constantly to ensure a smooth texture. Cook for 3 minutes or until mixture is smooth and has thickened.

Add the wine and ¼ cup Parmesan cheese. Season with salt and pepper to taste. Cook for 6 minutes or until sauce is smooth and heated through. Serve over fettuccine cooked according to package directions. Garnish with chopped parsley and serve with additional Parmesan cheese.

MAKES 2 SERVINGS.

Buddy Cianci's Marinara Sauce

Vincent "Buddy" Cianci is the infamous former mayor of Providence. He held the office on and off for almost three decades before he was convicted in 2002 of racketeering and was sentenced to almost six years in jail. Before his fall from grace, the charismatic Cianci was credited with the renaissance of Providence. He also created a line of Italian food products, whose proceeds from sales go to a scholarship fund that has helped more than a hundred Providence students go to college. Cianci's marinara sauce, still found in major supermarkets and small gourmet shops throughout Rhode Island, is an all-natural fresh sauce that can be used as the base for a meat sauce, or a pink sauce, or in Clams Zuppa. The secret to this sauce, according to Cianci, is the carrots. Cianci may be a political rascal, but his marinara sauce is totally honest.

---

6 garlic cloves, crushed

¼ cup extra-virgin olive oil

2 large red onions, chopped

10 pounds plum tomatoes, blanched

2 large carrots, chopped

½ cup finely chopped fresh parsley

½ cup chopped fresh basil

½ cup dry red wine (optional)

½ cup grated Parmesan cheese

Salt and freshly ground black pepper, to taste

In a heavy saucepan over medium heat, sauté the garlic in the olive oil just until tender. Add the onions. Sauté until the onions are translucent. Process the tomatoes through a food mill and add to the onion mixture. Add the remaining ingredients. Mix well. Lower heat and simmer for 2 to 6 hours or until thickened. Adjust the seasonings to taste. Serve over cooked pasta.

MAKES 16 CUPS, ENOUGH FOR 2 POUNDS OF PASTA.

Pesto Sauce

Drive through almost any suburban neighborhood in Rhode Island in the summer, and you will see many home gardens, small and large. No self-respecting Italian American would let the season go by without growing at least a few tomato plants and some fresh basil. I start harvesting my fresh basil leaves in August to make pesto, which I place in small jars in the refrigerator. It keeps indefinitely as long as there's enough olive oil in the jar to completely cover the pesto. By October I've made enough pesto to get through the coming winter and spring. I even have enough to give to friends and family. We like to add pesto to cooked pasta, which can be served warm or chilled as a salad. I also like to spread a generous layer of pesto on boneless pork cutlets or chicken breasts for baking in the oven, which fills the kitchen with a lovely aroma. I remember the first time I tasted pesto, back in 1983 during a food writers' conference. Now I can't imagine life without it.

2/3 cup olive oil

2 large garlic cloves, coarsely chopped

1/2 teaspoon salt

1/4 teaspoon freshly ground black pepper

2 tablespoons pignoli (pine nuts)

2 cups loosely packed fresh basil leaves

1/2 cup grated Parmesan cheese

In an electric blender or food processor, combine the olive oil, garlic, salt, pepper, pignoli, and basil. Cover and blend until smooth, scraping down the sides of the container as needed. Pour mixture into a bowl. Stir in the grated cheese. Serve over pasta, vegetables, chicken, pork, or pizza.

MAKES 1 1/4 CUPS.

White or Red Clam Sauce

Almost every Italian restaurant in Rhode Island offers pasta with either white or red clam sauce, and the best chefs always use fresh—never canned—clams. Littleneck clams are recommended. Be careful not to overcook them. The following recipe makes a white clam sauce. To make red clam sauce, use the same ingredients along with 1 cup crushed canned Italian brand tomatoes. Add the tomatoes when you add the clams. Some cooks also add ½ cup dry white wine along with the clam juice for extra flavor.

---

6 dozen fresh clams in their shells

3 tablespoons olive oil

3 tablespoons butter

2 garlic cloves, minced

2 tablespoons minced fresh parsley

Salt and freshly ground black pepper, to taste

Scrub the clams with a stiff brush. Rinse well under cold running water. In a large stockpot, steam the clams in 1 inch of water for 5 minutes, or until the shells open. Discard any clams that do not open. Remove meat from clamshells and chop finely. Set clam meat aside. Strain clam juice from pot.

In a large frying pan, heat the oil and butter. Add the clam juice to the frying pan. Add the parsley, salt, and pepper. Bring to a boil. Reduce heat to a simmer. Cover and cook over low heat for 10 minutes.

Add the chopped clams to the skillet to warm thoroughly. Pour this sauce over hot cooked linguine.

MAKES 4 CUPS.

Italian Meat Sauce or "Gravy"

Like many Italian Americans, especially those who can trace their roots to southern Italy, my family referred to the basic meat sauce that my mother made every Sunday morning as "gravy." She made it without thinking about the ingredients or measurements. She did it instinctively, probably while she thought about more important issues. On rare occasions we would have an all-American roast beef with mashed potatoes and gravy for Sunday dinner, but macaroni with "gravy" was absolutely essential at most family gatherings. Even on Thanksgiving, amid the turkey and stuffing, a pasta dish could always be found, perhaps stuffed jumbo shells or lasagna, and always with that rich meaty sauce we called "gravy."

Quahog Sauce

Custy's is another one of those legendary Rhode Island restaurants that people still talk about even though the establishment has long been closed. Located in North Kingstown, Custy's was famous for its reasonably priced all-you-can-eat buffet that included everything from lobster to prime rib. A well-known professional wrestler known as Andre the Giant holds the all-time lobster-eating championship title at Custy's—he consumed 40 lobsters at one sitting. Custy's Quahog Sauce was a staple at that groaning buffet table, served atop as much linguine as you could consume. Dieters, beware!

---

10 pounds quahogs

1 medium-size onion, diced

2 garlic cloves, crushed

2 tablespoons chopped fresh parsley

3 tablespoons vegetable oil

$\frac{1}{2}$ teaspoon hot pepper seeds

$\frac{1}{2}$ teaspoon white pepper

$\frac{1}{4}$ cup dry white wine

In a large stockpot, steam quahogs in 2 cups of water until shells open. Discard any that do not open. Remove meat from clamshells; chop clam meat and set aside, reserving juice.

In a large frying pan, sauté the onion, garlic, and parsley in the vegetable oil over medium-high heat, stirring constantly, for 3 to 5 minutes. Stir in the hot pepper seeds and white pepper. Add the chopped quahog meat, juice, and white wine. Bring mixture to a boil. Remove from heat. Serve this sauce over hot cooked linguine.

MAKES 2 CUPS.

CASSARINO'S, FEDERAL HILL

Garlic-and-Herb-Crusted Prime Rib

Years ago Rhode Islanders were content with a classic prime rib that was simply roasted in the oven. Nowadays, thanks in part to local grilling guru Don Hysko, they prefer a garlic-and-herb-crusted prime rib slowly smoked over a wood fire. The beef gets extra flavor from smoldering hickory wood and fresh herbs—just wonderful for a buffet table or an elegant sit-down dinner. *Note:* It's wise to grill foods that take longer than 25 minutes, such as roasts, over indirect heat. This means that the fire is arranged on either side of the food, not directly beneath it. With the grill's lid closed, heat swirls around the inside of the grill and caramelizes the surface of the roast, creating rich juices and succulent meat. A drip pan can be placed under the roast on the cooking grate to collect drippings.

¼ **cup chopped fresh basil**

¼ **cup chopped fresh oregano**

¼ **cup chopped fresh parsley**

¼ **cup chopped fresh rosemary**

3 **tablespoons olive oil**

1 **tablespoon kosher or sea salt**

1 **tablespoon freshly ground black pepper**

1 **prime rib roast, 12 to 14 pounds**

¼ **cup finely chopped garlic**

Soak hickory wood chips or chunks in water for at least 30 minutes.

In a bowl, combine the basil, oregano, parsley, rosemary, oil, salt, and pepper to make a moist rub. Mix well.

Trim the roast of any excess fat. Press the chopped garlic into the top and sides of the roast. Spread the rub over the top and sides of the roast. Allow to stand at room temperature for at least 30 minutes before grilling.

Prepare the grill for indirect low-heat cooking, placing the hickory over the wood fire on the hot side of the grill. Place the roast on the cool side of the grill and close the lid. Grill the roast until a meat thermometer inserted into the roast indicates an internal temperature of 135 degrees for medium rare, approximately 3 to 4 hours. Keep the grill temperature constant, adding charwood and hickory chips as needed throughout the cooking time.

Remove the roast from the grill. Cover the roast loosely with aluminum foil. Allow the roast to rest for at least 20 minutes before carving. The internal temperature of the roast will rise 5 to 10 degrees during this carry-over cooking time.

Using a very sharp knife, remove the bones from the roast. Cut the meat into ½-inch slices. Serve warm.

MAKES 12 SERVINGS.

Wild about Wood Grilling

While much of America is cooking outdoors on gas grills, Rhode Islanders are passionate about their aromatic, crackling wood fires. Perhaps that's because they learned from the master of the wood fire who lives right here in Lincoln. Don Hysko spent more than twenty years providing chefs and restaurants with freshly cut wood, wood chips, and hardwood charcoal for grilling through his business, Peoples Woods. Hysko sold his business to a local meat purveyor, A. J. Martin, who is continuing to spread the word about the merits of cooking over real wood fires, minus the chemical additives and lighter fluid normally associated with charcoal briquettes.

Three types of wood—basic, fruity, and specialty—are used in grilling. The basic woods are white and red oak, pecan, hickory, maple, and mesquite. The fruity woods include apple and cherry. Specialty woods consist of the woody stems of herbs, lilac, olive, grapevine, and seaweed.

Hysko still likes to demonstrate how to make Dirty Steak, a dish created at the Al Forno restaurant in Providence. He recommends using a Kansas City strip steak that's at least an inch thick. Allow the meat to come to room temperature, and then coat it with olive oil. Place it right on the red-hot coals (yes, right on the coals, not on the grate) for 4 to 5 minutes, then turn it over for another 3 to 4 minutes. Transfer the steak to a plate and let it rest for 5 minutes before serving.

Rhode Island's Best Burgers

The mother of all burgers in Rhode Island is the three-pounder offered at the funky, hole-in-the-wall Classic Café in Providence. The most expensive is the Mount Everest Burger offered at $29.95 at the Mews Tavern in Wakefield. The best gourmet burger can be found at the XO Steak House in Providence, where the 10-ounce burger is stuffed with barbecued duck confit and fresh, shaved black truffles, rubbed with Danish salt and Madagascar pepper, then sautéed in butter to a medium state of doneness. Finally, it is topped with pâté de foie gras and micro greens, and served on a toasted brioche roll. A wonderful tomato jam comes on the side, along with house-made potato chips served warm and drizzled with Gorgonzola cream.

STANLEY'S, CENTRAL FALLS

The Chanler in Newport offers a $25 Kobe beef burger that was listed in *GQ* magazine's "20 Hamburgers You Must Eat Before You Die," an article by the noted restaurant critic Alan Richman. Three local casual restaurant chains offer the basics and then some: Newport Creamery, Gregg's, and Johnny Rockets. The wackiest (and probably the healthiest) burgers in the state are at the Crazy Burger Café & Juice Bar in Narragansett. And who could forget the smothered-with-onions Stanleyburger at Stanley's in Central Falls? It's been on the menu since the joint opened in 1932.

But to be perfectly honest, my very favorite burger in all of Rhode Island is the one my husband cooks in our outdoor kitchen on a wood-burning grill. Our secret? We use hamburger meat with a high fat content, much of which drips into the fire, and our half-pound "patties" are at least an inch thick. The result is always a very juicy, flavorful burger. I like mine cooked medium (pink, not bloody), topped with lots of cheese (any kind), and served on a sesame seed bun with sautéed onions on the side.

Marsala Burger

When I started asking who makes the best burger in Rhode Island, more people told me about the Marsala Burger at Bullock's in Warren over in the East Bay than any other restaurant in the state. Like everyone said, it is "decadently juicy" and "sublime." With this recipe you can make your own at home. The Portuguese muffins are available in Portuguese markets and in the bread section of many supermarkets.

---

1 package Bolos Levedos
(Portuguese muffins)

2 pounds ground beef

12 bacon slices, cooked until crisp
and drained on paper towels

1 tablespoon butter

1 pound sliced mushrooms

1 large garlic clove

Freshly ground black pepper, to
taste

$\frac{1}{2}$ cup Marsala wine

6 slices provolone cheese

Slice the muffins in half and warm them in a 250-degree oven.

With the ground beef, form 6 patties of equal size. Cook as desired, preferably on the grill.

In a large frying pan, melt the butter and sauté the mushrooms, garlic, and pepper. Increase the heat and add the wine, flaming the mixture to burn off the alcohol.

Place 2 strips of cooked bacon on each cooked burger. Add some of the sautéed mushrooms and a slice of provolone cheese. Place the burgers on a baking sheet under the oven broiler just until the cheese is melted. Place the burgers on the warmed muffin halves. Serve immediately.

MAKES 6 SERVINGS.

Haven Brothers

The state's most famous diner is Haven Brothers, opened for business in 1893 by the widow Anna Coffey Haven with the help of her eight children. Haven Brothers gives new meaning to the phrase "meals on wheels." Every night, usually between 5:00 and 6:00 P.M., this stainless-steel trailer is hauled into its landmark spot next to City Hall in the heart of downtown Providence. Climb up the shaky stairs into this tiny "diner" and you enter another world. It almost seems haunted by more than a century of customers seeking a bit of hot food, a cup of java, or perhaps even a frosty glass of coffee milk.

When you order a burger at Haven Brothers, the man behind the counter will ask "Regular?" Say yes, and that will get you a burger topped with mustard, pickles, onions, relish, and ketchup. Until the wee hours of the morning, Haven Brothers serves a diverse clientele that includes Harley Davidson bikers, college kids, and politicians. With only five stools, Haven Brothers is almost always busy until it closes at 3:00 or 4:00 in the morning.

Meatballs alla Giardino

Years ago, when a non-Italian woman married into an Italian family, it was the custom for the new wife to learn how to cook in the style of her mother-in-law. This is how my mother made her meatballs and sauce, as she was taught by Maria Giardino, my father's mother. And it is still the way all my female relatives on the paternal side of my family make their meatballs.

TOMATO SAUCE

1 tablespoon olive oil

1 small to medium onion, cut into thin slices

Salt and freshly ground black pepper, to taste

2 (4-ounce) cans tomato paste

2 (8-ounce) cans tomato sauce

1 (8-ounce) can crushed tomatoes

MEATBALLS

1½ cups bread crumbs

Milk, as needed

1½ pounds lean ground beef

2 eggs

½ cup grated Parmesan cheese

Handful parsley (about ¼ cup chopped)

2 teaspoons fresh minced garlic, more or less to taste

Freshly ground black pepper, to taste

First make the sauce. In a large saucepan, heat the oil and brown the onions. Add the tomato paste, a dash of salt, and two dashes of pepper. Add water, using the 2 tomato paste cans for measure. Add the tomato sauce. Add water, using the 2 tomato sauce cans for measure. Finally, add the crushed tomatoes (but no more water). Bring to a boil on high heat, then lower the heat and simmer for 4 to 6 hours. Stir occasionally until the sauce cooks down and thickens.

To make the meatballs, in a large bowl, combine the bread crumbs with approximately ½ cup of milk, using a fork to mix. Add ground beef and incorporate together.

In a mug, crack open the eggs and add milk—up to about 1 inch from the top of the mug. Beat with a fork. Add to the bread crumb and meat mixture. Add the grated cheese, parsley, garlic, and black pepper. Using your hands, mix well and form into meatballs. Add to the tomato sauce.

Simmer the sauce and meatballs on top of the stove or in a Crock-Pot for 4 to 5 hours or until done, stirring occasionally. Do not stir the meatballs until they have cooked in the sauce for at least 1 hour, because they need to get firm before they are stirred or they'll break up.

MAKES 24 MEATBALLS.

Dynamites

Ever since I was a little kid, Dynamites have been on the table whenever a large crowd needed to be fed. I remember my mother cooking a big pot of Dynamite filling on the wood-burning stove in the cellar when everyone lost electric power during the famous blizzard of 1978. I'm not sure of the origin, but Dynamites are similar to Sloppy Joes, which virtually do not exist in this part of the country. Dynamite sandwiches are the kind of food you continue to eat even when you're full, just to get another bite, one more taste. So, while this recipe may seem to be for a crowd, you will be surprised at how fast it goes. Fresh torpedo rolls, also known as grinder rolls, are available at bakeries and supermarkets throughout Rhode Island. Almost any kind of roll will do, as long as it is substantial enough to hold a serious amount of the Dynamite mixture.

---

5 pounds ground beef

5 pounds green peppers, diced

5 pounds red peppers, diced

5 pounds yellow onions, diced

5 garlic cloves, crushed

4 (28-ounce) cans tomato sauce

2 bay leaves

1/2 cup chopped fresh parsley

Hot pepper flakes, to taste

Salt and freshly ground black pepper, to taste

Italian seasoning, to taste

20 fresh torpedo rolls

In a very large stockpot over medium-high heat, brown the ground beef, stirring often. Add the chopped green and red peppers, onions, and garlic. Mix well. When the vegetables begin to soften, add the tomato sauce, bay leaves, parsley, hot pepper flakes, salt, black pepper, and Italian seasoning. Cover and simmer, stirring occasionally, for 2 to 3 hours.

This filling tastes best if made a day or two ahead of time. Allow the pot to cool and then refrigerate it. Reheat slowly, stirring often. Serve in fresh torpedo rolls. Leftovers freeze very well.

MAKES 20 SERVINGS.

Italian Sausages with Creamy Polenta

One of the fondest food memories I have is of soft, creamy polenta, surrounded by plump, juicy Italian sausages that kept the polenta from spilling over, all served on a large wooden board in the middle of the dining room table. The polenta was cut with a taut string into thick slices that were topped with a robust tomato sauce. Home cooks, especially in the southern part of Rhode Island, prefer to use Fortuna's Fresh Italian Sausage, made in Charlestown. Fortuna's biggest fan is television celebrity Jay Leno, host of the *Tonight Show*, who says "Fortuna's is the best." Fortuna's is especially known for its dry-cured soppressata, known locally as Soupy. Four generations have been making Fortuna's Soupy, which is ready to slice and eat in salads, pastas, or sandwiches, or as an appetizer with cheese.

2 tablespoons olive oil

1 pound Italian sausages

1 pound mushrooms, sliced

2$\frac{1}{2}$ cups canned tomatoes (San Marzano strongly recommended)

Salt, to taste

$\frac{1}{4}$ teaspoon freshly ground black pepper

3 cups water

1 teaspoon salt

1 cup yellow cornmeal

1 cup cold water

Grated Parmesan cheese for sprinkling (optional)

In a heavy frying pan, heat the oil. Add the sausage and mushrooms to the pan and cook over medium heat until they are lightly browned. Stir in the tomatoes, salt, and pepper. Simmer for 30 minutes.

In a saucepan, bring the 3 cups of water and 1 teaspoon of salt to a boil. Combine the cornmeal and cold water. Gradually add the cornmeal mixture to the boiling water in the saucepan, stirring constantly, until the mixture becomes thick. Cover, lower the heat, and cook gently for another 10 minutes.

Transfer the cooked cornmeal (polenta) to a large cutting board or a warm serving platter. Surround with the cooked sausages, mushrooms, and tomato mixture. If desired, sprinkle with grated Parmesan cheese.

MAKES 2 SERVINGS.

Shepherd's Pie

The British who settled in Rhode Island brought over recipes for what the Brits do best: English-style fish-and-chips, pork pies, and old-fashioned shepherd's pie. No one can agree on how shepherd's pie got its name, though many hold that a shepherd's pie should be made with lamb, for obvious reasons. Nevertheless, many Rhode Island children grew up on this beefy version that was served in school cafeterias.

1 pound lean ground beef

1/2 cup finely chopped onion

1 teaspoon thyme

1/4 teaspoon freshly ground black pepper

2 tablespoons flour

1/2 teaspoon powdered beef bouillon

1/2 cup hot water

1/2 cup evaporated skim milk

1 large can peas or corn kernels

4 cups mashed potatoes

Preheat oven to 350 degrees.

In a large frying pan over medium-high heat, brown the ground beef and onions. Drain off fat. Add the thyme and pepper. Stir in the flour. Cook for another 2 minutes.

Dissolve the powdered beef bouillon in 1/2 cup hot water. Add to meat mixture. Cook for another 2 minutes, stirring occasionally. Add evaporated skim milk. Mix well.

Transfer meat mixture to a casserole dish. Top with a layer of peas or corn, then with a layer of mashed potatoes. Bake for 30 minutes, or until heated through.

MAKES 4 SERVINGS.

Tourtiere (French Meat Pie)

French meat pies are a staple for families of French-Canadian descent, but it seems that during the holidays almost everyone in Rhode Island has a meat pie on hand to serve company. The recipe varies slightly from family to family. This is my family's recipe. Meat pies freeze easily (but it's unlikely you'll have any leftovers). The best way to reheat them is in a microwave oven, one slice at a time. If you are reheating a whole pie in a standard oven, be careful not to bake it too long or it will be very dry.

4 medium-size potatoes, peeled

1$\frac{1}{2}$ pounds lean ground pork

$\frac{1}{2}$ pound lean ground beef

2 medium-size onions, chopped fine

Poultry seasoning, to taste

Salt and freshly ground black pepper, to taste

2 (9-inch) two-crust prepared pie shells (store-bought is fine)

In a pot of boiling water, cook the potatoes until tender. Sauté the pork and beef in a large frying pan, breaking up all the chunks of meat.

In a large bowl, mash the cooked potatoes. Combine with the cooked pork, beef, and onions. Season to taste with poultry seasoning, salt, and pepper.

Preheat oven to 350 degrees.

Divide the meat filling equally into the pie shells. Place the top crust on each pie. Crimp edges and cover the edges with aluminum foil. Cut 3 slits in each top crust. Bake the pies for 20 to 30 minutes, or until the top crust is light brown. Serve immediately.

MAKES 2 MEAT PIES, 6 SERVINGS PER PIE.

Angelo's Tripe Marinara

Definitely not for everyone, tripe is a dish that my parents—like many immigrants—always ordered when we ate at their favorite Italian restaurant. Tripe is the stomach of a cow, sheep, or pig, and it has never really caught on with Americans even though it is reportedly buttery tasting and exceptionally tender. Tripe can still be found on the menus of some Rhode Island restaurants, such as Mike's Kitchen, an old-fashioned Italian restaurant located inside a VFW hall in Cranston, and Angelo's Civita Farnese, which has been in business on Federal Hill in Providence since 1924. Here is Angelo's recipe.

---

5 pounds tripe

¼ cup vegetable oil

½ tablespoon freshly chopped garlic

1 cup minced onions

2 cups canned ground Italian plum tomatoes

1 tablespoon oregano

¼ teaspoon crushed red pepper

1½ tablespoons salt

¼ tablespoon black pepper

¼ cup water

In a large pot of boiling water, cook the tripe for 2 hours. Drain and allow to cool. Cut the tripe into strips 1½ inches by ½ inch in size. Set aside.

In a large pot over high heat, combine the oil, garlic, and onions. Sauté until light brown in color. Add the ground tomatoes. Rinse the tripe and add to the tomato mixture. Lower the heat and simmer, stirring occasionally, for 1 hour, adding 1 cup of water if mixture becomes dry.

Add remaining ingredients and simmer for an additional 30 minutes. Serve immediately.

MAKES 10 SERVINGS.

Porcetta (Italian-Style Roast Pork)

Porcetta is Italian for "roast pork," a highly seasoned boneless pork shoulder or butt roast, available in Italian meat markets. In northern Rhode Island, a *porcetta* is also an event—the time for really good Italian food. In large halls, civic groups will offer a *porcetta* dinner with all the appropriate fixings as a way to raise funds. You can also make your own *porcetta*, as I learned from my mother. She always served it with potatoes roasted with garlic and rosemary.

---

1 (4-pound) boneless pork shoulder or butt roast

1 teaspoon whole fennel seeds

1 teaspoon dried rosemary

Zest of 1 orange, minced

1/2 cup finely minced fresh fennel

Salt and freshly ground black pepper, to taste

4 garlic cloves, minced

1 tablespoon dry white wine

1 tablespoon olive oil

2/3 cup dry white wine

In a mortar or small bowl, combine the fennel seeds, rosemary, and orange zest. Using a pestle, pound these ingredients into a coarse mixture. Add the minced fennel, salt, pepper, garlic, white wine, and olive oil. Mix well.

Using a small sharp knife, cut small deep slits into the pork. Push some of the fennel seed mixture into the slits. Rub the rest of the mixture all over the surface of the pork, coating it well. Roll the pork into a tight cylinder. Tie with butcher's twine to hold the roll together. Place the pork in a roasting pan. Cover and refrigerate overnight.

The next day, preheat oven to 350 degrees.

Allow the pork to come to room temperature. Place the pork in the middle of the oven. Roast for 30 minutes. Add the remaining 2/3 cup white wine. Roast for 1 hour, basting occasionally, or until a meat thermometer reads 150 degrees when inserted into the middle part of the pork.

Allow pork to rest, covered, at room temperature for at least 10 minutes before serving.

Cut into thick slices. Serve immediately, drizzled with pan juices.

MAKES 8 SERVINGS.

Canadian Pork Chops

While I grew up in a home where mostly Italian food was served, most of my childhood friends were of French-Canadian descent. Being invited to their homes for dinner was an adventure. Back then, I thought these Canadian pork chops were the most exotic food on earth.

---

4 green scallions, finely chopped

2 garlic cloves

1/3 cup maple syrup

1 1/2 tablespoons ketchup

1 cup apple juice

1/8 teaspoon chili powder

1/8 teaspoon cinnamon

1 teaspoon salt

Pinch black pepper

4 pork chops, each 1-inch thick and trimmed of excess fat

1/2 cup finely crushed walnuts

Chopped fresh parsley, for garnish

In a large shallow dish, combine the scallions, garlic, maple syrup, ketchup, apple juice, chili powder, cinnamon, salt, and pepper.

Pierce the pork chops on both sides. Place the pork chops in the shallow dish, coating both sides. Cover with plastic wrap and refrigerate for at least 2 hours, turning the chops occasionally.

Prepare your grill. Over medium heat, grill the chops for 20 minutes on each side. Garnish with crushed walnuts and parsley.

MAKES 4 SERVINGS.

Hartley's Pork Pies

Thomas Hartley, an English immigrant, established the first Hartley's Pork Pies store in Fall River, Massachusetts, back in 1902. In 1954 his son Everett set up a pork pie shop in a tiny triangular-shaped brick building on Smithfield Avenue in Lincoln. Now owned by Dan and Colene Doire, Hartley's is still a Rhode Island institution. The little shop on the corner is open only Wednesday through Saturday, from 7:00 A.M. to 2:00 P.M., or until the pies run out—which is quite often. More than once I have been greatly disappointed to pull up in front of the store and see the sign Sorry—Sold Out Today. The Doires bake hundreds of pies daily, especially during the winter holiday season. And it's strictly takeout.

Five kinds of pies are available: pork, beef, meat-and-potato, chicken, and salmon (the latter available only on Fridays). Inside the flavorful pie crust is the steaming, spiced meat and the secret ingredient, the gravy. The individual-serving deep-dish pies fit into the palm of your hand. The top crust on each pie is stamped with the letter H—for Hartley. That's about all the advertising the Doires have to do.

Porco com Ameijoas a Alentejana (Pork with Clams)

Ethnic restaurants are popping up all over the Providence area. Among the most popular are the eateries serving Portuguese food. They typically serve multiple combinations of meats and starches, such as a grilled steak served with fries, rice, ham, and a fried egg. Here's one classic Portuguese dish, utilizing little-neck and cherrystone clams from Narragansett Bay.

1$\frac{1}{2}$ pounds lean pork, cut into 1-inch cubes

1 cup dry white wine

2 teaspoons paprika

1 bay leaf

2 whole cloves

Salt and freshly ground black pepper, to taste

6 garlic cloves, minced

2 tablespoons butter

2 medium-size onions, sliced

4 medium-size tomatoes, chopped

2 pounds littleneck or cherrystone clams

4 tablespoons fresh coriander

2 tablespoons chopped fresh parsley

1 lemon, cut into quarters

In a large casserole or glass baking dish, combine the pork with the wine, paprika, bay leaf, cloves, salt, pepper, and half of the minced garlic. Cover and refrigerate overnight, turning occasionally.

In a large saucepan, melt 1 tablespoon of butter. Add the onions, tomatoes, and remaining garlic. Cook over low heat until the onions are tender. Season to taste with salt and pepper.

Rinse the clams in cold water. Discard any clams that are already open. Add the clams to the saucepan. Cover and cook on high heat until they have opened, about 5 minutes. Discard any clams that do not open after cooking.

Drain the pork. Set the marinade aside. In a large frying pan, heat the remaining tablespoon of butter. Add the pork to the frying pan. Brown on all sides over medium-high heat. Add the marinade. Continue to cook over medium heat until most of the marinade has evaporated.

Pour the pork onto a serving platter. Pour the clams and onion-tomato sauce over the pork. Sprinkle with the coriander and parsley. Garnish with the lemon quarters. Serve immediately.

MAKES 4 SERVINGS.

Saugy Dawgy

Many Rhode Islanders grew up in families where this hearty, one-pan meal was served every Saturday night.

2 pounds Saugy frankfurters

3 medium-size onions, chopped

3 tablespoons olive oil

¼ cup honey

¼ cup brown sugar

1 bottle chili sauce (Heinz recommended)

1 (28-ounce) can baked beans (B&M recommended)

Garlic bread

Slice the frankfurters into 1-inch pieces. In a large, deep frying pan, sauté the frankfurters with the chopped onions in the olive oil for about 10 minutes. Add the honey, brown sugar, chili sauce, and baked beans. Cook over medium to low heat for another 15 minutes. Serve with garlic bread on the side.

MAKES 8 SERVINGS.

Saugy Hot Dogs

Saugy Inc., Rhode Island's historic frankfurter company, was started in Providence in 1869 by Augustus and Alphonse Saugy, who used a recipe brought over from Germany. Saugy franks are natural casing hot dogs that really do snap when you bite into them, as compared to skinless dogs that have no snap. A couple of million pounds of Saugys are sold annually to local supermarkets and restaurants. They also are available nationally, especially in Florida where so many Rhode Islanders retire. Saugys, as they are called, are as much a part of Rhode Island as seafood shacks and Del's frozen lemonade. No Rhode Island clambake would be complete without Saugy hot dogs mixed in with the fish, steamers, mussels, sausage, and potatoes.

Saugy Casserole

This recipe can easily be doubled, always using equal amounts of the grape jelly and ketchup.

1 pound Saugy frankfurters

1 tablespoon olive oil

Celery salt, to taste

1 (16-ounce) jar grape jelly

1 (16-ounce) bottle ketchup

Cut the frankfurters into 1-inch pieces. Sauté them in a large frying pan in the oil until slightly browned. Season with celery salt.

Place the frankfurters in a Crock-Pot. Add the grape jelly and ketchup, mixing well. Cook in the Crock-Pot on high, stirring occasionally, for 1 to 2 hours, or until the desired taste is achieved.

Serve warm with toothpicks as an appetizer.

MAKES 4 SERVINGS.

Man Bites Dog

Much good-hearted debate goes on in Rhode Island over who makes the best hot dogs. On the restaurant side of options, the New York System wiener topped with its special sauce is a hard-core favorite, followed by the new kid on the block, the flavorful Spike's Junkyard Dogs. Both of these hot dog concepts have locations throughout the state. When it comes to cooking your hot dogs at home, Saugy hot dogs have a very loyal following, followed by Little Rhody hot dogs, which are a bit bland in comparison, but they plump up nicely when cooked.

Saugys with Italian Sausages

This recipe gives the German frankfurters an Italian twist. Add a can of Italian tomatoes if you desire a "gravy." This dish can also be prepared in a 9x13-inch dish in the oven. Broil the meat until it browns, then add the rest of the ingredients, and bake at 375 degrees for 40 minutes.

1 pound Saugy frankfurters, cut in half

1 pound hot or sweet Italian sausages, cut into 2-inch pieces

1 tablespoon olive oil

1 large red or green pepper, sliced

1 large onion, sliced

5 large garlic cloves, sliced

3 unpeeled red potatoes, sliced and par-cooked in the microwave

Salt and freshly ground black pepper, to taste

Garlic powder, to taste

Dried basil, to taste

6 fresh sandwich rolls

In a large frying pan, brown the frankfurters and sausage in the olive oil. Add the sliced pepper, onion, and garlic. Sauté for a few minutes. Add the sliced potatoes. Season with salt, pepper, garlic powder, and basil. Cover and cook over medium heat for about 20 minutes. Serve with fresh rolls to make excellent sandwiches.

MAKES 6 SERVINGS.

Remembrance of Things Past

Walter Zuromski of Lincoln is now a research chef, working on special projects for major food companies across the nation. But his roots are deep in Rhode Island—his family used to own the Modern Diner in Pawtucket. His mother has especially fond memories of a time long gone, back when coffee was 15 cents a cup.

Among her keepsakes is an old menu featuring Meatloaf, French Meat Pie, Turkey Pot Pie, Salisbury Steak, Native Baked Stuffed Bluefish, New England Boiled Dinner, Fish and Chips in Beer Batter, Liver and Slab Bacon with Onions, and Walter's favorite dish as a kid—the hot dogs and beans dinner, with the hot dogs cooked in the baked beans and served with fluffy white bread and margarine.

Walter's father and his two uncles spent more than half a century shaping the taste buds of Rhode Islanders. In addition to the Modern Diner, the Zuromski family was involved with several restaurants that went on to become Rhode Island institutions—the old Lindsay Tavern, Twin Willows, Shepard's Tea Room, Chelo's, and Gregg's.

Kielbasa with Caraway-Dill Cabbage

Kielbasa, a pork sausage seasoned with garlic, is a close cousin to the hot dog. Polish friends taught me how to make this hearty kielbasa dish that goes so well with boiled new potatoes. I recommend preparing the cabbage in advance. It reheats in a snap while you're making the zesty accompanying sauce. Authentic Polish kielbasa is available in several Polish markets in the northern part of Rhode Island.

3 tablespoons butter

1 medium-size onion, diced

1 medium-size head cabbage, cored, and sliced thin

1 green apple, peeled, cored, and sliced thin

1 cup dry white wine

2 tablespoons white wine vinegar

1 teaspoon caraway seeds

¼ cup chopped fresh dill, plus additional sprigs for garnish

1 cup chicken broth

1 pound Polish kielbasa

Mustard Sauce (recipe follows)

In a large, deep frying pan, melt the butter over medium-high heat. Sauté the onion until tender, about 5 minutes. Add the sliced cabbage, tossing to coat well in the melted butter. Add the apple slices, wine, vinegar, caraway seeds, fresh dill, and chicken broth. Cook, uncovered, until the cabbage is tender, about 20 minutes.

Cut the kielbasa into 4 equal portions. In a separate, large, deep frying pan, cook the kielbasa in 2 to 3 inches of simmering water for 10 to 12 minutes.

Place a generous mound of cooked cabbage on each dinner plate. Top with a portion of the kielbasa. Drizzle with the mustard sauce. Garnish with dill sprigs, if desired.

MUSTARD SAUCE

3 tablespoons butter

3 tablespoons all-purpose flour

1 cup chicken broth

1 cup milk

½ cup white wine

2 teaspoons Dijon mustard

1 bunch scallions, chopped

In a small frying pan, melt the butter. Add the flour, blend well, and cook until the flour begins to turn golden in color. Set aside.

In a saucepan, combine the chicken broth, milk, wine, and mustard over medium-high heat. Bring to a simmer. Stirring constantly, add the butter-flour mixture gradually to thicken the sauce to a desired consistency. Add the scallions just before serving.

MAKES 4 SERVINGS.

French Lamb Stew

When it came to cooking, my mother excelled at stews. Her French-Belgian heritage no doubt came into play when she cooked such dishes instinctively. This lamb stew is perfect for a crowd, served simply with loaves of crusty bread and a salad of mixed greens.

---

3 tablespoons olive oil

2 pounds lean lamb chunks, trimmed of excess fat

1 medium-size onion, chopped

1 garlic clove, minced

2 tablespoons flour

2 cups chicken broth

Salt and freshly ground black pepper, to taste

1 bay leaf

¼ teaspoon marjoram

½ cup dry white wine

8 small white onions, peeled (about 1 inch in diameter)

4 carrots, peeled and sliced diagonally

1 cup fresh green beans, snapped in half

8 medium-size potatoes, peeled and cut into bite-size pieces

1 tablespoon finely chopped fresh parsley

In a large heavy pot, heat the oil. Brown the lamb on all sides over medium-high heat. Remove the lamb from the pot and set aside in a bowl.

In the same pot, sauté the chopped onion and garlic until golden brown. Return the lamb to the pot and sprinkle it with the flour. Add the broth, salt, pepper, bay leaf, marjoram, and wine. Stir to mix well. Cover and simmer over low heat for 30 minutes. Skim off any fat that comes to the surface. Add the white onions, carrots, green beans, and potatoes. Simmer for another 30 minutes, or until the lamb and vegetables are tender. A few minutes before serving, add the parsley to the stew.

MAKES 8 SERVINGS.

Chicken Beaulieu

One of the most surprising things that ever happened to me was the creation of this recipe by the chefs at CAV, an extraordinary restaurant in Providence. Owner Sylvia Moubayed named the dish in my honor. It is now one of my specialties when I have a dinner party in my home. CAV, by the way, stands for Cocktails, Antiques, and Victuals, and all that awaits you in this restaurant, located in the city's Jewelry District. At CAV, Chicken Beaulieu is served with mashed sweet potatoes, and all the sauce is drizzled on top of the chicken breast.

1 (10-ounce) boneless, skinless chicken breast

2 tablespoons butter, divided

1 tablespoon slivered almonds

1 small red onion, cut into julienne strips

1 Red Delicious apple, cut into julienne strips

¼ cup hazelnut liqueur, such as Frangelico

½ tablespoon Dijon mustard

1 teaspoon finely chopped fresh parsley

Salt and freshly ground black pepper, to taste

Preheat oven to 375 degrees.

Place a frying pan over high heat. When it is smoking hot, pan-sear the chicken breast. Transfer it to a baking dish and finish cooking it the oven, approximately 20 minutes.

In the same frying pan, melt 1 tablespoon of butter. Add the almonds and toast until light brown in color. Add the onion and cook until golden brown and tender. Add the apple and cook for 2 minutes. Deglaze the pan with the hazelnut liqueur. Add the Dijon mustard, remaining tablespoon of butter, and parsley. Allow the sauce to reduce slightly. Season to taste with salt and pepper.

MAKES 1 SERVING.

It's a Family Affair

Rhode Island, a state with two chickens named after it (Rhode Island Red and Rhode Island White), is also known for its family-style, all-you-can-eat chicken dinners served at very affordable prices.

Chicken dinner restaurants began to appear in northern Rhode Island during the Great Depression. Chicken farmers found themselves with more chickens than they could sell in the markets, so some farmers—with the help of their wives in the kitchen—opened small restaurants that sold only chicken dinners. This new type of restaurant flourished as the depression came to an end. People came from great distances for the chicken dinners, and seventy years later they are still a big draw.

How the chickens are cooked is a bit of a secret. Some chefs submerge whole chickens in olive oil to bake until golden brown. Others "broast" their chickens, which is a combination of broiling and roasting. Still others claim cooking the birds in a pressure cooker is what makes them so special.

Some chefs specialize in "berched" chicken. Whole chickens are split in half and layered on top of one another in deep rectangular pans. Water is added to the pans, as well as a "special seasoning." The pans are covered and placed on top of the stove to parboil gently and slowly, which allows the seasoning to saturate each bird. The pans of precooked chicken are then set next to a flat-top grill, where each chicken half is cooked to order, sometimes with a heavy weight pressing down on each bird. The skin gets crispy while the inside of the chicken stays moist and tender.

At these chicken dinner restaurants, platters of food are brought to the table for everyone to share. Side dishes include a simple salad of iceberg lettuce dressed in olive oil, macaroni in a red tomato sauce, french fries or roasted potatoes, and sweet sticky buns.

The most famous of these family-style chicken dinner restaurants is Wright's Farm in Nasonville, a Rhode Island landmark since 1972, still owned by the Galleshaw family. This is a big restaurant, able to serve 1,200 people at a time in six dining rooms with seventy-five ovens cranking out the famous chicken. The last time we went to Wright's, there were hundreds, perhaps even a thousand people in line ahead of us, and the wait was ninety minutes for a table. Well worth it, in my mind. Wright's tomato sauce and salad dressing are so popular, bottles of the stuff are sold at the restaurant and at local supermarkets.

Many other restaurants in northern Rhode Island offer family-style chicken dinners as part of their menu. For decades this chicken and macaroni combination has been served at wedding receptions and banquets in that part of the state. This is down-home food at its best.

Chicken with Artichokes and White Wine

When Rhode Island Supreme Court Chief Justice Frank J. Williams isn't in chambers, he's either in the kitchen or shopping for kitchen gadgets and quality ingredients up on Federal Hill. One of the most famous home cooks in the state, Judge Williams is quite proud of his Italian-American heritage and often demonstrates recipes such as this one for fund-raising efforts. He has even appeared on local TV, wearing his judicial robes as he whips up one of his gourmet dishes and seasons it—judiciously, of course.

---

4 chicken cutlets

All-purpose flour, as needed for coating chicken

10 tablespoons butter, divided

1 pound mushrooms, sliced

1 to 2 (14-ounce) cans artichoke hearts, drained and cut up

¼ cup white wine

Dip each chicken cutlet in the flour. Heat 2 tablespoons of the butter in a large ovenproof frying pan. Sauté the chicken breasts in the melted butter, then set aside.

Preheat oven to 350 degrees.

In the same frying pan, heat the remaining 8 tablespoons of butter. Sauté the sliced mushrooms and cut-up artichoke hearts in the melted butter. Add the wine and reserved chicken cutlets to the mushroom-artichoke mixture. Simmer for 10 minutes.

Place the frying pan in the oven and bake for another 10 minutes. Serve immediately.

MAKES 4 SERVINGS.

Chicken a la Providence

Since the 1920s, home cooks have been making Chicken a la Providence, an old-fashioned homey serving of chicken and vegetables in a rich sauce. Back then it was a gourmet dish. Today it's pure comfort food.

1 whole chicken (about 4 pounds), cleaned

8 cups boiling water

Salt and freshly ground black pepper, to taste

2 tablespoons butter

2 tablespoons flour

2 cups chicken broth (from cooked chicken)

2 egg yolks, slightly beaten

1/2 cup cooked sliced carrots

1/2 cup cooked peas

1 teaspoon chopped fresh parsley

In a large stockpot filled with the boiling water, simmer the chicken gently on low heat until tender. Season to taste with salt and pepper. Remove the cooked chicken from the pot and set aside. Measure 2 cups of broth from the pot.

To make the sauce, melt the butter in a small saucepan. Add the flour and blend smoothly. Add the chicken broth, stirring constantly. Cook for 5 minutes.

Pour about 1/2 cup of the sauce into the egg yolks, mixing well to prevent lumps, and then add the eggs to the remainder of the sauce. Stir in the carrots and peas. Season to taste with salt and pepper. Cut the chicken into serving pieces and arrange on a platter. Top with the sauce and sprinkle with the parsley. Serve immediately.

MAKES 4 SERVINGS.

South County Chicken Potpie

No one seems to know for sure if Rhode Island can be credited with creating the first potpie, but this dish dates back locally to 1792. More than likely, the idea for the American potpie came over with early English settlers. This pie is filled with chicken and vegetables, making good use of leftovers. Turkey can be substituted for the chicken.

6 tablespoons butter

6 tablespoons flour

2 cups chicken broth

1 cup whole milk or heavy cream

Salt to taste

$1/2$ teaspoon freshly ground black pepper

4 cups cubed chicken (or turkey)

$1/2$ cup diced carrots, cooked

$1/2$ cup baby peas, cooked

1 cup finely chopped onions

1 (9-inch) prepared pastry crust

Preheat oven to 425 degrees.

In a saucepan, melt the butter and stir in the flour with a whisk to make a roux. Cook for 2 minutes. Slowly add the broth, milk or cream, salt, and pepper, stirring constantly to prevent lumps. Cook for 5 minutes until the sauce is thick and smooth.

Lightly grease a deep pie plate or casserole. Place the cubed chicken in the pie plate. Add the carrots, peas, and onions. Cover completely with the sauce. Place the prepared pie crust over the pie plate. Crimp the edges. Bake for 30 minutes, or until crust is golden brown.

MAKES 6 SERVINGS.

Chicken Parmigiana

For some unknown reason, Thursday is "chicken parm" day in Rhode Island, much as Wednesday has been nationally marketed for years as "Prince Spaghetti Day." Restaurants, especially in Providence, offer chicken parmigiana as the Thursday special. Workers pour out of their office buildings craving this boneless chicken breast topped with tomato sauce and a melted slice of Parmesan cheese, usually accompanied by pasta in a red tomato sauce. Chicken parm sandwiches are also quite popular.

---

2 whole chicken breasts, boned, skinned, and split

1 cup milk

1½ cups seasoned bread crumbs

½ cup grated Parmesan cheese

4 tablespoons butter

2 cups tomato sauce

4 slices mozzarella cheese

Preheat oven to 450 degrees.

To make the chicken breasts more tender, pound them with a meat mallet before preparing this dish. Place them between sheets of waxed paper or plastic wrap before pounding for easy cleanup.

Soak the 4 chicken breasts in the milk. In a shallow dish, combine the bread crumbs and Parmesan cheese. Dredge the breasts in the bread crumb mixture. Place the breasts in a well-greased baking dish. Top each breast with 1 tablespoon of butter.

Bake the chicken breasts for 25 minutes. Remove them from the oven, top each breast with ½ cup tomato sauce and 1 slice of mozzarella cheese, and return the baking dish to the oven. Continue baking for 10 more minutes, or until the tomato sauce is bubbly and the cheese has melted.

MAKES 4 SERVINGS.

Antonelli's Fresh Poultry

Antonelli Poultry has been a fixture on Federal Hill since before the Civil War. As you approach the tiny storefront, sandwiched between Italian restaurants on DePasquale Plaza, you can smell the live chickens on death row in the rear of the store.

You can hand-select the bird you want to purchase, giving your order to the man next to the hanging scale. Other men are busy killing, plucking, and cleaning the birds. Don't be surprised if a couple of chickens have gotten loose and are wandering around. It doesn't get any fresher than this.

Owner Chrls Morris took over the business "twenty or thirty years ago" from his father-in-law, Frank Antonelll. Back then, most of the customers were of Italian descent, shopping for fresh chicken. These days, first-generation Asian and Hispanic customers frequent the shop more than those of any other ethnicity. But all kinds of folks shop at Antonelli's. During the holidays, German-Americans seek fresh geese. Home cooks come in for Muscovy duck or pheasant. Guinea hens, pigeons, rabbits, and even chicken feet are also available.

Shopping at Antonelli's will remind you of the outdoor markets you find in Italy and France. During the week, you can get your fresh chicken in fifteen minutes. On a bustling Saturday it can take an hour. If your timing is right, your purchase will still feel warm to the touch as you walk out the door.

Phillipe and Jorge Chicken

Phillipe and Jorge, columnists for the alternative *Providence Phoenix* newspaper, are known for mincing a shallot or two but never their words. This recipe was created in their honor by Linda Bigelow at Leo's back in the 1980s, when Leo's was the hip place to dine in Providence's Jewelry District. Leo's is long gone and sorely missed. At least we can still make this outrageously good chicken dish at home.

½ pound fresh fennel

2 sweet red peppers

6 boneless chicken breasts, skin on

¼ cup olive oil

2 shallots, minced

1 cup white wine

⅓ cup Pernod liqueur

2 teaspoons tomato paste

½ teaspoon dried thyme

1 cup black olives

1 cup green olives

Salt and freshly ground black
    pepper, to taste

Slice the fennel into ¼-inch strips, removing the leaves. Slice the peppers into ¼-inch strips.

In a large frying pan, sauté the chicken breasts in the olive oil until lightly browned. Remove the chicken from the pan and keep it warm.

Add the fennel to the frying pan. Cover and cook for 15 minutes or until tender. Add the peppers and shallots. Cook for 5 more minutes. Add the wine, Pernod, and tomato paste. Mix well. Cook for 10 minutes over high heat or until the sauce is slightly thickened. Reduce heat. Add the thyme, black and green olives, and chicken breasts to the frying pan. Cook until the chicken is cooked through, about 5 to 10 minutes. Season to taste with salt and pepper.

MAKES 6 SERVINGS.

Infornata di Pollo con Patate, Limone, e Rosmarino
(Baked Whole Chicken with Potatoes, Lemon, and Rosemary)

At Aquaviva, a Providence restaurant that specializes in clay cookery, chef-owner Walter Potenza offers cooking classes so that home cooks can duplicate his savory dishes, such as this baked chicken. The terracotta pot in which the chicken cooks is soaked in water for 15 minutes before using. The results? Probably the most succulent, moist chicken you've ever had. Clay cooking pots can be purchased in upscale gourmet shops.

---

1 (3-pound) whole chicken, boned, cut into pieces

10 fresh sage leaves

1 sprig fresh rosemary

4 garlic cloves, peeled

3 tablespoons olive oil

Juice and zest of 1 large lemon

2 teaspoons kosher salt

$\frac{1}{2}$ teaspoon freshly ground black pepper

1 large potato, peeled, sliced in $\frac{1}{4}$-inch rounds

$\frac{1}{2}$ cup dry white wine

$\frac{1}{2}$ cup chicken broth

Preheat oven to 400 degrees. Soak a large terra-cotta or clay pot in clean cold water for 15 minutes.

In a medium-size bowl, combine the chicken pieces with the sage, rosemary, garlic, half the olive oil, lemon juice and zest, 1 teaspoon kosher salt, and $\frac{1}{4}$ teaspoon black pepper. Toss gently. Set aside.

Empty the water from the clay pot. Using your fingers coat the interior of the pot with the remaining olive oil. Line the bottom of the pot with the sliced potatoes (do not overlap). Sprinkle evenly with the remaining kosher salt and pepper. Arrange the chicken pieces on top of the potatoes in a circular pattern.

To the bowl in which the chicken was seasoned, add the wine and chicken broth. Mix well. Using a rubber spatula, pour the liquid and the rest of the ingredients left in the bowl over the chicken.

Bake for 1 hour, or until the chicken is tender and juicy. Serve hot.

MAKES 4 SERVINGS.

Seafood

Steamers, Italian-Style

The holy trinity of Italian flavors—olive oil, garlic, and fresh parsley—will give your basic steamers an Italian flavor.

---

4 tablespoons olive oil

3 garlic cloves, crushed

3 tablespoons minced fresh parsley

1 tablespoon black pepper

3 dozen steamers, well scrubbed

In a large frying pan, heat the oil. Gently fry the garlic and parsley for about 3 minutes, being careful not to burn the garlic. Add the pepper. Add the clams, cover the pan with a tight-fitting lid, and simmer slowly until all the clams have opened. Discard any that do not open. Serve in warm soup plates with the juice from the frying pan poured over the clams.

MAKES 2 SERVINGS.

Clam Juice and Clam Broth

Is clam juice the same thing as clam broth? No.

Clam juice is the nectar, the briny liquid inside every clam.

Clam broth is easily made by combining 24 well-washed clams and 3 cups of water in a large pot over high heat. Boil for 6 minutes. Remove the clams from the pot. Strain the liquid in the pot through a fine cheesecloth, and that's clam broth.

Rhode Island Steamed Clams

Rhode Islanders call them "steamers." They are the soft-shell clams with rubbery necks that are steamed open, usually in water or beer. As soon as they are cool enough to handle, but hopefully still warm, you just pluck the full clams from their shells. Discard any that do not open fully after steaming—a sign that the clams are not fresh. Peel away and discard the black membrane covering the neck. Die-hard fans dip their steamers one at a time into a cup of the broth in which the clams were cooked to rinse off any grains of beach sand and to re-warm the clam. Nearly everyone dips the steamer into warm, melted butter and eats it whole, rubbery neck and all. You can go clamming for steamers for free—the beds at low tide along the Galilee Escape Road in Narragansett are quite productive—or you can purchase the costly clams at local fish markets. Figure on at least one pound of steamed clams (in the shell) per person—two pounds if people are crazy about steamers. Before cooking, if the clams seem sandy, soak them for a couple of hours or overnight in the refrigerator in a pot of salted water with a bit of vinegar, cornmeal, and cayenne pepper. Shake the pot occasionally to get the clams to spit out any sand they might contain.

---

1 pound steamers per person

1 yellow onion

1 cup water or beer

4 tablespoons butter per person

Rinse the clams thoroughly in clean, cold water. Discard any clams that are open or that have cracked shells. Place the clams and onion in a large stockpot and add the water or beer. Place the pot over high heat, cover it with a tight-fitting lid, and bring the pot to a boil. Reduce heat to a simmer and continue cooking until the clamshells have popped open, approximately 8 minutes.

While the clams are cooking, melt the butter in a saucepan over low to medium heat.

Remove the steamed clams from the pot. Place them in a large serving bowl or individual soup bowls. Strain the broth in which the clams were cooked. Pour the strained broth into individual cups or bowls to be served with the steamed clams and the melted butter.

Steamers, Portuguese-Style

Because of the addition of linguica, green peppers, and tomatoes, you'll want to have some crusty bread on hand to sop up the wonderful broth with these steamers.

---

5 pounds steamers, well scrubbed

1/2 pound linguica (Portuguese sausage), cut into 3/4-inch slices on the bias

1 large onion, cut into thin wedges

1 small green pepper, cut into thin strips

1 (14-ounce) can whole tomatoes, crushed

2 cups Vinho Verde (Portuguese wine) or dry white wine

1/4 cup Portuguese olive oil

Chopped fresh parsley, for garnish

Place the clams in a large stockpot with a tight-fitting lid. Add the linguica, onion, green pepper, tomatoes, wine, and olive oil to the pot. Cover tightly and set over high heat. Cook until all the clams have steamed open, shaking the pot often. Discard any clams that do not open.

Divide the steamed clams evenly into warm soup plates. Garnish with chopped parsley. Strain the broth in the stockpot and serve in bowls on the side for dipping.

MAKES 5 SERVINGS.

A Shore Thing

Classic Rhode Island seafood dishes are sometimes served together in what is called a Rhode Island shore dinner. Similar to a clambake, which is traditionally prepared and served outdoors, shore dinners used to be served in big halls or pavilions by the sea, with Rocky Point on Warwick Neck being the most famous. On summer weekends, thousands of people would fill row upon row of long tables in the huge dining room with an ocean view.

A typical shore dinner includes a steamed lobster, steamers, boiled red bliss potatoes, smoked sausage, corn on the cob, chowder, and watermelon for dessert.

The massive shore dinner halls of Rhode Island are long gone, but the tradition continues in a handful of seaside restaurants. One of the best is Aunt Carrie's in Narragansett, where Indian pudding (see recipe in Desserts chapter) is also available.

Rhode Island Quahog Pie

The recipe for Quahog Pie has been around for decades. Some Rhode Island home cooks believe the recipe originally came from Nantucket, but they say it comes out best when made with fresh quahogs from Narragansett Bay.

1 quart freshly shucked quahogs
(available in fish markets)

Pie dough, enough for bottom and
top crust (store-bought is fine)

Salt and freshly ground black
pepper to taste

2 tablespoons butter, cut into small
pieces

1 cup milk

1 teaspoon butter

Drain the quahogs, reserving 1 cup of the broth to use in the sauce. Using an old-fashioned meat grinder or a modern-day food processor, grind the quahogs. Season to taste with salt and pepper.

Preheat oven to 400 degrees.

Line a pie plate with the dough for the bottom crust. Pour the ground quahogs into the pie plate. Dot with the small pieces of butter. Cover the quahogs with the dough for the top crust.

Bake the pie until the crust begins to turn golden brown, approximately 10 minutes. Reduce heat to 350 degrees and bake for another 30 minutes.

Make a white sauce by combining the reserved quahog broth, milk, and 1 teaspoon butter in a saucepan over medium-high heat. Simmer until it thickens to the desired consistency. Serve the quahog pie with the sauce, mashed potatoes, and the vegetable of your choice.

MAKES 6 SERVINGS.

Quahog Chili

Duffy's Tavern in North Kingstown is famous for its fresh seafood, abundant servings, and low prices. One of the most enduring dishes on the menu is a unique chili created by the owner, Captain Stu Tucker. When fresh tuna is in season, Stu adds it to this recipe with delicious results.

3 tablespoons oil

1 green pepper, chopped

1 yellow onion, chopped

2 cups stewed tomatoes

1 tablespoon chili powder

Salt and freshly ground black
 pepper, to taste

1 pound chopped quahogs

1 (16-ounce) can red kidney beans

1 (16-ounce) can cannellini beans

1 pound sautéed fresh tuna
 (optional)

In a large saucepan, heat the oil. Add the chopped green peppers and onions. Sauté for 3 minutes. Add the stewed tomatoes and chili powder. Simmer until thick, about 1 hour. Season to taste with salt and pepper. Add the chopped quahogs, beans, and tuna, if desired. Simmer for 30 minutes.

MAKES 6 SERVINGS.

Thanks to the Indians . . .

Our culinary debt to American Indian tribes, such as the Narragansett in Rhode Island, is great. Many classic American dishes are of American Indian origin: Brunswick stew, steamed lobster, baked beans, clam chowder, chili con carne, spoon bread, and cranberry sauce, to name just a few.

Perhaps the greatest gift from the Narragansett tribe was the clambake. American Indians on the East Coast steamed their dinners in earthen pits, creating the first clambakes. Every clambake is presided over by the bakemaster. This method of cooking was passed on to an early settler, who became the first Rhode Island bakemaster. Since then the clambake tradition has been handed down from generation to generation.

Fried Clams

Clams that are already shucked are available at most fish markets. Be prepared for steep prices. You can also buy a packaged mix to make the batter for fried clams, or you can make it from scratch with the following recipe. In Rhode Island the entire clam—including the plump belly—is fried, unlike other parts of the country, where only clam strips minus the belly are served.

1 egg, separated

1/2 cup milk, divided

1/2 cup sifted flour

1/4 teaspoon salt

1 tablespoon melted butter

24 shucked clams

Cooking oil for deep-frying

Salt, as needed

Tartar sauce, as needed

In a bowl, beat the egg yolk and combine with $1/4$ cup of the milk. In another bowl, combine the flour and salt, and sift together into the egg-milk mixture. Beat until the batter is smooth.

In another bowl, beat the egg white until stiff peaks form.

Add the remaining 1/4 cup of milk and the melted butter to the batter. Fold in the beaten egg white. Dip each clam into the batter, and deep-fry the clams in a 4- to 6-inch pan containing hot oil until each clam is golden brown on all sides. Drain on paper towels. Serve immediately with salt and tartar sauce.

MAKES 2 SERVINGS.

STARBOARD GALLERY,
NARRAGANSETT

How to Cook a Lobster

Live lobsters should be cooked the day they are purchased. The ideal way to store lobsters until it is time to cook is in the refrigerator on a bed of seaweed. Do not keep lobsters in the sink; they die in fresh water.

To boil a lobster, bring an almost full pot of lightly salted water to a rolling boil. Drop the lobsters head first into the pot. When the water returns to a boil, cover the pot and time the cooking.

To steam a lobster, use a pot with a rack in the bottom of the pot. Add 1 to 2 inches of water to the pot. Add 2 teaspoons of salt to the water. Bring the water to a full boil. Place the lobsters on the rack in the pot, no more than 2 deep. When the water returns to a boil, cover the pot and time the cooking.

A basic 1¼-pound lobster will take 9 to 10 minutes to boil, 12 minutes to steam. Slightly larger lobsters will take 12 minutes to boil, 15 minutes to steam.

A 2-pound lobster will take 15 minutes to boil, 18 minutes to steam.

A 3-pound lobster will take 25 minutes to boil, 30 minutes to steam.

Lobsters on the Wood-burning Grill

Some home cooks brave enough to throw their lobsters on the grill prefer to parboil the lobsters, break them apart, and grill only the meaty tails. Call me crazy, but I choose to simply split the live lobsters in half (definitely not for the faint of heart) and cook the entire split lobsters on the grill, being careful that the claws don't burn.

Using a large chef's knife, I split lobsters in half lengthwise, brush them with a little olive oil, and place them on a wood-burning grill that has a hot side and a cold side. Using long metal tongs, I constantly turn the lobsters, moving them to the cool side of the grill if they appear to be cooking too fast. Within 5 to 7 minutes, the lobster meat will turn opaque. I brush the cooked lobster meat with a generous amount of melted butter, often flavored with herbs such as basil.

Point Judith Lobster Remoulade

A remoulade is usually associated with French cuisine in New Orleans, but Rhode Islanders have embraced all kinds of American regional dishes, including remoulade. It turns out that a remoulade is an ideal accompaniment to boiled, split lobster. A classic remoulade would include hot mustard, horseradish, cayenne pepper, chopped shallots, and Worcestershire sauce. Don't be afraid to experiment with these ingredients to make your own unique remoulade, but a basic recipe follows.

---

2 cups mayonnaise

2 garlic cloves, minced

1 tablespoon finely chopped fresh tarragon, or 1 teaspoon dried

1 teaspoon dry mustard

1 tablespoon capers

2 hard-boiled eggs, finely chopped

1 tablespoon finely chopped fresh parsley

1 teaspoon anchovy paste

3 lobsters, boiled and split in half lengthwise

In a bowl, combine all the remoulade ingredients (everything but the lobster). Mix well. Cover and refrigerate for at least 2 hours before serving. Ideally it should be made a day ahead of time. One hour before serving, remove the remoulade from the refrigerator so that it can come to room temperature.

Serve each person a boiled half lobster with the remoulade on the side.

MAKES 6 SERVINGS.

Native Lobster and Potato Hash with Artichoke Cream

Only Casey Riley, executive chef at the Castle Hill Inn & Resort in Newport, would think to turn lobster into hash and then garnish it with a sour cream sauce flavored with artichokes. This versatile dish can be served as an appetizer, a light lunch or dinner entrée, or even a breakfast item, topped with poached eggs.

---

4 large white potatoes, diced, with skin

1 pound cooked lobster meat, roughly chopped

1 cup finely diced scallions

4 garlic cloves, minced

2 tablespoons chopped fresh tarragon

$1/2$ cup crème fraîche

$1/2$ cup dry bread crumbs

Salt and freshly ground black pepper, to taste

Lemon juice, to taste

6 medium-size oil-cured artichoke hearts

1 cup sour cream

Cornmeal, as needed for dredging

Vegetable oil, as needed for pan-frying

In a pot of salted water, cook the potatoes over medium-high heat until fork tender. Do not boil. Once cooked, drain the potatoes very well and place them in a large bowl. Allow them to cool to room temperature.

Add the lobster, scallions, garlic, and tarragon to the potatoes. Toss together. Add the crème fraîche and bread crumbs. The mixture should be wet but still able to hold its shape when formed into a mass. Add more bread crumbs if necessary. Season to taste with salt, pepper, and lemon juice.

For the artichoke cream, cut the artichoke hearts into small chunks and mix into the sour cream. Season to taste with salt, pepper, and lemon juice.

Form the lobster mixture into even-size cakes, about the size of a silver dollar and a half inch thick. Dredge each cake in cornmeal. Heat a large frying pan over medium heat. Add $1/2$ inch of oil to the pan and gently place the cakes in the oil. Panfry until golden brown on each side. Remove the cakes from the frying pan, pat off excess oil, and serve immediately with a dollop of the artichoke cream.

MAKES 8 SERVINGS.

Twin Oaks Baked Stuffed Shrimp

Twin Oaks is described by its third-generation owners, the DeAngelus family, as "a poor man's country club." The Cranston restaurant opened in 1933 and is now considered a Rhode Island institution, serving more than half a million meals a year. Regular customers dine there three and four times a week. Many of the waiters have been there for decades. It's the kind of place where everyone knows your name, your favorite cocktail, and what you like to eat. Always crowded, the 650-seat Twin Oaks offers all-American fare and is well known for its baked stuffed shrimp. Many of the menu items, including a secret-recipe pasta sauce, are bottled and sold on the premises.

---

5 pounds fresh jumbo shrimp

2 pounds butter

1 garlic clove, chopped

2 tablespoons chopped fresh parsley

1¾ pounds round buttery crackers (such as Ritz), ground fine

¼ pound fine bread crumbs

Peel the shrimp, split the underside, and remove the black vein. Set the shrimp aside.

In a large saucepan, melt the butter over medium-high heat. Add the garlic and sauté for 5 minutes. Remove the garlic before it turns brown. Add the parsley, cracker crumbs, and bread crumbs. Mix well.

Preheat oven to 400 degrees.

Place the shrimp on an ungreased baking sheet. Spoon the stuffing mixture into the split underside of each shrimp. Bake for 15 minutes. Serve immediately.

MAKES 16 TO 20 SERVINGS.

Mussels Baked with Potatoes and Fresh Tomatoes

One of my absolute favorite seafood dishes is this mussel dish, which I learned how to make from Giuliano Hazan, son of the famed Italian cook and author Marcella Hazan. For a time Giuliano had an Italian food shop on the East Side of Providence, where he gave cooking classes. Like his mother, Giuliano believes in fresh ingredients and uncomplicated recipes. Most of the mussels available in Rhode Island come from American Mussel Harvesters in North Kingstown, one of the largest producers of mussels in North America.

---

3 pounds fresh mussels

1 pound potatoes, unpeeled

6 tablespoons olive oil, plus extra to coat baking dish

3 tablespoons chopped fresh parsley

1 tablespoon chopped garlic

¼ cup toasted plain bread crumbs

¼ cup freshly grated Parmesan cheese

Salt and freshly ground black pepper, to taste

6 ripe plum tomatoes

Soak the mussels in cold water. Remove the wiry "beard" from each mussel and discard. Rinse the mussels several times in clean, cold water, rubbing them against one another or scrubbing them with a brush.

Place the mussels in a large stockpot with a tight-fitting lid. Cook the mussels quickly over medium-high heat. As soon as the shells open, drain the mussels and set them aside to cool. Discard any that do not open.

Rinse the potatoes and cook them, whole and unpeeled, in boiling water.

When the mussels are cool enough to handle, detach the meat from each shell. In a large bowl, combine the mussel meat with 4 tablespoons of the olive oil, the parsley, garlic, 2 tablespoons of the bread crumbs, 2 tablespoons of the grated Parmesan cheese, salt, and pepper. Mix well.

Rinse the tomatoes and skin them with a vegetable peeler. Cut them in half lengthwise, remove the seeds, cut them lengthwise into ¼-inch wide strips, and place them in a colander to drain.

When the potatoes are cooked, drain and peel, and cut them into ¼-inch-thick slices.

Preheat oven to 450 degrees.

Coat the inside of a 9x13-inch baking dish with some of the remaining olive oil. Cover the bottom of the dish with a layer of potato slices without too much overlapping. Sprinkle with salt. Cover the potatoes with a layer of mussels and all the seasonings in the bowl. Sprinkle lightly with salt. Top with the tomato strips. Sprinkle with the remaining bread crumbs and grated Parmesan cheese. Drizzle the remaining olive oil over the entire dish.

Bake in the upper part of the oven for 15 to 18 minutes, or just until the top begins to form a pale brown crust. Remove from the oven. Allow to stand for 5 minutes before serving.

MAKES 6 SERVINGS.

CHAMPLIN'S SEAFOOD, POINT JUDITH

Cornmeal-Dusted Scallops with White Wine

Scallops that glisten like huge pearls don't need a whole lot of fussing with when it comes time for cooking. This recipe couldn't be simpler. The cornmeal gives the scallops just a bit of crunch. The butter enriches the flavor, and the wine keeps the scallops moist. Note that sea scallops are large, sometimes almost 2 inches wide and an inch thick, while bay scallops are much smaller. For the best results with this recipe, sea scallops are recommended.

---

2 pounds fresh sea scallops

**Rhode Island cornmeal, as needed
    for coating**

4 tablespoons butter

4 tablespoons white wine

In a shallow dish, dredge the scallops in the cornmeal just enough to coat lightly.

In a large frying pan, melt the butter over medium heat. One at a time, shake the excess cornmeal off the scallops and place the scallops in the frying pan. Sauté for 1 minute without stirring, then turn each scallop over and cook for another 3 minutes.

Add the wine. Cover the pan. Cook for another 3 minutes, or until the scallops are just done. Serve immediately.

MAKES 4 SERVINGS.

Fish Stock

Seafood recipes often call for fish stock as a key ingredient. It's easy enough to make. You can get fish bones from any seafood market.

2 tablespoons vegetable oil or olive oil

2 shallots, chopped

10 garlic cloves, peeled

$\frac{1}{2}$ cup chopped fennel stalks

6 black peppercorns

1 carrot, chopped

Fish bones from 1 or 2 fish, chopped

$2\frac{1}{2}$ cups water

$\frac{1}{2}$ cup white wine

In a large saucepan over medium heat, combine the oil, shallots, garlic, fennel, peppercorns, and carrot. Sauté for 5 minutes. Add the fish bones and continue to cook for 5 more minutes. Add the water and wine. Bring to a boil, then reduce to a simmer for 20 minutes. Strain into a bowl through a fine sieve or cheesecloth. Save the liquid, which is the fish stock. Discard the rest. Use the fish stock immediately or store in a covered container in the refrigerator or freezer.

MAKES 3 CUPS.

Boquerones (Portuguese-Style Smelts)

A smelt is a small, slender, silver-colored fish found in oceans, rivers, and lakes, with the rainbow smelt commonly found along the Atlantic coast. It takes about a dozen smelts to make a pound. Smelts are a popular fish among the various ethnic populations in Rhode Island. The Italians are big fans of the small fish, as are the Portuguese. This recipe comes from Robert LaMoia, executive chef and owner of LaMoia Restaurant and Tapas Bar in Providence.

1/3 cup corn flour (*masa* in the Hispanic section of supermarkets)

1/3 cup wheat flour

1 tablespoon salt

1 egg

1/4 cup milk

3/4 cup water, more or less

3 cups cornflakes (unsweetened)

2 pounds smelts, heads removed

Vegetable oil, as needed for frying

2 to 3 tablespoons olive oil

1 tablespoon chopped garlic

1/2 teaspoon crushed red pepper

1/3 to 1/2 cup sherry wine vinegar

Mix corn and wheat flours with the salt, then add the egg and milk. Slowly add the water until you have the consistency of a thin pancake batter.

In a food processor or blender, grind the cornflakes until they are 1/8 inch in size (not a powder).

Wash the smelts thoroughly and blot dry with paper towels. Dip the smelts in the batter, then roll them in the dry cornflakes, lightly packing the crushed cornflakes onto the battered smelts. At this point, you can fry the smelts, refrigerate them, or freeze them for cooking at a later date.

To cook the smelts, pour 2 to 3 inches of vegetable oil into a deep, heavy saucepan. Heat the oil to 350 degrees. Working with small batches, drop the smelts in, making sure each one is submerged. Cook until golden brown. Remove the smelts from the oil and drain on a plate lined with paper towels.

In a very hot frying pan, heat the olive oil. Add the garlic and red pepper. Let it swizzle, but do not brown, constantly swirling the ingredients in the pan. Add the smelts a few at a time, and swirl them around the pan.

Very carefully, add the sherry wine vinegar and allow it to flame up, burning off all the liquid in the pan. The pan should be dry when you are finished cooking. Serve the smelts immediately.

MAKES 4 SERVINGS.

Spicy Block Island Swordfish with Crab and Sweet Potato Hash

At the height of the summer season, Block Island swordfish is much in demand. Easily recognized by its long, sharp-edged, pointed sword, this is a large fish that is marketed usually as steaks. The meat is firm and white. Executive Chef Joe Melanson of Blackstone Caterers in Newport likes to spice it up and then soften the heat with a crab and sweet potato hash on the side.

$1/2$ pound sweet potato, peeled and cut into $1/2$-inch dice

2 tablespoons salt

2 tablespoons freshly ground black pepper

1 tablespoon cayenne pepper

2 tablespoons garlic powder

2 tablespoons smoked paprika

2 tablespoons unsalted butter

1 shallot, diced fine

$1/4$ cup diced red bell pepper

$1/4$ cup heavy cream

1 tablespoon tomato paste

2 tablespoons Worcestershire sauce

$1/2$ cup jumbo lump crabmeat

1 tablespoon chopped fresh parsley

Salt and freshly ground black pepper to taste

2 (6-ounce) fresh Block Island swordfish steaks

4 tablespoons olive oil

Preheat oven to 350 degrees.

Place the diced sweet potato on a baking sheet and roast in the oven until tender.

In a bowl, combine the salt, black pepper, cayenne pepper, garlic powder, and paprika. Mix until well incorporated. Set aside.

Place a frying pan on medium heat and melt the butter. Add the diced shallot. When the shallot pieces are translucent, add the roasted sweet potato and bell pepper, and cook for 2 minutes. Add the cream, tomato paste, Worcestershire sauce, and crabmeat. Toss gently in the frying pan, and continue to heat for another 2 minutes. Add the chopped parsley, salt, and pepper. Keep the hash warm on low heat.

Heat a separate, heavy frying pan over high heat. Brush the swordfish with olive oil and coat with the spice mixture. Add the swordfish to the hot pan and cook for 4 minutes on each side. Place a scoop of hash on a plate and top with the swordfish steak.

MAKES 2 SERVINGS.

Grilled Block Island Striped Bass with Roasted Three-Pepper Salsa

Carol Connolly of the successful Catering Collaborative on the East Side of Providence reports that the Block Island striped bass they offer at special events always gets rave reviews. This prized fighting sport fish is usually 18 to 24 inches in length, with an olive green back and dark stripes running along its sides. The meat on a striped bass is white, flaky, and slightly oily.

2 tablespoons olive oil

2 tablespoons white wine

2 tablespoons lemon juice

Salt and freshly ground black pepper, to taste

1 cup (2 sticks) butter, melted

6 center-cut striped bass fillets, boneless and skinless

Roasted Three-Pepper Salsa (recipe follows)

Fresh dill for garnish

In a bowl, combine the olive oil, wine, lemon juice, salt, pepper, and melted butter. Let stand for 10 minutes at room temperature.

Add the striped bass fillets to the marinade in the bowl and let stand for 15 minutes prior to grilling.

Prepare a gas grill. The cooking surface on the grill should be slightly oiled to prevent sticking. Preheat the gas grill on high, covered, for 10 minutes, and then reduce heat to moderately high.

Preheat oven to 350 degrees.

Grill the striped bass for a total of 5 minutes, 2 to 3 minutes per side. Remove the fish to a baking pan and bake in the oven for approximately 10 minutes or until cooked through.

Top the cooked fish with Roasted Three-Pepper Salsa just before serving. Garnish the fish with a sprig of fresh dill and a scattering of chopped raw red, yellow, and green peppers.

ROASTED THREE-PEPPER SALSA

1 sweet red pepper, finely chopped

1 yellow pepper, finely chopped

1 green pepper, finely chopped

1 red onion, finely chopped

1 teaspoon crushed garlic

1 tablespoon finely chopped
cilantro

1 tablespoon finely chopped
jalapeños

1 drop Tabasco sauce

Salt and freshly ground black
pepper, to taste

Set aside a small amount of the chopped peppers to use as a garnish on the fish. Mix all the remaining ingredients together, seasoning to taste. Chill for approximately 1 hour before serving. Drain off excess liquid before topping fish. Sprinkle reserved chopped peppers on fish.

MAKES 6 SERVINGS.

Block Island Beckons

Summertime visitors to Block Island are drawn to the natural beauty of its ocean cliffs, sandy beaches, quiet coves, winding roads lined with fragrant bayberry and wild roses, and old farmhouses that have become expensive summer rentals. The rich and the famous have discovered Block Island, now a favorite getaway for celebrities. One of the nicest ways to spend a perfect summer day is to sail completely around beautiful Block Island. Boaters call this "going around the Block."

The most fun on Block Island happens every Labor Day weekend when hundreds of boaters lament the end of summer by throwing the biggest Christmas party you can imagine. Just about every pleasure boat at every marina is decked out with holiday lights, and carols fill the air. At some docks, cabin cruisers and bow riders are rafted up seven deep. That means if you're the last boat tying up, you have to climb across as many as six other boats to reach the dock—which isn't so bad when you realize there is food and frivolity available on almost every boat.

CHAMPLIN'S SEAFOOD, POINT JUDITH

Baked Block Island Halibut with Green Peppercorn Cream Sauce

The atmosphere in the Hotel Manisses on Block Island reflects an elegant era of long ago—the 1870s, to be exact—and the food served at the summer hotel today is equally elegant. *Manisses* is the original Native American name for Block Island, meaning "God's little island." This recipe from the Hotel Manisses makes good use of the native halibut caught in Block Island Sound. Eastern halibut, the largest member of the flounder family, is one of the most desirable white-flesh fishes. Costly halibut steaks are usually sold with the skin on so that customers can be sure of what they are getting. The black lateral line on the halibut, known as "the devil's thumbprint," is what smart shoppers look for.

2 (7-ounce) halibut fillets or steaks

1 tablespoon butter

1 tablespoon green peppercorns

2 tablespoons brandy

1 tablespoon dry vermouth

1 cup heavy cream

Salt and freshly ground black
    pepper, to taste

Preheat oven to 350 degrees.

Place the halibut in a glass baking dish, and bake for 15 to 20 minutes or just until the fish flakes when touched with a fork.

In a saucepan, heat the butter and sauté the green peppercorns for 1 minute. Add the brandy and vermouth. Reduce by half. Add the cream and reduce by half. Season with salt and pepper. Serve drizzled over the halibut.

MAKES 2 SERVINGS.

The Beauty of Block Island

About 12 miles off the Rhode Island coast, Block Island is just 3 miles across at its widest point, yet it is dotted with more than 300 ponds and is home to 200 endangered animal and plant species. Its redbrick Southeast Light atop Mohegan Bluffs is the tallest lighthouse in New England and was originally dedicated by President Ulysses S. Grant in 1875. The Nature Conservancy has declared Block Island to be "one of the last 12 great places in the Western Hemisphere."

Some call Block Island the Bermuda of the North. When Italian explorer Giovanni da Verrazano reported on the island, he likened its size and character to that of the Greek isle of Rhodes, comments that led to the state eventually being named Rhode Island.

Block Island Monkfish Wrapped in Bacon

Monkfish, also known as the anglerfish, is one of those underutilized fish species that smart chefs are making the most of—especially in this case, because monkfish tastes like lobster. The tail end of the monkfish is the part most often sold. Wrap it in bacon, and you surely won't be disappointed. This recipe comes from the Providence Oyster Bar on Federal Hill. Executive chefs Craig Tragni and Aaron Thorpe recommend serving it over a gnocchi cassoulet. You can make gnocchi from scratch or buy it freshly made at an Italian market.

---

2 (10-ounce) Block Island monkfish tail ends

Salt and freshly cracked black pepper, to taste

6 strips apple-smoked bacon

2 tablespoons olive oil

Apple-Shallot Jam (recipe follows)

Season the monkfish with salt and pepper. Wrap 3 strips of bacon around each piece of fish and secure with toothpicks.

Preheat oven to 350 degrees.

In an ovenproof frying pan over high heat, sear the fish on all sides in the olive oil, about 1 minute per side. Place the skillet in the oven and bake for 6 to 8 minutes. Serve immediately with a dollop of Apple-Shallot Jam.

APPLE-SHALLOT JAM

1 cup sugar

4 shallots, chopped

4 Cortland apples, peeled and diced

1/2 cup port wine

2 cups apple cider

2 tablespoons maple syrup

In a saucepan over low heat, cook the sugar until it becomes caramel in color. Add the shallots, apples, port wine, apple cider, and maple syrup. Cook until thick and reduced by half.

MAKES 2 SERVINGS.

Broiled Native Bluefish Dijon

Maureen Pothier and Paul Inveen created this dish when they owned and operated the Bluepoint in Providence, a wonderful seafood restaurant with the tiniest kitchen imaginable. Maureen always emphasized the need for native Rhode Island bluefish, not the Boston variety. The strong-flavored bluefish is a great sport fish, known as "the bulldog of the ocean" because of its tenacity. The Bluepoint's kitchen may have been small, but its aromas and flavors were huge.

DIJON SAUCE

1 cup white wine

3/4 cup fish broth

1/2 teaspoon dried thyme leaves

1 small bay leaf

A few parsley stems

1 cup heavy cream

1 tablespoon butter

1/3 cup sliced scallions

2 teaspoons minced garlic

1 tablespoon grated fresh ginger

1/3 cup Dijon mustard

1 teaspoon freshly ground white
   pepper

4 (8-ounce) skinless native Rhode
   Island bluefish fillets

1/2 cup fresh bread crumbs

Lemon wedges, for garnish

In a nonreactive saucepan, such as glass or enamel, combine the wine, fish broth, thyme, bay leaf, and parsley stems. Bring to a boil and simmer until the mixture is reduced to 1/4 cup. Add the cream gradually and continue to simmer and reduce until thick but not separating. You should have 3/4 to 1 cup left at this point. Strain into a bowl.

Preheat the oven broiler.

In a frying pan over medium-high heat, melt the butter. Sauté the scallions, garlic, and ginger for 3 minutes. Mix the scallion mixture, Dijon mustard, and white pepper into the cream mixture.

Broil the bluefish fillets skin side down in the broiler until almost done, approximately 5 to 10 minutes depending on the thickness of the fish. Spread a generous amount of sauce on each fillet and dust with bread crumbs. Return the fillets to the broiler and continue to cook until the sauce is bubbling and crumbs are golden brown. Serve immediately, garnished with lemon wedges.

MAKES 4 SERVINGS.

Point Judith Fish Roll-Ups

Generation after generation of home cooks in Rhode Island have been preparing this dish, named for the commercial fishing village of Point Judith down on the south coast of the state. Cooking the fish in aluminum foil packets makes for moist and perfectly cooked fish as well as quick and easy cleaning. Just about any fish fillet will do here, including cod, haddock, hake, whiting or pollock—whatever looks good at your favorite seafood market.

---

1 cup packaged bread stuffing

1 cup cracker crumbs

4 tablespoons chopped fresh parsley

1/4 cup chopped onion

1/4 cup chopped celery

1/4 teaspoon salt

Freshly ground black pepper, to taste

Boiling water, as needed to moisten stuffing

4 fish fillets, your choice

4 tablespoons butter, melted

1 tablespoon lemon juice

Cheese Sauce (recipe follows)

Combine the bread stuffing with the cracker crumbs, parsley, onion, celery, salt, and pepper. Add just enough boiling water to moisten the stuffing. Set aside.

Preheat oven to 400 degrees.

Place each fish fillet on a large square of aluminum foil, large enough to form a packet. Place a scoop of the stuffing on each fillet. Roll up the fillet, tying it with butcher's twine or securing it with a toothpick. Brush the fish roll-up with the melted butter and drizzle with the lemon juice. Fold the foil around each fillet and fasten securely to make a packet.

Place the 4 packets in a shallow baking pan. Bake for 30 to 40 minutes. Remove the packets from the oven. Open the packets and transfer the cooked fish to a serving dish. Serve the fish with Cheese Sauce.

CHEESE SAUCE

2 tablespoons butter

½ teaspoon salt

Freshly ground black pepper, to taste

2 tablespoons flour

Paprika, to taste

1 cup milk

¼ cup grated cheese, your choice

2 tablespoons lemon juice

In a saucepan, combine the butter, salt, pepper, flour, paprika, and milk. Cook over medium-low heat, stirring constantly, until sauce thickens. Add the grated cheese and lemon juice just before serving.

MAKES 4 SERVINGS.

English-Style Fish-and-Chips

English-style fish-and-chips is quite popular in Rhode Island, especially in the northern part of the state, where Ye Olde English Fish & Chips restaurant has been in business since 1922 in Woonsocket. Founded by an émigré from Yorkshire, Ye Olde—as it is called by the locals—is known for making a rich batter that offsets the slight sweetness of the fish.

Fans claim the chips, or french fries, have just the right mix of soft and crisp potato. Rhode Islanders love to sprinkle vinegar on them, as it is done in England. The cafeteria-style restaurant also offers an unusual fish cake—a thin piece of fish is placed between slices of potato, dipped in batter, and then fried together in one piece. The potatoes almost melt into the fish, blending the flavors.

The only complaint people have is the restaurant's short hours—closed Sunday and Monday and most evenings by 5:00 or 6:00 P.M., although it's open on Fridays until 8:00.

Native Flounder, Shrimp, and Broccoli Rabe with Sweet Potato Ravioli

Casey Riley is one of the top chefs in Rhode Island, most recently at the Castle Hill Inn in Newport. He is truly devoted to creating flavorful dishes made with ingredients indigenous to the area. In this dish he turns paper-thin slices of sweet potato into ravioli that are served with native flounder. There are many types of flounder, with winter flounder being the most common species found in fresh-fish markets. It is the thickest and meatiest of flounders caught in Rhode Island waters, and the flesh is white and firm.

CHARDONNAY JUICE

1 small onion, diced

10 garlic cloves, crushed

3 cups Chardonnay wine

1 bunch sweet green grapes

SWEET POTATO RAVIOLI

1 cup farmer's cheese (cow or
   goat milk)

6 garlic cloves, minced

2 tablespoons chopped fresh herbs
   (such as basil, rosemary, and
   oregano)

Zest from an orange or lemon

Salt and freshly ground black
   pepper, to taste

3 sweet potatoes, peeled, sliced
   lengthwise paper-thin, and
   blanched for 3 minutes

First, make the Chardonnay Juice. In a small saucepan, sauté the onion until golden brown. Add the crushed garlic. Sauté for 2 minutes. Add the wine and grapes. Bring to a simmer and reduce by half. Strain through a fine mesh strainer, pressing lightly to extract all the juice. Return the juice to a fresh saucepan. Set aside.

Next, make the Sweet Potato Ravioli. Preheat oven to 400 degrees.

Mix the cheese with the minced garlic, herbs, and citrus zest. Season with salt and pepper. Lay out the slices of sweet potato on a clean work surface. Properly blanched, the paper-thin slices of the sweet potato are just right for folding and sealing in the ravioli filling. On one half of each slice, spoon a dollop of the cheese mixture. Fold the other half over and lightly press edges together. Place ravioli on a lightly greased baking sheet. Bake for 3 minutes. Keep warm.

To finish the dish: In a frying pan, cook the broccoli rabe in the olive oil until tender, but not soft. Add minced garlic, lemon juice, salt, and pepper. Remove from heat and allow to cool to room temperature.

FLOUNDER

2 bunches broccoli rabe

3 tablespoons olive oil

Minced garlic, to taste

Lemon juice, to taste

Salt and freshly ground black
    pepper, to taste

12 (4-ounce) flounder fillets

12 medium-size shrimp

1/4 cup chopped fresh herbs

2 teaspoons white truffle oil

Lay the fish fillets on a clean work surface. Place a little broccoli rabe and 1 shrimp on each fillet. Roll the ends of each fillet together tightly to make a roulade. Place each roulade with its open end down in a casserole dish.

Heat the Chardonnay juice to a simmer. Add the 1/4 cup of chopped fresh herbs, truffle oil, and salt and pepper to taste. Pour over the fish fillets, covering them halfway. Place a sheet of greased waxed paper or baking paper over the fish. Bake for 5 to 10 minutes at 400 degrees or until the fish flakes with a fork.

Place 2 fillets on each plate with 4 ravioli on either side of the fish. Ladle some juice onto each plate. Garnish with additional fresh herbs. Serve immediately.

MAKES 6 SERVINGS.

A Quick Look at the Smallest State

Providence serves as the heart of the state, almost like the hub of a wheel, with every other town and city serving as a suburb—another indication of how small Rhode Island really is. To the north is the Blackstone River Valley, where America launched its Industrial Revolution in Pawtucket. The northwest corner of the state, known for its apple orchards and rural farmstands, is called Apple Valley.

East Bay is the name given to the region that lies east of Narragansett Bay. It includes well-to-do Barrington, historic Warren, and quaint Bristol. The easternmost part of the state consists of Tiverton and Little Compton, where lush farmland rolls down along the coast. Likewise, West Bay is the area to the west of the bay; it includes the cities of Cranston and Warwick, known best for their many shopping centers. Farther west are the sparsely populated suburban towns of Coventry and West Greenwich.

Directly on Narragansett Bay are the diverse communities of wealthy East Greenwich, the island town of Jamestown, and touristy Newport.

South County is the nickname residents have conferred upon the southern third of the state, especially when referring to the seaside communities along the coast from Narragansett down to Westerly.

South County Paella

I was fortunate to know the late Jean Hewitt, food editor for *Family Circle* magazine for many years. British by birth and New Yorker by choice, Jean spent most of her free time at her stylish home in Watch Hill, a seaside village in Westerly near the Rhode Island–Connecticut border. For this author of ten cookbooks, the kitchen was the most important room in the house. We spent one perfect summer afternoon together in that kitchen, cooking on her six-burner Garland stove and talking about food. Here is the dish she created that day, a classic paella featuring Rhode Island seafood.

4 garlic cloves, finely chopped

1 teaspoon chopped fresh thyme leaves, or $\frac{1}{2}$ teaspoon dried thyme

$\frac{1}{2}$ teaspoon salt

$\frac{1}{4}$ teaspoon freshly ground black pepper

3 tablespoons olive oil

2 tablespoons balsamic vinegar or red wine vinegar

6 chicken legs with thighs, separated, or 2 small chickens, cut up

$\frac{1}{2}$ pound lean boneless pork, cut into 1-inch cubes

$\frac{1}{2}$ pound chorizo, linguica, or other spicy hot sausage, skinned and cut into $\frac{1}{2}$-inch slices

1 pound large shrimp, shelled and deveined

In a shallow glass dish, mix together the garlic, thyme, salt, pepper, olive oil, and vinegar. Add the chicken pieces, turning to coat well. Let stand 30 minutes at room temperature, or refrigerate for up to 3 hours.

In a paella pan or very large, deep frying pan, brown the chicken pieces. Remove them from the pan, drain, and set aside on a large serving platter.

Add the pork cubes and chorizo to the same frying pan. Cook, stirring often, until no pink remains. Remove, drain, and add to the serving platter.

Add the shrimp to the frying pan. Cook, stirring often, until they turn pink. Remove, drain, and reserve in a separate bowl.

1 large onion, finely chopped

2 1/2 cups uncooked rice

5 cups chicken broth

1/2 cup dry white wine or dry
    vermouth

1 teaspoon saffron leaves, or
    1/2 teaspoon powdered saffron

4 plum tomatoes, skinned and
    chopped

18 cherrystone clams

18 mussels, scrubbed, with beards
    removed

2 cups frozen baby peas

1 (2-ounce) jar pimentos, drained

Add the onion to the frying pan. Cook until soft but not browned. Add the rice and cook, stirring for 3 to 4 minutes. Add the chicken broth, wine, saffron, and tomatoes. Bring to a boil. Add the reserved chicken, pork, and chorizo. Bring back to a boil. Cover and simmer for 15 minutes.

In a stockpot, steam open the clams and mussels in 1/4 cup water, about 4 minutes. Discard any unopened shells. Reserve the cooking liquid.

Preheat the oven to 350 degrees.

Add the reserved shrimp, the peas, and the pimentos to the frying pan. Arrange the clams and mussels, still in their opened shells, on top. Add the liquid in which the shellfish was cooked. Cover and reheat in the oven for 5 to 10 minutes. If necessary, this dish can be held in a 200-degree oven for up to 30 minutes.

MAKES 6 SERVINGS.

What Is South County?

You won't find it on any map, but South County is defined as the southernmost edge of Rhode Island extending along the coastline down to the Connecticut border. This waterfront area consists of serene farmland rolling down to the sea, with more than 100 miles of shoreline waiting to be explored. Quaint seaside villages, white sandy beaches, and world-class salt-water fishing make South County a vacation hot spot in the summer.

South County is not really a county, but more a state of mind. Little Rhode Island has only five counties: Bristol, Kent, Newport, Providence, and Washington. All the towns considered part of South County are actually in Washington County, which used to be called Narragansett County. Confused? It gets better. Strangely enough, there is no North County in Rhode Island, though people do refer to the upper part of the state as the North Country.

Narragansett Strudel

Made popular at the Richards' Bed & Breakfast in Narragansett, this is an easy-to-make strudel, especially if you get your seafood salad already made at a local fish market. If the seafood salad is on the runny side, allow it to drain through a fine strainer. A good seafood salad will include lobster, fish, shrimp, celery, and peppers. A slice of strudel can be a light lunch, served with a garden salad, or the first course at a dinner party.

12 sheets phyllo pastry

1 cup (2 sticks) butter, melted

1 cup fine, dry bread crumbs

1 pound seafood salad

Preheat oven to 400 degrees.

Lightly dampen a clean cotton towel, and spread the towel on a clean work surface. Lay a sheet of phyllo pastry on the towel. Brush the sheet with melted butter and sprinkle lightly with bread crumbs. Repeat 4 times, ending with the sixth sheet of phyllo.

Place half of the seafood salad on the narrow edge of the phyllo, leaving a 2-inch border on each side. Fold in the sides and roll up the pastry. Place the roll on a buttered baking sheet. Brush with melted butter.

Repeat these steps, using the remaining filling and phyllo to make a second strudel. Bake both strudels for 20 minutes.

MAKES 2 STRUDELS, OR 8 SERVINGS.

La Vigilia—The Feast of Seven Fishes

The number seven has always had magical connotations. According to the Bible, it took seven days to create the world, and our lives revolve around the seven days in a week. We marvel at the Seven Wonders of the World, and the world as we know it consists of seven continents. But nothing is more magical than the Feast of the Seven Fishes on Christmas Eve, an old Italian tradition that is alive and well in Rhode Island.

In Italy it is known as *La Vigilia* (*lah vee-gee-lyah*). Like the English word vigil, it comes from the Latin word for wakefulness and watching. In Roman Catholicism Christmas Eve is the time of the final vigil before the dawn that brings the birth of Jesus Christ. Many Catholic Italians serve at least seven courses of fresh seafood dishes on Christmas Eve. The symbolism of this seafood makes for great conversation in Rhode Island homes that still observe La Vigilia.

Over the years the number of courses served by most Italian-American families on Christmas Eve has decreased as newer generations shy away from tradition. The older family members still shop for silvery smelts, slabs of salted cod, and coils of dark-colored eels, while the youth prefer more modern, Americanized cuisine—jumbo shrimp, lobster, and scallops. Captain's Catch, a seafood market in North Providence, typically sells 250 pounds of eel and 4,000 pounds of shrimp during the holidays. The eel, by the way, has a special religious symbolism attached to it. Eating eel is thought to cleanse the body of evil.

One restaurant in Providence is determined to see that this unique custom continues. Every year Mediterraneo on Federal Hill offers its customers the opportunity to participate in an authentic *La Vigilia,* held a few weeks before Christmas so as not to interfere with family plans on Christmas Eve. The two chefs who run the kitchen at Mediterraneo, Michele Calise and Gianfranco Campanella, both come from families where the Feast of Seven Fishes is a tradition. Every year their *La Vigilia* at Mediterraneo is as spectacular as ever. The two chefs always begin the dinner with a marinated seafood salad of baby squid, shrimp, and scallops. Next a fish soup is served, followed by spaghetti with clam sauce, then baked cod, mixed fried fishes, and baked sole in lemon and oil. The last fish course is oven-roasted eel.

Frutti di Mare (Marinated Seafood Salad)

This marinated seafood salad—the first course in a *La Vigilia feast*—can be served at room temperature, or it can be prepared ahead of time and kept chilled until just before it's served. You can also serve this as a dinner appetizer any time of the year.

1 pound shrimp, peeled and deveined

1 pound squid, cleaned and sliced

1 pound bay scallops

12 mussels, cooked, with beards removed

½ cup extra-virgin olive oil

3 tablespoons fresh lemon juice

1 garlic clove, chopped

1 tablespoon chopped fresh Italian parsley

Salt and freshly ground black pepper, to taste

Lettuce and lemon wedges (optional)

Bring a pot of salted water to a boil. Add the shrimp and cook just until bright pink and cooked through, about 3 minutes. Using a slotted spoon, transfer the shrimp to a colander to drain. Add the squid to the boiling water and cook until opaque, about 2 minutes. Using a slotted spoon, transfer the squid to the same colander to drain. Add the scallops to the boiling water and cook for about 3 minutes. Using a slotted spoon, transfer the scallops to the colander to drain.

In a large bowl, combine the shrimp, squid, scallops, and cooked mussels. Add the olive oil, lemon juice, garlic, chopped parsley, salt, and pepper. Toss all the ingredients until well mixed. Serve over a bed of lettuce with lemon wedges and grilled Italian bread, if desired.

MAKES 6 SERVINGS.

Zuppa di Pesce (Fish Soup)

Seafood lovers will appreciate this soup that is swimming with shrimp, lobster, scallops, and fresh fish. It's the proposed second course of a *La Vigilia* feast.

$\frac{1}{3}$ cup extra-virgin olive oil

2 cups diced onions

1 cup diced celery

$\frac{1}{2}$ cup finely chopped fresh
parsley

$\frac{1}{2}$ cup finely chopped fresh thyme

$\frac{1}{2}$ cup finely chopped fresh
oregano

2 cups chopped quahogs

4 ounces crabmeat

4 ounces shrimp, peeled, deveined,
and diced

4 ounces lobster meat, diced

4 ounces scallops, chopped

4 ounces fresh fish (such as cod or
haddock), diced

Salt and freshly ground black
pepper, to taste

1 cup dry white wine

46 ounces clam juice (or seafood
broth if available)

1 (28-ounce) can peeled Italian
tomatoes, with juice

2 cups peeled and diced potatoes

In a medium-size stockpot, combine the oil, onions, and celery. Sauté until the vegetables become translucent. Add the parsley, thyme, oregano, and all the seafood. Season to taste with salt and pepper. Deglaze the bottom of the pot with the white wine.

Add the clam juice and tomatoes. Bring to a simmer. Taste for salt and pepper, adjusting if necessary. Allow the soup to reduce down to half of its original amount, and then add the potatoes. Cook until the potatoes are tender. Once again, taste for salt and pepper, adjusting if necessary.

MAKES 6 SERVINGS.

Spaghetti alla Vongole (Spaghetti with Clams)

A classic Italian dish, Spaghetti with Clams can be found on the menu of many restaurants in Providence, especially on Federal Hill. The dish is served at the Mediterraneo restaurant in Providence as the third course in *La Vigilia*.

---

2 large garlic cloves, finely chopped

1 small dried red chile pepper, crushed, or a pinch of red pepper flakes

1/3 cup olive oil

3 pounds small hard-shelled clams (cherrystones or littlenecks)

1 cup clam juice

1/2 cup dry white wine

Salt, to taste

1 pound spaghetti or linguine

1/2 cup finely chopped fresh Italian parsley

In a large saucepan over medium heat, warm the garlic and chile pepper in the olive oil until the garlic is golden, about 1 minute. Add the clams, clam juice, and wine; cover and cook over medium heat, shaking the pan occasionally until all the clams open.

Meanwhile, bring a large pot of salted water to a boil. Add the pasta and cook, stirring frequently, until al dente. Drain and transfer the pasta to a warm serving bowl. Add the clams and parsley; toss well. Serve immediately.

MAKES 4 SERVINGS.

Italian and French Holiday Traditions

Some northern Rhode Island families that have both French-Canadian and Italian ancestry pay homage to both nations on Christmas Eve. The night typically begins with the traditional Italian seafood feast, based in the Catholic custom of abstaining from meat on certain holy days. Homemade pasta with clam sauce, baked fish, and antipasto are served, after which some family members might take a nap in preparation for the late-night holiday festivities. Later the families attend the midnight Mass held at Catholic churches throughout the area. After the church services the families resume their holiday merry-making, observing the traditional French-Canadian *reveillon* to celebrate the birth of Jesus. Pork pies, boiled potatoes, and pickles are served into the wee hours of the morning, with some Italian cookies thrown in for good measure and for dessert.

Baccala alla Napoletano (Baked Cod)

Baccala is dried salted cod that must be refreshed in several changes of water before being eaten. You should be able to find *baccala* at any seafood market.

---

1 large onion, sliced

2 garlic cloves, chopped

2 tablespoons olive oil

1 cup diced fresh tomatoes

½ cup dry white wine

2 cups Italian plum tomatoes,
    with juice

2 tablespoons caperberries
    (available in gourmet shops)

20 kalamata olives

8 green olives, sliced

1 cup clam juice or fish broth

Salt and freshly ground black
    pepper, to taste

2 pounds cod or *baccala* (dried
    salted cod that must be
    refreshed in several changes
    of water)

1 teaspoon chopped fresh oregano

6 basil leaves, cut into thin strips

In a frying pan over medium heat, cook the onions and garlic in the olive oil. Add the diced tomatoes and cook for 2 minutes. Add the wine and let it reduce for 2 minutes. Add the plum tomatoes, caperberries, kalamata and green olives, fish broth, salt, and pepper. Simmer over medium heat for 5 minutes.

Preheat oven to 375 degrees.

Place the fish in a roasting pan. Top the fish with the sauce. Sprinkle with the oregano and basil. Cover with aluminum foil and bake for about 20 minutes. Serve hot, with grilled Italian bread, if desired.

MAKES 6 SERVINGS.

Sogliola Limone (Sole in Lemon and Oil)

The marriage of fresh lemon juice and rich olive oil makes this delicate fish dish quite memorable.

1 tablespoon olive oil

2 tablespoons butter

1 small shallot, chopped

$\frac{1}{2}$ cup dry white wine

Juice from 2 lemons

Salt and freshly ground black
   pepper, to taste

1 teaspoon capers

$\frac{1}{2}$ cup fish broth or clam juice

$1\frac{1}{2}$ pounds sole fillets

1 tablespoon chopped fresh Italian
   parsley

Lemon wedges for garnish
   (optional)

In a frying pan over low heat, heat the oil and butter and add the chopped shallot. Add the wine and reduce for 2 minutes. Add the lemon juice, salt, pepper, capers, and fish broth.

Preheat oven to 350 degrees.

Roll up each fillet of sole and place in a roasting pan. Pour the butter sauce over the sole. Sprinkle with chopped parsley. Cover the pan with aluminum foil. Bake for 15 minutes. Serve hot, with lemon wedges, if desired.

MAKES 4 SERVINGS.

VENDA RAVIOLI, FEDERAL HILL

Side Dishes

Baked Antipasto

Chef Nancy Carr Starziano from East Side Market in Providence offers this locally popular recipe. It's a wonderful side dish on an Italian buffet. Leftovers—if there are any—are perfect the next day for lunch along with a salad of mixed greens.

2 packages crescent dinner rolls

¼ pound provolone cheese, thinly sliced

¼ pound salami, thinly sliced

¼ pound ham, thinly sliced

¼ pound pepperoni, thinly sliced

¼ pound mozzarella cheese, thinly sliced

¼ pound any other desired Italian cold cuts

3 eggs, beaten

Grated Parmesan cheese, to taste

Italian seasoning, to taste

1 (7-ounce) jar roasted red peppers

1 (2-ounce) can sliced black olives

Preheat oven to 350 degrees.

Spray a 9x13-inch glass baking dish with vegetable oil spray.

Open the first package of crescent rolls. Unroll the dough and place it on the bottom of the glass baking dish, pressing the seams together, to make the bottom crust.

Begin to layer each thinly sliced item in the order as listed.

In a bowl, combine the eggs, grated cheese, and Italian seasoning. Mix well. Pour this mixture over the layered meats and cheeses. Top with an even layer of roasted red peppers and black olives.

Open the second package of crescent rolls. Unroll the dough and place it over the top of the glass baking dish, covering as much of the layered ingredients as possible.

Bake for 30 to 35 minutes, or until golden brown. Serve immediately.

MAKES 12 SERVINGS.

Suggested pairing: Chicken Parmigiana, page 122.

Arancini (Sicilian Fried Rice Balls)

If you grew up in a Sicilian family, you were blessed with *arancini* as part of the antipasto prepared for relatives and friends at special gatherings. Today these flavorful rice balls can be purchased at the prepared food counter inside Italian gourmet shops on Federal Hill in Providence. Traditionally they are between 1 and 2 inches in diameter. If you prepare them yourself, you can make them smaller—just the right size to pop in your mouth.

---

4 cups cooked rice, at room temperature

Salt and freshly ground black pepper, to taste

1/2 cup chopped fresh basil leaves

1/2 cup grated Parmesan cheese

3 tablespoons butter

1 egg, beaten

1/2 cup fresh mozzarella, cut into 1/2-inch cubes

1/4 cup baby peas, cooked

3/4 cup tomato sauce (Bolognese recommended)

3 large eggs, beaten

2 cups bread crumbs

2 cups olive oil, for frying

Place the cooked rice in a large mixing bowl. Season with salt and pepper. Add the chopped basil and Parmesan cheese. Blend well. Add the butter and beaten egg, and combine. Season to taste with additional salt and pepper, if needed.

Scoop about 2 tablespoons of the seasoned rice mixture into a smooth ball. Keep a bowl of warm water handy to rinse your hands as you shape the balls. Place the shaped balls on a sheet of waxed paper or parchment.

One at a time, hold a rice ball in your hand. With your finger, make a hole in the center, being careful not to go all the way through the ball. Fill the hole with a cube of cheese, a couple of peas, and a teaspoon of the tomato sauce. Close up the hole by compressing the rice to enclose the filling and make a perfectly sealed *arancini*.

Place the 3 beaten eggs in one bowl, and the bread crumbs in a second bowl. Dip each rice ball into the eggs and then in the bread crumbs. Pack the bread crumbs evenly around the entire *arancini* for even frying.

In a large, deep skillet, heat the oil to 375 degrees (an electric skillet is recommended). Fry the balls in batches of 4 to 5 at a time, cooking them for about 3 to 4 minutes, or until golden brown. Drain well on paper towels.

Serve immediately, or keep them warm in a 225-degree oven for 10 to 15 minutes. *Arancini* will keep in the refrigerator for about 5 days. They also can be frozen before they are coated in bread crumbs. Freeze them separately on a sheet pan and then store in sealable plastic bags.

MAKES 12 LARGE OR 24 SMALL *ARANCINI*.

Infornata di Riso Asparagi e Gorgonzola
(Baked Rice with Asparagus and Gorgonzola Cheese)

As the master of clay cookery, chef Walter Potenza is always looking for interesting dishes that can be prepared in terra-cotta (or clay) cookware. This is one of those recipes that he includes in the many culinary classes he teaches. If you choose to use frozen asparagus, add it halfway through the cooking process. The Gorgonzola cheese can be the domestic variety, which is much harder in texture and milder in taste. If using store-bought vegetable or chicken broth, always check the saltiness; you may not need to add salt to the rice mixture.

3 tablespoons olive oil

1 large onion, minced

1 cup rice, Italian Arborio or
   Carnaroli variety

2 cups fresh asparagus, cut into
   ¼-inch pieces

6 fresh whole sage leaves

1 teaspoon kosher salt

½ teaspoon freshly ground black
   pepper

½ cup dry white wine

3 cups vegetable or chicken broth

1 cup crumbled Gorgonzola cheese

Soak a terra-cotta pot in clean, cold water for 15 minutes. Preheat oven to 375 degrees.

In a medium-size mixing bowl, combine the olive oil, onion, rice, asparagus, sage leaves, salt, pepper, wine, and broth. Mix well. Remove the terra-cotta pot from the water and pour the mixture into it, spreading it out evenly. Bake for 30 minutes. Do not stir the rice; it will absorb most of the liquid during the cooking process.

Remove the pot from the oven. Top the rice with the crumbled Gorgonzola. Return to the oven for another 5 minutes to melt the cheese.

Serve immediately from the pot. Keep in mind that terra-cotta pots are great conductors of heat, and the food in them will continue to cook even after the pots are removed from the oven.

MAKES 4 SERVINGS.

Suggested pairing: Chicken with Artichokes and White Wine, page 119.

Mike Lepizzera's Polenta

Mike Lepizzera is the "chef" at Mike's Kitchen, a Rhode Island institution located in a VFW hall in Cranston. Mike's restaurant is a slice of Italian-style Americana and wonderfully stuck in the 1950s, especially when it comes to prices. It's not unusual to wait for a table in a line that stretches out beyond the glass-plated doors into the parking lot. The place is noisy, and the waitresses are no-nonsense. But don't go on a Saturday night—the place is closed. How many restaurants dare to do that? One of Mike's most famous dishes is polenta served with a rich tomato sauce, sweet sausages, and the best meatballs around.

¼ cup olive oil

1 cup (2 sticks) unsalted butter

1 to 2 tablespoons chopped garlic

2 cups chicken broth

1½ quarts half-and-half

2½ cups water

1 to 2 teaspoons kosher salt

12 turns of a pepper grinder

1 teaspoon crushed red pepper flakes

2 cups cornmeal

Pinch sugar

1 to 2 cups freshly grated Pecorino Romano cheese

Tomato sauce of your choice

In a large, heavy stockpot, heat the oil and butter. Add the garlic and sauté over low heat until it is golden.

Add the chicken broth, half-and-half, water, salt, pepper, and red pepper flakes. Stir to combine. Bring to a boil.

Very slowly add the cornmeal, stirring constantly. Lower the heat to maintain a gentle boil. After all the cornmeal has been added, continue to stir until it is thick and creamy, about 20 minutes.

Remove the stockpot from the heat. Stir in the sugar and grated cheese. Serve immediately with your favorite tomato sauce. If desired, serve with Italian sausages and meatballs.

MAKES 12 SERVINGS.

Suggested pairing: Meatballs alla Giardino, page 103.

Garlic Mashed Potatoes

Rhode Island is the land of garlic mashed potatoes, sometimes referred to as "smashed" potatoes, with virtually every restaurant in the state offering this savory side dish. One bite and you just can't stop eating these potatoes that go with just about everything, from steak to seafood. Local restaurant chefs say the best version is made with potatoes grown on farms found along the southeast coastline.

6 whole garlic heads

Olive oil, as needed

5 pounds potatoes, quartered, with or without skins

$1/2$ cup (8 tablespoons) butter, at room temperature

$1/2$ cup cream

Salt and freshly ground black pepper, to taste

Preheat oven to 350 degrees.

Peel the garlic and coat each clove with olive oil. Place the garlic cloves in an ovenproof dish. Cover and bake for 1 hour.

In a large pot of boiling salted water, cook the potatoes until tender. Drain.

In a large mixing bowl, mash the potatoes with the butter, cream, and baked garlic until smooth. Season to taste with salt and pepper.

MAKES 10 SERVINGS.

Suggested pairing: Garlic-and-Herb-Crusted Prime Rib, page 98.

Quebec-Style French Fries

I really did think I had died and gone to heaven when I first went to Stanley's in little Central Falls. Only 1 square mile in size, densely populated Central Falls is the smallest community in the nation's smallest state. I went there for the famous fresh beef Stanleyburger. Since 1932 the honest and affordable Stanley-burger (today a mere $1.69) has been served up with its trademark grilled onions and pickles on a steamed bun that's buttered and then lightly grilled. What came as a surprise was the menu item listed as Quebec-Style Fries or *poutine* (pronounced "poo-TEEN").

I had heard about these artery-clogging fries but had never found them on any American menu. According to the American-French Genealogical Society, *poutine* was created in the early 1950s, when a customer walked into a restaurant in Warwick, Quebec, and made a special request for a pile of *frites* with cheese and gravy. The chef remarked, "That's a real mess," using the local slang word for mess, which is *poutine*. Nonetheless, he dished up his first order of *poutine*, added it to his menu, and to this day is credited with the innovative side order. French Canadians brought the recipe with them when they moved to northern Rhode Island to work in the textile mills.

In Quebec the classic version consists of a heaping pile of golden french fries topped with cheese curd, then smothered with hot beef gravy. The fries are large and freshly made, not the frozen variety, and the cheese curd is called *fromage en grain*. More of this cheese is dumped on top of the fries, and then the entire "mess" is covered with a dark brown beef gravy, preferably homemade and piping hot.

At Stanley's—a retro lunch and dinner spot that is best described as "the Jetsons meet Art Deco"—the fries are adorned with shredded mozzarella cheese and brown gravy. Close enough, I thought as I took my first bite. I almost expected my heart to stop beating, but it didn't, so I kept on eating.

Variations on this theme also exist—*poutine* with chopped beef and fried onions, *poutine* with spaghetti sauce, and *poutine* with chunks of chicken and green peas. The one thing *poutine* fans can agree upon is that it must be accompanied by lots of beer.

Rhode Island Baked Beans

Bruce Tillinghast, chef-owner of the New Rivers restaurant in Providence, credits his mother, Barbara, with creating this recipe for baked beans—the one he uses in his tiny jewel of a restaurant. He has shared this recipe with other chefs, and they agree that these are the best. Instead of the pea beans or navy beans associated with Boston baked beans, the Tillinghasts use yellow-eyed beans or red kidney beans, which are more flavorful. Making old-fashioned baked beans is an all-day (or overnight) process, but it requires only a little prep work and not much attention. The Tillinghasts have always made their baked beans in a traditional bean pot, but they suggest that a heavy pot like Le Creuset porcelain-enameled cast-iron cookware will suffice. An industrial-strength Crock-Pot can also be used.

---

1 pound bag dry yellow-eyed beans
or red kidney beans

¼ pound lean salt pork

1 medium-size onion, quartered
(leave stem end on so onion
quarters hold together)

3 tablespoons sugar

4 tablespoons dark (robust)
molasses

1¼ teaspoons salt

1 teaspoon dry mustard (Coleman's
recommended)

Put the beans in a large saucepan, checking for stones as you pour them in. Cut the salt pork into 4 pieces and put it in the pan with the beans. Pour enough water into the pan to cover the beans by 2 inches. Bring to a boil and simmer for 15 minutes. Strain the beans and reserve the water.

Place the beans in a bean pot in two layers, with 2 onion quarters and 2 pieces of salt pork between the layers and also on top.

Preheat oven to 350 degrees.

Add the sugar, molasses, salt, and dry mustard to 2 cups of the hot bean juice. Stir to dissolve. Pour the seasoned bean juice over the beans. Add more bean juice if necessary to just cover the top level of beans. Cover the pot and place in the preheated oven. Cook for 1 hour and lower the heat to 250 degrees. Cook for another 4 hours. Check once or twice during the cooking process and add more bean juice if necessary—the liquid and bean levels should be even.

Remove the cover during last half hour of cooking. The beans can be served when done but do benefit by sitting awhile in the pot with the cover off. Reheat in the pot in a 200-degree oven. Properly baked beans will hold their shape but get meltingly soft when done.

MAKES 8 SERVINGS.

Suggested pairing: An old-fashioned traditional clambake.

Favas

In some Portuguese families in Rhode Island, favas are made with hot Portuguese sausage and canned fava beans. The sausage is precooked to release much of its fat, then peeled and ground up to be added to the bean mixture. Fans of this version claim it tastes even better when reheated the next day. Here is the vegetarian version of favas, from my good friend, Nancy Sandbach.

1 pound fava beans

3 large onions, chopped

2 tablespoons olive oil

Crushed red pepper, to taste

1 teaspoon salt

2 tablespoons chopped fresh parsley

1 bay leaf

¼ teaspoon allspice

¼ teaspoon cinnamon

1 cup vinegar

1 (29-ounce) can tomato sauce

Soak the fava beans in water for 3 days, changing the water every day. On the fourth day, drain the beans and put them in a large stockpot. Cover the beans with fresh salted water. Bring to a boil. Reduce heat to simmer. Cook until tender. Do not drain.

While the fava beans are cooking, make the sauce. In a large frying pan, sauté the chopped onions in the olive oil until tender. Add the remaining ingredients. Mix well. Simmer 30 minutes.

Add the sauce to the stockpot containing the cooked fava beans. Simmer for 3 hours. If the sauce is too thick, add water. Taste and adjust seasonings to your liking.

MAKES 12 SERVINGS.

Suggested pairing: Portuguese Pork with Clams, page 111.

The Original Baked Beans

There are countless variations of this colonial classic, all of which contain pork of some sort and beans, usually navy or pea beans. But the original baked beans, those of the Narragansett Indians, never contained pork. Baked in earthen pits, the beans were flavored with venison drippings. The early settlers of Rhode Island learned how to bake beans from the Narragansetts. For the deeply religious early American settlers, who did not cook on Sundays, the baked beans were a blessing. The beans were baked every Saturday and served that night and again on Sunday.

Succotash

Old Yankee families in Rhode Island count this side dish as one of their favorites, especially at Thanksgiving. Legend has it that the Indians greeted Roger Williams, founder of Rhode Island, with a meal of succotash and fresh fish. The Indians taught the early settlers how to combine corn and beans for one of the most colorful dishes on their table. Tomatoes somehow got thrown into the mix in the nineteenth century. Succotash may be old-fashioned, but it's still delicious.

---

2 (10-ounce) packages frozen lima beans

2 (10-ounce) packages frozen corn

4 tablespoons butter

1 cup finely chopped yellow onion

1 teaspoon sugar

1 cup light cream

2 cups chopped tomatoes, fresh or stewed

2 tablespoons chopped scallions

Salt and freshly ground black pepper, to taste

2 tablespoons chopped chives

Cook the lima beans and corn according to package directions. Drain and combine in a large bowl.

In a large, deep frying pan, melt the butter. Sauté the onions until tender. Stir in the cooked vegetables and sugar. Add the light cream. Simmer 5 minutes. Add the tomatoes and scallions. Season to taste with salt and pepper.

Pour the cooked mixture into a serving bowl. Garnish with chopped chives. Serve warm.

MAKES 8 SERVINGS.

Suggested pairing: A traditional Thanksgiving Day turkey dinner.

Roman Green Beans with Fontina Cheese

When you buy locally grown produce, you help farmers earn a livelihood and you preserve an agricultural heritage. The Rhode Island Division of Agriculture provided this recipe to help consumers become more familiar with locally grown products such as green snap beans, which were once called string beans. Today's beans are really stringless, so you just need to break off the ends as you wash them. Cooked beans should have a crunchy texture; if yours don't snap, they're probably overdone. Many Italian families in Rhode Island make a simple cold string bean salad, flavoring the beans with black pepper, garlic, parsley, and olive oil. Here is a fancier version.

1 pound string beans, trimmed, or snap beans

1/2 pound Fontina cheese, cut into 3-inch strips, 1/4-inch wide

1 garlic clove, minced

1/2 teaspoon Dijon mustard

1/4 cup lemon juice

1/2 cup olive oil

Salt and freshly ground black pepper, to taste

In a pot of boiling salted water, cook the beans until tender-crisp, about 2 minutes. Rinse under cold running water. Drain. Combine with the cheese in a large serving bowl.

In a small bowl, combine the garlic with the mustard. Stir in the lemon juice. Slowly whisk in the oil. Pour the dressing over the beans and cheese. Toss well. Season to taste with salt and pepper. Serve at room temperature or slightly chilled.

MAKES 4 SERVINGS.

Suggested pairing: Baked Whole Chicken with Potatoes, Lemon, and Rosemary, page 125.

Broccoli Rabe

Without a doubt, broccoli rabe is a favorite vegetable in Rhode Island's Italian community. It is often served on the side, affectionately known as an order of "rabes" (pronounced "rob-bees"). The somewhat bitter broccoli rabe is also served in sandwiches with thick slices of provolone cheese. When you purchase broccoli rabe, look for bunches that are bright green in color with many small bud clusters. It is essential that you rinse it thoroughly before cooking to remove all traces of grit.

---

1 large bunch broccoli rabe

4 tablespoons olive oil

4 large garlic cloves, minced

Salt, to taste

Carefully rinse the broccoli rabe in several changes of clean, cold water. Cut off the tough, stringy stems.

In a large pot of boiling water, cook the broccoli rabe for about 5 minutes. This will help reduce the bitterness. Using a large strainer, drain it and allow it to cool. When it's cool enough to handle, you may opt to cut the broccoli rabe into 2-inch-long pieces. However, some people prefer to leave it intact.

In a large frying pan, heat the olive oil. Add the garlic and cook over medium heat until golden. Add the drained broccoli rabe and sauté, stirring often, for 5 minutes. Serve immediately.

MAKES 4 SERVINGS.

Suggested pairing: Mussels Baked with Potatoes and Fresh Tomatoes, page 136.

Grilled Vegetables with Balsamic Dressing

In the summer it seems like all of Rhode Island is grilling vegetables and then drizzling them with balsamic dressing just before serving. This bounty of summer can be served hot or allowed to cool to room temperature—the perfect side dish on a hot summer night. In cooler weather you can adapt this recipe by roasting the vegetables in your oven.

18 asparagus stalks, trimmed

6 carrots, trimmed and peeled

6 small zucchini, trimmed

6 small yellow squash, trimmed

2 large green peppers, cut into strips

2 large red peppers, cut into strips

2 large yellow onions, cut into thick slices

1 large eggplant, cut into 1/2-inch rounds

1/2 cup olive oil

Kosher salt, to taste

Freshly ground black pepper, to taste

1 cup balsamic vinegar

Place all the prepared vegetables in a large baking dish or roasting pan. Drizzle them with the olive oil, tossing gently to coat well. Season to taste with salt and pepper.

On a prepared grill, with a hot side and a cold side, place the vegetables on the hot side. After just a few minutes, start to turn the vegetables, being careful they do not begin to burn. If the fire is too hot, move the vegetables to the cooler side of the grill. As the vegetables finish cooking, move them from the grill to a serving platter. Cover the vegetables with a sheet of aluminum foil to keep them warm.

While the vegetables are cooking (or this could be done ahead of time), bring the balsamic vinegar to a boil in a saucepan over medium-high heat. Allow the vinegar to reduce to a thick syrup.

When all the vegetables are cooked, drizzle them with the balsamic dressing.

MAKES 6 SERVINGS.

Suggested pairing: Grilled Block Island Striped Bass with Roasted Three-Pepper Salsa, page 142.

Grilled Asparagus Wrapped with Prosciutto

The first time I saw this dish, I was mesmerized first by the presentation, then by the taste, and finally by the simplicity. It's almost always on the menu at Salvatore's Caffe inside Venda Ravioli on Federal Hill in Providence, and it's now often duplicated by home cooks at summer dinner parties.

18 asparagus stalks

¼ cup olive oil

18 extra-thin slices prosciutto

Parmigiano-Reggiano cheese, for garnish

Trim the woody ends off the asparagus stalks. Blanch the asparagus by parboiling the stalks for 3 to 4 minutes in a pan of boiling water. Place the asparagus in a shallow baking dish. Drizzle with the oil, tossing the asparagus gently to coat well.

When the asparagus is cool enough to handle, wrap 1 slice of prosciutto around each stalk. Place the wrapped stalks on a prepared grill over medium heat. Make sure the stalks are lying horizontally on the grill so they don't fall through the grates. Turn the stalks constantly, making certain they do not burn.

After 2 to 3 minutes, remove the stalks from the grill and place them on a serving platter. Garnish with shaved Parmigiano-Reggiano cheese.

MAKES 6 SERVINGS.

Suggested pairing: Portuguese-Style Smelts, page 140.

Too Many Vegetables?

Well-meaning social workers were sent to Italian-American homes in Rhode Island during the 1930s to educate the immigrants on the right way to eat. The prevailing nutritional opinion of that day was that the Italian Americans were eating too many vegetables and that they needed to increase their dietary intake of meat. The families were taught that meat should accompany starch at every meal. Inexpensive Italian restaurants began to open up, and they served entrees with a side order of spaghetti, or spaghetti and meatballs on the same plate—even though this simply was never done in Italy. Italian cooks also began to substitute meat in traditional vegetable dishes. Thus veal Parmesan—an American creation—evolved from eggplant Parmesan.

Zucchini Ribbons with Tomatoes and Black Olives

By late summer Rhode Islander home gardeners usually have more zucchini than they know what to do with—in fact, there is an official day in August when folks leave zucchini on the porches of all their neighbors who don't have gardens. So this is a delicious way to serve it. The ribbons are made by using a vegetable peeler. The results? A colorful, elegant side dish. Choose smaller zucchini that have tinier seeds and less moisture.

2 pounds zucchini

Salt, to taste

1 to 2 tablespoons olive oil

1 garlic clove, minced

1 plum tomato, cored and diced

¼ cup small black olives, pitted

8 basil leaves, cut into thin strips

½ cup grated Parmesan cheese

Using a vegetable peeler, peel the zucchini lengthwise into thin ribbons. Continue to peel the zucchini until you reach the inner core of seeds. Save this core for another dish, or discard it.

Sprinkle the zucchini ribbons with salt. Set aside for 5 minutes. Squeeze the excess moisture from the zucchini.

In a large frying pan over medium-high heat, heat the olive oil. Add the garlic and allow it to cook for about 30 seconds, then remove the garlic from the pan and discard it. Add the zucchini ribbons and diced tomatoes. Cook for 2 to 3 minutes, stirring often, or until the zucchini becomes limp. Add the black olives and basil. Toss gently. Sprinkle with the Parmesan cheese. Serve immediately.

MAKES 4 SERVINGS.

Suggested pairing: Twin Oaks Baked Stuffed Shrimp, page 135.

Doing Zucchini Right

Because of its high moisture content, zucchini can easily turn to mush if it's overcooked. Slice your zucchini, sprinkle it with salt, and set it aside for 30 minutes, which will release some of its water. Rinse well and dice, then toss the zucchini into a really hot frying pan with olive oil and sliced onions. In just a few minutes, the zucchini will be bright green and ready to eat. Rinsed well and cut into thin strips, zucchini can also be eaten raw.

French-Canadian Turkey Stuffing

The ingredients in this stuffing recipe are similar to those in the classic French Meat Pie (see recipe on page 107). We always make extra stuffing that we bake in a casserole dish for the finicky eaters at our family gatherings who do not like their stuffing cooked inside the bird. I pour a little turkey broth over the casserole stuffing to give it more real turkey flavor.

---

1 tablespoon butter

1 large onion, chopped fine

2 large potatoes, peeled and quartered

1 pound lean ground pork

1 pound lean ground beef

Salt and freshly ground black pepper, to taste

In a large frying pan, melt the butter and cook the onion until tender.

In a pot of boiling water, cook the potatoes until tender. During this time, add the ground pork and beef to the frying pan, breaking up all the chunks of meat. Cook until all the pink is gone from the meat.

Drain the cooked potatoes. Add them to the frying pan, mashing well into the meat mixture. Season with salt and pepper.

Allow the stuffing to cool completely before stuffing the turkey.

MAKES ENOUGH STUFFING FOR A 20-POUND BIRD.

A History Lesson

Much of Rhode Island's unique food subculture is tied to history. The oldest Rhode Island company is the Kenyon Corn Meal Company, founded in 1656 and still operating in the quaint village of Usquepaugh. The state's second oldest still-operating business is the White Horse Tavern in Newport, which first opened its doors in 1673 and is now considered one of the finest restaurants in the state. The Mills Coffee Roasting Company in Providence has been operating since 1860. John Hancock once wrote in a letter to his cousin: ". . . if you see anything good at Providence, do buy it for me . . . "

Sausage-Chestnut Stuffing

French-Canadians in Rhode Island also make this stuffing for their holiday turkey. The most time-consuming step involves the chestnuts that have to be pierced or cut open with a small X, otherwise they just might explode as they cook. Then they are so hot to handle, you have to wait for them to cool before you can start peeling, so plan ahead accordingly.

½ cup (1 stick) butter

1 cup chopped celery

¾ cup chopped onions

1 pound breakfast sausage links, casings removed

3 cups chicken or turkey broth

1 (8-ounce) package stuffing mix

2 eggs, beaten

1 cup peeled and chopped cooked chestnuts

Salt and freshly ground black pepper, to taste

In a large frying pan, melt the butter and sauté the celery and onion until tender. In a separate frying pan, brown the sausage, breaking the links into small pieces. Add the cooked sausage to the celery-onion mixture.

Heat the broth in the same frying pan you used to cook the sausage. In a large bowl, combine the hot broth, the package of stuffing mix, and the cooked mixture of celery, onions, and sausage. Mix well. Allow to cool.

Add the beaten eggs and cooked chestnuts. Mix well.

MAKES ENOUGH STUFFING FOR A 20-POUND BIRD.

Vadenais Family Dressing

One of my dearest friends, from high school and college days, is Mary Vadenais Dexter, whose parents were in the fish-and-chips business. In fact, they made the best fish-and-chips in the area. That recipe, I'm afraid, is long gone, but "Mom's Famous Family Dressing" is still with us. The Vadenais family makes it in a variety of guises—as an accompaniment for turkey, a stand-alone meat dish, the filling for a French-Canadian meat pie, or as the bottom layer of *port-de-chinois,* the French-Canadian version of shepherd's pie. This recipe makes enough to serve a holiday crowd, but if you cut the recipe in half, you'll still have enough dressing for 12 people. If desired, leftover boiled or mashed potatoes can be added to the dressing to make it go further.

4 large onions

$\frac{1}{2}$ package celery

$\frac{1}{2}$ cup (1 stick) butter

$\frac{1}{4}$ cup olive oil

$4\frac{1}{2}$ pounds lean ground beef

$4\frac{1}{2}$ pounds ground veal

2 pounds ground pork

1 (12-ounce) package mild breakfast sausage

1 (14-ounce) package seasoned stuffing mix

1 cup, or more, chicken broth

Ground sage, to taste

Using an old-fashioned hand-turned grinder, if possible (otherwise mince these ingredients as finely as possible), grind the onions and celery. In a very large black cast-iron frying pan, heat the butter and oil together, and sauté the onions and celery until soft. Transfer the cooked onions and celery to a bowl and set aside.

In the same frying pan, sauté all four of the meat ingredients—this may have to be done in batches.

Combine the sautéed meat with the onion and celery mixture, the stuffing mix, and enough chicken stock to make a moist consistency. Add a pinch of sage, or more to taste.

Move the entire mixture into a large Crock-Pot to keep warm for at least 30 minutes, then serve. Or it can be made in advance and reheated at mealtime.

MAKES 24 SERVINGS.

Breads & Pizzas

Rhode Island Indian Meal Corn Bread

The black specks in Rhode Island stone-ground whitecap cornmeal are actually nutrients and minerals. Commercial mills use soft dent corn. They remove the specks and add preservatives to extend shelf life. Real Rhode Island meal has no preservatives or additives. It should be stored in an airtight container in a refrigerator or freezer to preserve its nutty, somewhat sweet flavor. Originally from an old Rhode Island family cookbook, this recipe came with few directions.

1 cup Rhode Island stone-ground whitecap cornmeal

1 cup flour

$1/8$ teaspoon salt

2 teaspoons baking powder

$2/3$ cup sugar

1 egg, beaten

¾ cup milk

1 tablespoon butter, melted

Preheat oven to 375 degrees.

In a mixing bowl, combine the dry ingredients. Mix well. Add the egg, milk, and melted butter. Beat by hand until well mixed. Spoon into an 8-inch square baking pan. Bake for 20 to 25 minutes, or until golden brown. Serve immediately. This corn bread can be frozen and reheated in a 250-degree oven for 10 minutes.

MAKES 8 SERVINGS.

Oaklawn Corn Bread

This simple corn bread recipe comes from the *Oaklawn Grange Cookbook*, published in 1914. Oaklawn is now a section in the city of Cranston filled with shopping centers and strip plazas, a far cry from the Oaklawn of 1914.

---

2 cups flour

3 teaspoons baking powder

1/2 cup sugar

1 cup cornmeal

3/4 cup melted butter

1 cup milk

3 eggs, well beaten

Preheat oven to 425 degrees.

Sift the flour, baking powder, and sugar together into a large mixing bowl. Add the cornmeal to the bowl.

In a separate bowl, combine the melted butter and milk with the beaten eggs. Stir into the flour mixture just until well blended. Do not overmix. Pour into a greased 9x9-inch square pan. Bake for 20 minutes.

MAKES 9 SERVINGS.

Scialo Brothers Bakery

Scialo Brothers on Federal Hill is the quintessential Italian bakery. Luigi and Gaetano Scialo opened the shop in 1914 with sweets as their specialty. Huge brick ovens were soon added so the Scialo brothers could make breads and pastries. Luigi's daughters now own the business. Sisters run it, but it's still called Scialo Brothers.

Time seems to have stood still in the small shop where glass cases display Italian pastries, colorful cookies, and aromatic rum cakes on shelves lined with white paper doilies. A wall of shelves is stocked with Italian bread in all shapes and sizes.

Fans claim Scialo Brothers has bread that you can't find anywhere else. The bread is made with flour, water, salt, and yeast—basically the same dough for all the breads. The way the dough is aged and how it is shaped make the difference. The dough is allowed to sit after it is mixed, which affects the texture and taste. "Sicilian" is an elongated braid. "Italian" is a crusty oval or round.

***Warning:* You have to eat this bread the day it's baked. With no preservatives, the bread will harden by the next day. Stored in plastic, the crust gets soft. The folks at Scialo Brothers will tell you to wrap the bread in foil and freeze it if you can't eat it on the day it's purchased.**

Portuguese Sweet Bread

Sweet and yeasty, Portuguese sweet bread is surprisingly easy to make. Most home cooks will be pleased to find that they probably have on hand everything they need to make this Rhode Island favorite. Still warm from the oven and spread with a little apricot jam, this golden loaf is beyond wonderful.

½ cup mashed potatoes

¼ cup lukewarm "potato water"

1 tablespoon sugar

1 package dry yeast

⅛ teaspoon ground ginger

½ cup milk

1¼ teaspoons salt

¼ cup butter

3 eggs

¾ cup sugar

4 to 5 cups all-purpose flour

Save some of the water used to boil the potatoes. Measure ¼ cup of this potato water. Combine the 1 tablespoon of sugar and the dry yeast with the potato water, stirring until dissolved. Blend in the mashed potatoes and ginger. Set aside in a warm area. Allow the mixture to double in size, which should take 30 to 45 minutes.

In a saucepan, scald the milk. Add the salt and butter. Allow the mixture to cool to a lukewarm state.

In a bowl, beat the eggs. Set aside 1 tablespoon of the beaten eggs to use as a glaze. Add the ¾ cup of sugar to the bowl. Beat until light and fluffy.

In a large mixing bowl, combine the yeast mixture with the milk and egg mixtures, using an electric mixer set at low speed. Blend thoroughly. Stir in 2 cups of the flour and beat until well blended, about 5 minutes. Stir in the remaining flour with a spoon, adding just enough to make a soft dough.

Turn the dough out onto a floured work surface. Knead until smooth and elastic, about 5 minutes. Add only enough flour to prevent sticking. Place the dough in a greased bowl, turning to completely coat the surface of the dough. Cover the bowl with a clean cotton towel and set it aside in a warm area. Allow the dough to double in size, about 1½ hours.

Punch down the dough and place it in a greased 10-inch tube pan, or divide it equally into 2 greased casserole dishes. Cover the container and allow the dough to double in size again, which should take another 1½ hours.

Preheat oven to 350 degrees. Brush the loaves with the reserved tablespoon of beaten egg. Bake for about 30 minutes, or until golden brown.

MAKES 1 LARGE LOAF OR 2 SMALLER LOAVES.

Grilled Italian Bread

Several recipes in this book call for grilled Italian bread as an accompaniment. Nothing could be easier, or as satisfying. Any kind of Italian bread can be used, even if it's a day old. If you don't have a grill, you can achieve similar results by placing the slices of bread under the broiler of your oven for a few minutes. Be careful not to burn the bread.

---

1 loaf Italian bread, any kind, any shape

Olive oil, as needed

Whole garlic cloves (optional)

Prepare your grill as usual.

Cut the loaf of Italian bread into slices that are just slightly less than 1 inch thick. Drizzle a little olive oil on both sides of every slice. If possible, use a pastry brush, dip it in olive oil, and then spread the oil lightly and evenly over every bread slice. If desired, you can also rub each slice with a whole garlic clove to impart a subtle hint of garlic.

Place the bread slices on the grill with tongs. Watch over them carefully so that they do not burn. Check to see how brown the underside of the bread is getting. When golden brown, or when grill marks begin to appear on the bread, turn the slices over and continue grilling for another minute or so. Transfer the grilled Italian bread slices to a serving platter. Serve immediately.

MAKES ABOUT 8 SERVINGS PER LOAF.

SCIALO BROTHERS BAKERY, FEDERAL HILL

Sticky Buns

If you're accustomed to sticky buns as a breakfast or Sunday brunch goodie, you'll be surprised to learn that Rhode Island restaurants, especially in the northern part of the state, are known for serving sticky buns with their big family-style chicken dinners. This recipe, however, comes from Martha Murphy, whose sticky buns were legendary at her Murphy's B&B, just a short walk from the seawall along Ocean Road in Narragansett. Pillowy soft and just sweet enough, they're impossible to resist.

1$\frac{1}{2}$ cups milk

2 packages dry yeast

2 eggs

1 cup (2 sticks) butter or
   shortening, melted

1 cup sugar

1 teaspoon salt

1 tablespoon cinnamon

6 to 8 cups flour

TOPPING

1 cup brown sugar

$\frac{1}{2}$ cup honey

4 tablespoons butter

$\frac{1}{2}$ cup chopped pecans

$\frac{1}{4}$ cup butter, melted

$\frac{1}{2}$ cup sugar combined with
   2 tablespoons cinnamon

1 cup raisins

Scald the milk and pour into a large bowl. Allow it to cool to lukewarm. Add the yeast and allow it to dissolve. With an electric mixer, beat in the eggs, 1 cup melted butter, 1 cup sugar, salt, 1 tablespoon cinnamon, and just enough flour to make a stiff batter. When the mixer can no longer handle the dough, turn the dough out onto a floured work surface and knead, adding flour as needed, until the dough is smooth and elastic. Cover the dough with a clean, dry cotton towel. Let it rise for 20 minutes.

Combine all the topping ingredients in a saucepan. Heat, stirring, until the butter melts. Spread over the bottom of 2 9x13-inch baking pans.

Divide the dough in half and roll out each half into a rectangle about 12x18 inches in size and $\frac{1}{4}$ inch thick. Brush the rectangles with the $\frac{1}{4}$ cup melted butter. Sprinkle with the cinnamon sugar. Distribute the raisins evenly over the dough. Starting with the long edge of the dough, roll it up like a jelly roll.

Using a sharp serrated knife, cut the roll into 2-inch sections, being careful not to flatten the dough. Place the sections, with their spiral design facing up, in the prepared baking pans, spacing them about $\frac{3}{4}$ inch apart.

Cover the pans with plastic wrap and refrigerate overnight or at least 8 hours before baking.

Preheat oven to 350 degrees. Bake the buns, uncovered, for 20 to 30 minutes. When they are done, immediately invert them onto a serving plate. The topping will be very hot. Allow the buns to cool slightly before serving.

MAKES ABOUT 24 BUNS.

Life in South County

My brother always said I was blessed, and I'm beginning to believe him. For I have a summer home in South County—Narragansett, to be exact. It really is hard to explain, but a wonderful feeling comes over many people as they exit over Interstate 95 and head south into this land of farms that roll down to the ocean, with horses at play in fields of wildflowers, and almost magical places to visit. My three favorite food places in South County are:

Schartner Farm: Acres of strawberry patches and corn fields surround Schartner Farm in Exeter. Quaint baskets of just-picked fruits and vegetables—the most perfect specimens I've ever seen—immediately catch your eye. Then the nose detects the aromas of fruit pies (blueberry is the best) and rustic breads coming from the oven. In adjacent greenhouses are acres of colorful plants and flowers intermingled with antiques. "People can see where their food is being grown and who is growing it. That's important to them, and part of why we've been around for so long," says co-owner Nancy Schartner.

The Fantastic Umbrella Factory: This rambling old farmstead, in continuous use since 1760, now houses a just plain weird assortment of shops where you can buy anything from a kite to jewelry. Summer vacationers with children flock to this Charlestown site on rainy days. The ramshackle buildings are overgrown with vines, and spotted guinea fowl roam freely. Duke's Umbrella Café is the creation of David "Duke" Deery, a South County icon who has cooked at the legendary Duke's in Middlebridge, Peppers in Narragansett, and Ocean Mist in Matunuck. Duke's food reflects his travels through the Southwest, and Native American artifacts serve as part of the eclectic decor. "Sustenance comes in many forms, not only food," says Duke. "This is a place where people can discuss anything they want and feel fulfilled."

The Towers: Straddling scenic Route 1A, with the sea pounding against the mile-long seawall, are the Towers of Narragansett—all that remains of the town's casino that burned to the ground in 1900. Like something out of a fairy tale, the twin stone towers arch across a busy street. It's no wonder that weddings often take place on the upper level. Sitting on the deck of the nearby Coast Guard House restaurant offers one a bird's-eye view of this architectural jewel as well as a seafaring panorama that stretches from Newport to Block Island—a perfect perch for wining and dining on a sunny day.

Cavacas (Portuguese Popovers)

A Portuguese treat, *cavacas* puff up like popovers even though there is no baking powder or baking soda in the recipe. If desired, a bit of vanilla extract and sugar icing turn *cavacas* into a dessert.

---

8 jumbo eggs

1 cup vegetable oil

2 cups flour

Drizzle of vanilla extract (optional)

Confectioners' sugar icing (optional)

Preheat oven to 375 degrees.

In a bowl, beat together the eggs, vegetable oil, flour, and, if desired, the vanilla to make a thin batter. Pour into greased muffin cups or ovenproof custard cups, filling ¾ full. Bake for 30 to 35 minutes.

Turn the *cavacas* out of the cups. Allow to cool. If desired, drizzle with a thin confectioners' sugar icing.

CONFECTIONERS' SUGAR ICING

½ cup confectioners' sugar

Drizzle of lemon juice

Milk to thin icing

Combine the sugar, lemon juice, and enough milk to make a thin icing.

MAKES ABOUT 18 POPOVERS.

The Honor System

Daddy's Bread in Matunuck is a ramshackle old house, overgrown with beach roses, where some of the best baked goods around are offered on the honor system. Inside the house are shelves and shelves of multi-grain breads, fruit-laden muffins, and oversize cookies. The prices are posted on the wall, and customers are on their own to drop their money into a chute that sends the money to who knows where? And if you don't have the money, it's okay to leave an IOU that you can pay the next time you visit Daddy's Bread.

Pizza Dough

While the following recipe is a basic one, you can be creative with toppings. Possibilities include chopped canned tomatoes in a heavy puree and fresh basil leaves; spinach, Gorgonzola, and raisins; tomato, olives, jalapeños, and mozzarella; prosciutto, egg, and Parmigiano-Reggiano; Roman style with garlic mashed potatoes and fresh rosemary; or bean puree, olive puree, and tomato.

1 package active dry yeast

1 cup warm water

Pinch sugar

2¼ teaspoons kosher salt

¼ cup johnnycake meal or fine-ground white cornmeal

3 tablespoons whole wheat flour

1 tablespoon virgin olive oil

2½ to 3½ cups unbleached white flour

In a bowl, dissolve the yeast in the warm water with the sugar. After 5 minutes, stir in the salt, johnnycake meal, whole wheat flour, and oil. Gradually add the white flour, stirring with a wooden spoon until a stiff dough has formed. Place the dough on a floured work surface, and knead it for several minutes. Add only enough additional flour to keep the dough from sticking.

When the dough is smooth and shiny, transfer it to a bowl that has been brushed with olive oil. Brush the top of the dough with additional olive oil to prevent a skin from forming. Cover the bowl with plastic wrap. Allow the dough to rise in a warm place, away from drafts, until it has doubled in size, approximately 2 hours.

Punch down the dough and knead once more. Let the dough rise again for about 40 minutes. Again, punch down the dough. If it is sticky, knead in a bit more flour. Store the dough, well coated in olive oil, at room temperature for at least 30 minutes before baking.

MAKES ABOUT 24 OUNCES OF DOUGH, ENOUGH FOR 4 (10-INCH) PIZZAS.

Grilled Pizza with Garden Tomato Sauce

The secret to grilled pizza is olive oil. The pizza dough, either made from scratch or store-bought, is divided into 6-ounce balls, then coated generously with olive oil and left to sit for at least 30 minutes in a shallow sheet pan. The oil reacts to the intense heat of the wood-burning grill and is seared into the dough, almost like frying it. The balls of dough can sit in the olive oil for hours and, as a result, are soft and pliable.

6 ounces pizza dough (homemade or store-bought)

1/2 cup virgin olive oil

1/2 teaspoon minced fresh garlic

1/2 cup mixed chopped fresh herbs (oregano, thyme, chives, and basil)

1/2 cup loosely packed shredded Fontina cheese

2 tablespoons freshly grated Pecorino Romano cheese

1 cup Garden Tomato Sauce (recipe follows)

Prepare a hot fire on one side of your grill, using wood or hardwood lump charcoal. This is absolutely essential. A gas grill will not do—it will not get hot enough. Set the grill rack 4 inches above the hot coals. A wood fire or one made with hardwood lump charcoal is considered to be "hot" when you can hold your hand over the coals for 3 to 4 seconds at a distance of 5 inches. If you can hold your hand over the hot coals for longer than 4 seconds, it isn't hot enough to grill a pizza.

On a large, well-oiled, inverted baking sheet, spread and flatten the pizza dough, using your hands, into a 10-inch free-form shape, 1/8 inch thick. Do not make a lip around the pizza, and try not to stretch the dough so thinly that holes appear. An even thickness is recommended.

When the fire is hot, gently lift the dough off the sheet pan with your fingers and drape it onto the grill. The dough will not fall through the grates. Within 1 minute, the dough will puff up slightly, and its underside will stiffen, with grill marks appearing.

With tongs, flip the pizza over onto the cooler side of the grill. Brush the grilled top of the pizza with olive oil. Sprinkle on the minced garlic, fresh herbs, shredded Fontina, and grated Pecorino Romano. Add small dollops of the tomato sauce to various parts of the pizza. Do not overload the pizza with toppings; if you do, the pizza will burn before the toppings are heated through. Drizzle the top of the pizza with more olive oil.

Using tongs, slide the pizza back toward the hot coals, rotating the pizza frequently so that different sections are exposed to the heat. Check the underside often to make sure it is not burning. The pizza is done when the cheese is melted, about 6 minutes. Serve at once, with additional olive oil, if desired.

GARDEN TOMATO SAUCE

3 tablespoons virgin olive oil

1 teaspoon minced fresh garlic

12 to 15 Italian plum tomatoes, peeled, seeded, and chopped

1/2 teaspoon kosher salt

In a heavy frying pan, heat the olive oil. Add the garlic and sauté until golden. Add the tomatoes and cook over moderate heat, stirring frequently, for about 10 minutes, or until the sauce begins to thicken. Add the salt. Use immediately, or allow to cool, cover and refrigerate or freeze. This makes about 2 cups of sauce.

MAKES 1 MAIN-COURSE SERVING OR 4 APPETIZER SERVINGS.

TONY'S COLONIAL, FEDERAL HILL

Cosimo's Famous Pizza

Every day around lunchtime you can find a large wicker basket on the checkout counter at Venda Ravioli up on Federal Hill in Providence. In the basket are oversize pieces of Cosimo's Famous Pizza selling for a dollar a slice. No matter how much Cosimo Dellatore makes, it always sells out. If you can't get to Venda, you can try to make this thick, chewy pizza at home with Cosimo's recipe.

---

4 pounds pizza dough (homemade or store-bought)

1 tablespoon Crisco

1 (32-ounce) can San Marzano Italian peeled tomatoes

1 teaspoon salt

1 teaspoon dried oregano

1 teaspoon finely chopped garlic

1/2 cup extra-virgin olive oil

Pinch of freshly ground black pepper

2 pounds shredded mozzarella cheese

First prepare the dough. Coat a large baking sheet (approximately 18x24 inches in size) with the Crisco. Place the dough in the center of the pan, working it out to the outside edges of the pan. The dough should be about 1/2 inch thick, except for the border, which should be about 1 inch thick. Place the pan in the refrigerator for 30 minutes.

Next prepare the sauce. Place the canned tomatoes in a large bowl. Using your hands, break up the tomatoes. Add the salt, oregano, garlic, olive oil, and pepper. Using a spoon, blend until all the ingredients are mixed well.

Preheat oven to 400 degrees.

Remove the sheet pan from the refrigerator. Pour the sauce in the center of the dough and spread it out, covering almost the entire pizza but leaving a half-inch border. Sprinkle the mozzarella cheese generously over the entire pizza.

Place the baking sheet in the oven and cook for 45 to 60 minutes, depending on your oven. When the pizza is done, the cheese will be bubbly and the crust around the edges golden brown.

MAKES 16 SERVINGS.

Pizza: Past and Present

Ahhh, pizza. For many Rhode Islanders, pizza is the perfect food, having it all in one bite—bread, vegetable, and dairy. Most of us grew up on pizza, and some of us still search for that perfect pizza from our childhood. I remember the pizza served at the Sons of Italy Lodge in Woonsocket back in the 1950s, when my father and I would sneak into the kitchen for a bite of the mozzarella cheese used to make the best pizza I ever had. The lodge is now Savini's Restaurant, serving wonderful Italian food, but alas, no pizza can be found on the menu.

Restaurants specializing in pizza are as common as doughnut shops in Rhode Island. It's hard to drive down any city street without seeing a sign for pizza. There's thin crust, thick crust, even stuffed pizzas like those made at Geppetto's on Federal Hill in Providence. Some people claim Palmieri's Pizza is one of the "true wonders" of Rhode Island—strips of soft bread–type dough topped with a pungent tomatoey sauce laced with olive oil (note the absence of any cheese). But if there is one kind of pizza Providence is best known for, it would have to be grilled pizza.

I wonder what my Italian-born father would think of grilled pizza, made famous in recent years by Al Forno, arguably Providence's most famous restaurant. I'm sure this chewy, crisp pizza would confound him. You'd think that something like grilled pizza would be a California concoction, but no—it was conceived by George Germon of Al Forno fame.

George and his wife, Johanne Killeen, opened Al Forno in 1980. Since then they have been serving extraordinary food, most of it prepared over real wood fires. Their pizza is legendary—a thin, crisp dough in a free-form shape, topped with dollops of this and that, offering testimony that less really is more, especially when it is intensely flavored. Glistening with a final drizzle of spicy olive oil, the Al Forno pizza is brought whole to the table, where it is not cut into wedges but usually torn apart as it is eaten.

George and Johanne have been very generous in sharing their grilled pizza technique with the world. I was fortunate to spend a Sunday afternoon with them at Al Forno, learning their well-worked-out method of making grilled pizza, which I now make for friends and family all summer long on the wood-burning grill in our outdoor kitchen. It is definitely a technique worth mastering.

Johnston-Style Sausage and Pepper Pizza

Antonio DePetrillo of Johnston is the king of pizza in Rhode Island. This home cook has created hundreds of recipes, many reflecting a specific Italian neighborhood in the state. This is how the folks in Johnston like their pizza.

1 pound pizza dough (homemade or store-bought)

¾ pound sweet or hot Italian sausage links

2 tablespoons olive oil

1¼ cups canned Italian crushed tomatoes

1½ cups chopped red bell pepper

⅛ teaspoon salt

¼ teaspoon black pepper

1 tablespoon dried oregano

⅓ cup diced pepperoni

⅓ cup chopped prosciutto

1¼ cups shredded mozzarella cheese

Spread the dough evenly over a 12- or 13-inch pan, and let it rise for 30 minutes in a warm place.

In a skillet over medium-high heat, sauté the sausage in the olive oil until brown. Remove the sausage to drain and cool on paper towels. Brush some of the sausage drippings evenly over the pizza dough.

Preheat oven to 450 degrees.

Drain off any remaining drippings from the skillet. Over medium heat, add the crushed tomatoes and red pepper, and sauté for 7 or 8 minutes. Season with salt, pepper, and oregano, blending well. Spread the tomato and pepper mixture over the pizza dough, and bake for about 7 minutes.

Cut the sausage into ¼-inch slices. Remove the pizza from the oven and place the sausage slices evenly over the pizza.

Combine and blend together the pepperoni, prosciutto, and mozzarella cheese, and sprinkle the mixture over the pizza. Return the pizza to the oven, and bake until the bottom has turned golden brown and the cheese has melted. Remove the pizza from the oven, let cool slightly, then slice and serve.

MAKES 8 SERVINGS.

TONY'S COLONIAL, FEDERAL HILL

Federal Hill Pizza

So many pizzas, so little time. This is an original recipe from Antonio DePetrillo, named in honor of the Little Italy section of Providence.

1 medium-size onion, sliced thin

1 teaspoon minced garlic

3 tablespoons olive oil

1 medium-size red bell pepper, cut into rings

1 medium-size green bell pepper, cut into rings

1 pound pizza dough (homemade or store-bought)

1 cup crushed tomatoes

1 tablespoon dried parsley

1/2 teaspoon white pepper

1/2 pound thinly sliced pepperoni

1 1/2 cups shredded mozzarella cheese

In a large frying pan over medium heat, sauté the onion and garlic in the olive oil until tender. Add the red and green bell pepper rings to the pan and sauté for about 5 more minutes.

Spread the dough evenly over a 12- or 13-inch pan. Spread the crushed tomatoes evenly over the dough. Sprinkle the parsley and white pepper over the tomatoes, and let the pizza rise for 30 minutes.

Preheat oven to 425 degrees.

Place the thinly sliced pepperoni around the pizza in a circular pattern starting at the outside and working toward the center. Spoon the onion-garlic-pepper mixture over the pepperoni, covering the entire pizza with all the mixture.

Bake the pizza for 6 or 7 minutes. Remove it from the oven, spread the mozzarella cheese over the entire surface, and return the pan to the oven. Bake until the cheese has melted and the bottom is golden brown. Remove the pizza from the oven, let cool slightly, then slice and serve.

MAKES 8 SERVINGS.

Silver Lake Pizza

Created by Antonio DePetrillo, this recipe reflects the taste of Silver Lake, a predominantly Italian neighborhood in Providence. For a spicy hot pizza, sprinkle on a tablespoon of red pepper flakes just before adding the mushrooms.

1 pound pizza dough (homemade or store-bought)

1 stick pepperoni

1 pound hot or sweet Italian sausage links

1⅓ cups crushed tomatoes

3 tablespoons grated Parmesan cheese

1 cup sliced cooked mushrooms or 2 (4-ounce) cans sliced mushrooms, drained

1 tablespoon olive oil

1¼ cups shredded mozzarella cheese

1½ teaspoons Italian seasoning

1 tablespoon dried basil

Spread the dough evenly over a 12- or 13-inch pan, and let rise for 30 minutes.

Peel the outer skin off the pepperoni; dice the pepperoni into pieces about ¼-inch square. Grill the Italian sausages and dice into ¼-inch square pieces.

Spread the crushed tomatoes evenly over the pizza dough. Sprinkle the tomatoes with the Parmesan cheese. Place the mushroom slices evenly around the pizza. Sprinkle the pizza with the pepperoni and sausage cubes.

Preheat oven to 425 degrees. Drizzle the olive oil over the pizza and bake for about 7 minutes.

In a bowl, combine and blend the mozzarella cheese with the Italian seasoning and basil. Remove the pizza from the oven. Sprinkle the cheese mixture over the pizza. Return the pan to the oven, and bake until the cheese has melted and the bottom is golden brown. Remove the pizza from the oven, let cool slightly, then slice and serve.

MAKES 8 SERVINGS.

Rhode Island Pizza Strips

Louie Umberto, who has worked at Palmieri's Bakery in Johnston for more than twenty years, shares with us his recipe for Palmieri's famous Pizza Strips. There's but a teaspoon of cheese called for in the recipe, and that's enough to make two large pizzas.

---

2 pounds pizza dough (homemade or store-bought)

¼ cup olive oil

1 (28-ounce) can crushed or ground, peeled tomatoes in puree

3 teaspoons salt

½ teaspoon coarse ground black pepper

¾ teaspoon minced garlic

¾ teaspoon dried oregano

1 teaspoon grated Pecorino Romano cheese

Preheat oven to 400 degrees.

Divide the dough in half. Spread the dough onto 2 baking sheets, 18x24 inches each, that have been wiped with a little olive oil.

In a bowl, combine the remaining ingredients. Spread the mixture evenly over the dough. Sprinkle lightly with additional olive oil. Bake until the crust is crisp, approximately 15 to 20 minutes. Cut the pizza on each baking sheet into 16 strips, each approximately 9x3 inches in size.

MAKES 32 SERVINGS.

Spinach Pie

You know you're a Rhode Islander when you've eaten a Wimpy Skippy. That's the special spinach pie at Caserta's Pizzeria on Federal Hill, a Rhode Island institution since 1946. This "pie" isn't really a pie but more like a calzone stuffed with mozzarella cheese and sliced pepperoni, all wrapped in a chewy crust. The authentic Wimpy Skippy recipe is a family secret, but this recipe comes pretty close. By the way, the Wimpy Skippy was named after two old friends of the Caserta family, a guy called Wimpy and another guy known as Skippy.

---

2 packages frozen chopped spinach

1 (4-ounce) can chopped black olives

1 pepperoni stick, chopped into small pieces

$\frac{1}{2}$ cup shredded mozzarella cheese

Garlic salt or powder, to taste

Salt and freshly ground black pepper, to taste

2 pounds pizza dough (homemade or store-bought)

$\frac{1}{4}$ cup vegetable oil

Preheat oven to 350 degrees.

Cook the spinach according to package directions. Drain well. Combine with the black olives, pepperoni, mozzarella, garlic salt, salt, and pepper.

Roll out the pizza dough on a lightly floured work surface. Cut the dough into 12 equal pieces. Place a portion of the spinach mixture on each piece of dough. Close each piece of dough and seal to make a turnover. Brush each turnover with some of the oil.

Place the turnovers on a baking sheet. Bake for 30 minutes, or until golden brown. Serve immediately.

MAKES 12 SERVINGS.

Desserts & Beverages

SCIALO BROTHERS
BAKERY,
FEDERAL HILL

Apple Valley Pie

Back in 1989, Eileen Fochler of Greenville was a winner in the Best Two-Crusted Apple Pie in New England Cook-Off held at the historic Salem Cross Inn in West Brookfield, Massachusetts. When she won, Eileen said it was the Rhode Island apples that made her recipe taste better than the others.

PASTRY

2 cups flour (King Arthur flour preferred)

¾ cup shortening (Crisco preferred)

1 teaspoon salt

½ cup plus 2 tablespoons ice-cold water

FILLING

5 to 6 Mutszu apples, or newly picked Gravenstein or Cortland apples

¼ cup plus 1 tablespoon sugar

1 teaspoon cinnamon

1 teaspoon nutmeg

3 tablespoons melted margarine

2 tablespoons molasses

1 egg, beaten well

Sugar, as needed for sprinkling

To make the pastry, in a large bowl, work the flour, shortening, and salt with a pastry blender until the mixture is coarse like corn meal. Add just enough water to hold the dough together. Hold back 2 tablespoons of the water—you may not need it. Divide the dough into 2 balls. Set aside.

Peel, core, and thinly slice the apples. In a large bowl, combine the apples with the sugar, cinnamon, and nutmeg. Set aside.

Roll out one of the balls of dough to make the bottom crust for a 9-inch pie. Line a pie plate with the crust, leaving an overhang. Fill with the sliced apples.

In a small saucepan, combine the melted margarine and molasses. Drizzle over the apples in the pie plate. Preheat oven to 450 degrees.

Roll out the second ball of dough to make the top crust. Wet the rim of the dough with water. Place the top crust over the apples. Trim excess dough and flute the edge. Brush beaten egg all over. Sprinkle lightly with sugar. Cut air vents in the top crust and prick with a fork. Decorate with excess dough cut into the shape of an apple, if desired.

Bake at 450 degrees for 10 minutes, then reduce heat to 350 degrees and bake for another 30 to 35 minutes.

MAKES 6 SERVINGS.

Apple Crostata

The Italian version of apple pie is *crostata*, more rustic and easier to make because the crust is not fluted. The famed Al Forno restaurant in Providence introduced the free-form *crostata* to its many patrons, who quickly learned how to make the dish at home. My Italian grandmother used to make *crostata*, though she didn't have the luxury of a food processor, but the ingredients are the same as ever. *Crostata* can also be made with other fillings such as cranberries, walnuts, raspberries, and fresh figs.

DOUGH

3 cups all-purpose flour

1 tablespoon sugar

1 teaspoon salt

1 cup (2 sticks) plus 2
   tablespoons cold butter

9 tablespoons ice-cold water

FILLING

6 Granny Smith apples, peeled,
   cored, and quartered

Juice and zest from 1 lemon

Zest from 1 lemon

¾ cup sugar

½ teaspoon cinnamon

3 tablespoons butter, in small
   chunks

1 egg, beaten

1 tablespoon milk or cream

Confectioners' sugar (optional)

Vanilla ice cream, as needed

To make the dough in a food processor, combine the flour, sugar, and salt. Pulse for a few seconds. Add the butter and process for 30 seconds, or until the mixture resembles coarse corn meal. With the food processor running, add the ice-cold water in a steady stream. Pulse on and off until a ball forms. Be careful not to overwork the dough, or it will become tough. This process also can be done by hand.

Shape the dough into a large ball. Wrap in plastic wrap and refrigerate for at least 1 hour. The dough will keep for up to 3 days in the refrigerator.

Remove the dough from the refrigerator about 30 minutes before rolling it out. Dust a clean work surface with flour, and roll out the dough with a floured rolling pin until it is ¼-inch thick. Carefully fold the dough in half and place it on a lightly greased baking sheet.

In a large bowl, combine the apples, lemon juice and zest, sugar, cinnamon, and butter. Pile the mixture high in the center of the rolled-out dough, allowing at least 3 inches of dough all around. Fold over the edges of the dough to keep the apples from spilling out. The apples in the center should be exposed.

Preheat oven to 350 degrees.

In a small bowl, combine the beaten egg and milk. Brush the dough with the egg-milk mixture. Bake for 40 minutes, or until the apples are tender.

Slide the *crostata* onto a serving platter. Sprinkle with confectioners' sugar, if desired. Serve warm with a scoop of vanilla ice cream, if desired. *Crostata* can be made ahead and frozen for up to 1 week. Allow the frozen *crostata* to thaw, then reheat it in the oven until warm.

MAKES 6 SERVINGS.

Applesauce Spice Cake

The secret ingredient in this cake recipe is Kenyon's barley flour, rather unusual when it comes to desserts. Known more for its cornmeal, Kenyon's Corn Meal Company is the oldest company in Rhode Island, founded in 1656 and still operating in the quaint village of Usquepaugh down near the University of Rhode Island in South County. The applesauce can be store-bought, or it can easily be made from scratch with local apples.

$^1/_2$ cup (1 stick) butter

1 cup honey

1 egg

$1^3/_4$ cups Kenyon's barley flour

$^1/_2$ teaspoon salt

1 teaspoon baking soda

1 teaspoon ground cinnamon

$^1/_4$ teaspoon ground nutmeg

$^1/_2$ teaspoon ground cloves

1 cup raisins

$1^1/_2$ cups slightly warm applesauce

1 cup chopped walnuts

Cream Cheese Frosting (recipe follows), or confectioners' sugar

Preheat oven to 350 degrees.

In a large bowl, whip the butter until creamy. Add the honey and continue to whip. Add the egg, and whip until smooth and well blended.

In another bowl, sift together the flour, salt, baking soda, cinnamon, nutmeg, and cloves. Dredge the raisins in some of the flour mixture. Add the remaining flour mixture to the batter. Stir in the applesauce, raisins, and walnuts. Beat well.

Bake in a greased tube pan or in a 9x13-inch pan for 50 minutes, or until a toothpick inserted in the center comes out clean. Allow to cool. If desired, frost with the cream cheese frosting or sprinkle with confectioners' sugar.

CREAM CHEESE FROSTING

3 cups confectioners' sugar

1 (8-ounce) package cream cheese, softened

2 tablespoons butter, melted

1 teaspoon vanilla

You can soften the cream cheese at room temperature or in the microwave oven. Remove the cream cheese from its wrapper and place the cheese on a microwave-safe dish. Microwave the cheese on a medium heat for 1 to 1 1/2 minutes.

In a large bowl combine all the ingredients. Beat until smooth.

MAKES 8 SERVINGS.

Rhode Island Apple Bits

The first orchard in Rhode Island was planted in 1635 by William Blaxton, a clergyman who had planted the first orchard in Massachusetts ten years earlier. Blaxton is given credit for growing the first named apple in America–Blaxton's Yellow Sweeting, which became known as Sweet Rhode Island Greening, now the official state fruit. Because its texture and flavor hold up to heat, most of the Rhode Island Greening crop is sold for commercial processing (applesauce, pies, etc.). It's also good for out-of-hand eating and can be found at roadside stands, especially in Apple Valley.

Applesauce Cornmeal Tarts

The folks at Kenyon's Grist Mill are often called upon to perform cooking demonstrations at fairs and festivals. These cornmeal tarts are one of their most popular. They are made with Kenyon's famous cornmeal (though another kind of cornmeal can be substituted), and the applesauce can be store-bought or made from scratch using Rhode Island apples.

1 cup all-purpose flour

1/2 cup Kenyon's cornmeal

2 teaspoons baking powder

1/2 teaspoon salt

1/2 teaspoon baking soda

1 3/4 cups buttermilk

2/3 cup applesauce

Confectioners' sugar, for sprinkling as needed

Whipped cream, for topping

In a bowl, stir together all the dry ingredients. Add the buttermilk. Mix until just blended.

Pour about 1/4 cup of the batter onto a hot, greased griddle or skillet, spreading into a 4-inch circle. Cook until golden brown, turning over once when cakes have a bubbly surface and slightly dry edge.

To serve, place 2 tablespoons of applesauce between 2 cornmeal cakes, sprinkle with confectioners' sugar, and top with whipped cream.

MAKES 6 SERVINGS.

Glocester Cranberry Apple Pie

The Glocester Heritage Society in Chepachet Village has a large collection of recipes that have been handed down from generation to generation. This one combines Rhode Island apples with cranberries from nearby Massachusetts to make the perfect fall dessert.

---

1 large seedless orange, unpeeled

2 cups cranberries, washed

3 cups peeled, diced apples, your choice

1 tablespoon lemon juice

8 teaspoons cornstarch

1/4 teaspoon salt

1 1/2 cups sugar (less if apples are sweet)

1/4 cup chopped walnuts

Pastry for a deep 2-crust 9-inch pie

1 tablespoon butter

1 tablespoon heavy cream

1 tablespoon sugar

Cut the orange into quarters. Using a food chopper or food processor, chop the orange quarters along with the cranberries. In a large bowl, combine the coarsely chopped fruit with the diced apples. Sprinkle with the lemon juice to prevent browning.

In a separate bowl, combine the cornstarch, salt, sugar, and nuts. Spoon the cornstarch mixture into the fruit mixture, mixing gently.

Place the pastry for the bottom crust into a deep pie plate. Flute the edges. Pour the filling into the pastry shell. Dot with butter.

Preheat oven to 425 degrees.

Roll out the other sheet of pastry for the top crust. Cut lengthwise into 1/2-inch strips. Place the strips in a lattice pattern on top of the pie, trimming the ends to fit within the fluted edge. Brush the strips with cream. Sprinkle with sugar.

Bake for 45 minutes or until the pastry is golden. Cool on a wire rack.

MAKES 6 SERVINGS.

Fruited Country Cobbler

Aaron Smith Farm, which dates back to 1730, is located in rural Mapleville, a center for wool manufacturing during the twentieth century. The owners of the farm offer gourmet dining workshops in their restored farmhouse. Guests are brought back in time as they work together to help prepare historically inspired meals. This fruit cobbler is made with local fruit when in season.

---

2 cups prepared fresh fruit
(chopped apples, blueberries,
sliced strawberries, and rhubarb)

1/2 cup whole-berry cranberry sauce

1/2 cup chopped walnuts

1/2 cup sugar

1/2 cup baking mix (such as
Bisquick)

1 egg

1 teaspoon cinnamon

1/2 cup light cream

1/4 cup melted butter

Preheat oven to 400 degrees.

In a large bowl, combine the prepared fruit, cranberry sauce, and walnuts. Pour into a generously greased 6x10-inch baking dish.

In another bowl, combine the remaining ingredients. Mix well. Drop by spoonfuls on top of the fruit mixture.

Bake at 400 degrees for 15 minutes, then reduce the heat to 350 degrees and bake for another 10 minutes. Serve warm topped with vanilla ice cream, if desired.

MAKES 4 SERVINGS.

Blueberry Cornmeal Cobbler

From Donna Lee, retired food editor of *the Providence Journal,* comes this cobbler recipe that makes use of two native products, blueberries and johnnycake meal. The cobbler can be made with fresh or frozen berries. Donna says she sometimes adds red raspberries or strawberries with the blueberries. The proportions don't really matter as long as the berries total four 4 cups. Donna picks blueberries in late summer at Rocky Point Farm, a small venture in Warwick, not far from the gone-but-not-forgotten Rocky Point Amusement Park and Shore Dinner Hall. Donna also says this easy cobbler is best served warm, with the juices bubbling up around the golden cakelike topping. The cornmeal adds a pleasant texture, but the topping is lighter than cornbread.

---

2 pints (4 cups) blueberries or 4 cups mixed berries (blueberries, raspberries, and/or strawberries)

1/3 cup sugar

3 tablespoons flour or 4 teaspoons cornstarch

TOPPING

1/3 cup sugar

4 tablespoons butter (1/2 stick), at room temperature

l large egg

2 tablespoons lemon juice

2 tablespoons milk

1 teaspoon vanilla

2/3 cup flour

1/3 cup cornmeal or johnnycake meal

2 teaspoons baking powder

1/4 teaspoon salt

Rinse the berries. Drain in a colander. Mix the first 1/3 cup sugar with the flour or cornstarch; combine lightly with the berries. Pour the berries into a buttered 8- or 9-inch square baking dish or a 2-quart casserole dish.

Preheat oven to 350 degrees.

Make the topping. With an electric mixer on high, beat together the second 1/3 cup sugar and the butter for 2 or 3 minutes. Beat in the egg. Beat 1 minute.

Mix the lemon juice with the milk and vanilla. Mix the flour with the cornmeal, baking powder, and salt.

Add the milk mixture to the butter mixture; beat in. Blend in the dry ingredients on low speed just until mixed. Drop the batter by spoonfuls over the berries and spread it over the batter. It does not have to completely cover the berries. Sprinkle with about a tablespoon of sugar, if desired.

Bake, uncovered, for about 40 minutes or until the fruit is bubbly and the top is golden and cooked through. It may take up to 1 hour, depending on the oven. Serve warm or at room temperature, plain or with cream or ice cream.

MAKES 6 TO 8 SERVINGS.

Prudence Island Blueberry Cake

Well over fifty years ago, this cake recipe was created by a home cook on Prudence Island, where wild blueberries are still plentiful today. The epitome of the simple life, Prudence Island is located in the center of Narragansett Bay, less than 2 miles from the mainland. It's next to Hog Island where my Italian relatives have simple summer homes, some still with outhouses. The only way to get to either island is by the small ferry out of Bristol that runs only in the summer, serving a state park there.

---

2 cups sifted flour

⅔ cup sugar

2 teaspoons baking powder

½ teaspoon salt

½ cup (1 stick) butter, at room temperature

2 eggs

½ cup milk

1 teaspoon vanilla extract

2 cups fresh or frozen blueberries

½ cup light brown sugar

1 tablespoon butter

½ teaspoon cinnamon

¼ cup coarsely chopped walnuts or pecans

In a large bowl, sift together the flour, sugar, baking powder, and salt. Cut in the ½ cup butter.

In another bowl, beat the eggs. Add the milk and vanilla extract. Pour the liquid mixture into the first bowl, mixing just enough to moisten. Add the blueberries and mix gently.

Preheat oven to 375 degrees.

Pour the batter into a greased 9-inch square pan. In a small bowl, combine the brown sugar, 1 tablespoon butter, cinnamon, and chopped nuts. Sprinkle this mixture over the top of the batter.

Bake for about 35 minutes, or until a toothpick inserted in the center of the cake comes out clean.

MAKES 6 SERVINGS.

Rhubarb Upside-Down Cake

Rhubarb grows almost everywhere in Rhode Island. It's also available at farmers' markets and in local supermarkets. As a child, I would snap off a stalk on hot summer days, dip it into a dish of sugar provided by my mother, and eat it raw. Walter Elwell from the Little Compton Grange over in the East Bay section of the state provided this recipe using the plentiful fruit in a moist and delicious cake.

---

3 cups sliced rhubarb

1 cup sugar, divided

$1/3$ cup butter

$1 1/2$ teaspoons baking powder

1 egg

1 teaspoon vanilla extract

$1/2$ cup milk

$1 1/4$ cups all-purpose flour

Preheat oven to 350 degrees.

In a large saucepan, combine the rhubarb and $2/3$ cup of the sugar. Cook over low heat, stirring frequently, until the sugar melts. Spread this mixture over the bottom of a well-greased 8- or 9-inch square baking pan.

In a mixing bowl, beat the butter with the remaining $1/3$ cup of sugar and the baking powder until the mixture is fluffy, and then beat in the egg and the vanilla extract. Gradually add the milk, alternating it with the flour, and blend the ingredients well. Spoon the batter evenly over the fruit layer.

Bake for approximately 35 minutes. Allow the cake to cool in its pan on a rack for about 5 minutes. Run a knife around the edges of the cake to loosen. Turn the cake out of the pan, upside down, onto a platter.

MAKES 8 SERVINGS.

Rhode Island Peach Slump

You can make a betty, buckle, clafouti, cobbler, crisp, crumble, grunt, pandowdy, or a slump—they are all old-fashioned fruit desserts, probably brought over by English settlers, that are baked and stewed. A slump was so named, in the mid-1700s, because its cooked fruit and raised dough slumped on the plate when served. This particular version makes use of Rhode Island peaches harvested in the late summer months.

6 cups peeled and sliced fresh ripe peaches

1 cup sugar

1½ teaspoons ground cinnamon

½ cup water

12 baking powder biscuits (about 1½ inches in size)

In a large frying pan, combine the peaches, sugar, cinnamon, and water over medium-high heat. Bring to a simmer and top with the biscuits. Cover and simmer for about 30 minutes. Serve with cream, if desired.

MAKES 6 SERVINGS.

Baked Fruit Compote in Peach Wine

A baked fruit compote goes from simple to sublime with the addition of peach wine from Diamond Hill Vineyards in Cumberland in the northern part of Rhode Island. The small winery specializes in making fruit wines with local peaches, apples, and blueberries. Owners Claire and Peter Berntson serve this dessert to family and friends as well as guests visiting the winery.

½ cup (1 stick) butter, at room temperature

1 pound cake, allowed to dry out and made into crumbs

1 can each pears, peaches, apricots, and cherries, drained

Brown sugar (about ½ cup)

Shredded coconut (optional)

½ bottle Diamond Hill Vineyards peach wine

Preheat oven to 350 degrees.

Butter a shallow ovenproof baking dish or pie plate. Spread generously with about ¾ of the cake crumbs. Arrange the drained fruit with hollow sides up. Dot with the remaining butter and the brown sugar. Sprinkle with the remaining cake crumbs and, if desired, the coconut. Add enough peach wine to cover the bottom of the dish to a depth of ½ inch.

Cover the dish tightly with aluminum foil. Bake for 20 minutes or until hot and bubbly. Remove the foil and place the dish under the broiler until the compote is golden brown on top. Serve in small bowls with heavy cream or ice cream.

MAKES 6 SERVINGS.

Native Pumpkin Cheesecake

Pastry chef Matthew Petersen at the Castle Hill Inn & Resort in Newport created this dessert to make use of native pumpkins in the fall. Instead of an ordinary crust, he adds ground almonds to the graham cracker crumbs for a slightly nutty flavor.

PUMPKIN PUREE

1 (5-pound) pumpkin

Your favorite ground spices (ginger, allspice, nutmeg, cloves, and cinnamon recommended), to taste

2 tablespoons butter

CRUST

1 1/2 cups graham cracker crumbs

1/2 cup ground raw almonds

4 tablespoons melted butter

First make the pumpkin puree. Preheat oven to 400 degrees.

Remove the stem from the pumpkin. Cut the pumpkin in half and remove all seeds, saving some for garnish.

Combine equal amounts of all your favorite ground spices. Rub the spice mixture into the flesh of the pumpkin, using generous amounts. Place 1 tablespoon of butter into each pumpkin half. Place pumpkin halves in a roasting pan and put them into the oven.

Bake the pumpkin for about 1 hour or until the flesh is very soft and brown on the outside. Allow it to cool to room temperature. Remove all flesh from the skin. Place the flesh in a food mill or food processor, and process until smooth. Measure 1 1/2 cups of puree for the filling; set aside.

Next make the crust. Preheat oven to 350 degrees.

In a mixing bowl, combine the crumbs, almonds, and melted butter. Mix well with a spoon. Press the mixture evenly into the bottom of a 10-inch spring-form pan. Bake for 5 to 10 minutes. Set side to cool.

FILLING

¹/₂ cup maple syrup

3 cups (24 ounces) cream cheese, softened

4 eggs

Finally make the filling. Preheat oven to 250 degrees.

In a mixing bowl with paddle attachment, combine the maple syrup and softened cream cheese. One at a time, add the eggs, scraping the bowl between each addition. Add the 1¹/₂ cups of pumpkin puree. Mix the batter until smooth. Pour the batter into the prepared springform pan.

Place the springform pan into a larger pan that can be filled with water when the cheesecake is placed in the oven. This allows the cake to bake more evenly from the edges to the center. Fill the outer pan with water just up to where the top of the cake is.

Bake for 45 minutes to 1 hour, or until the center is firm. The pumpkin seeds you saved can be roasted in the oven while the cake is baking to use as a garnish. Cool the cheesecake and refrigerate overnight before unmolding and serving.

MAKES 8 SERVINGS.

The Avondale Swan

Since 1916 the Olympia Tea Room has been a Watch Hill institution, especially in the summer when yachts pull into the harbor and people with perfect suntans stop by for lunch or dinner. This old-fashioned seaside restaurant still serves freshly squeezed lemonade and lime rickeys, as well as Point Judith lobsters and calamari made with local squid. The desserts are noteworthy, especially the raspberry bread pudding made with Portuguese sweet bread. But what makes the Olympia Tea Room unique is its World Famous Avondale Swan, named in honor of the local area of Avondale. An oversized cream puff shell is cut up and made to look very much like a graceful swan, thanks to a great deal of whipped cream. The swan, which is filled with golden French vanilla ice cream, seems to be floating in a pool of dark chocolate sauce.

Blote Kage (Rainbow Dessert)

Rhode Island First Lady Susan Carcieri, wife of Governor Don Carcieri, has made this dazzling dessert for many a big party, whether it was for family or political fund-raising. *Blote Kage* (pronounced *bloata kaga*) is Norwegian for "soft cake" and reflects her heritage. This spectacular sweet ending to a meal has fillings that offer a rainbow of colors. It all starts with a basic sponge cake or chiffon cake, which you can make from scratch or purchase at a supermarket.

---

1 large sponge cake or chiffon cake

3 cups whipping cream

6 tablespoons confectioners' sugar

PINEAPPLE FILLING

2 teaspoons unflavored gelatin

1 tablespoon pineapple juice

1 cup drained, crushed pineapple

Green food coloring, as needed

APRICOT FILLING

2 teaspoons unflavored gelatin

1 tablespoon pineapple juice

1 cup mashed apricot pulp

Cut the cake into four layers, each 1 inch thick. In a bowl, whip the cream and confectioners' sugar until stiff.

Prepare each of the fillings. For the pineapple filling, soften the gelatin in the pineapple juice. Dissolve in a double boiler over hot water. Stir into the drained, crushed pineapple. Tint as desired with green food coloring. Chill. When partially set, fold in 1 cup of the whipped cream.

For the apricot filling, soften the gelatin in the pineapple juice. Dissolve in a double boiler over hot water. Stir into the mashed apricot pulp. Chill. When partially set, fold in 1 cup of the whipped cream.

RASPBERRY FILLING

2 teaspoons unflavored gelatin

1 tablespoon pineapple juice

1 cup thick raspberry jam

Green pistachio nuts, blanched and finely chopped, as needed for garnish

Apricots, cut in half, as needed for garnish

Mint leaves, as needed for garnish

For the raspberry filling, soften the gelatin in the pineapple juice. Dissolve over hot water. Stir into the raspberry jam. Chill. When partially set, fold in 1 cup of the whipped cream.

Reassemble the cake using a different filling between each layer. Cover the top and sides of the cake with the remaining whipped cream. Sprinkle with the chopped pistachio nuts. Chill for at least 3 hours before serving.

Just before serving, arrange the apricot halves, rounded side out, around the base of the cake. Garnish with a few mint leaves. Serve at once.

MAKES 8 TO 12 SERVINGS.

The Milkman Cometh

Some of us in Rhode Island can still remember the local milkman delivering farm-fresh milk in glass bottles to our doors. Some Rhode Island dairies still offer home delivery. The biggest by far is Munroe Dairy in East Providence, which has been in business since 1881, but today they deliver a whole lot more than milk. The Munroe trucks, painted to resemble a black-and-white milking cow, are miniature grocery stores on wheels. What's especially interesting is that Munroe Dairy is a great source of unique local Rhode Island products.

These products include: Barney's Bagels from Cranston, Fortuna's Sausage from Greenville, Supreme cheese products from Warwick, ice cream cakes from the Ice Cream Machine in Cumberland, desserts from the Pastry Chef in Pawtucket, brownies and cheesecakes from Anita's in Providence, gourmet coffee from Newport Coffee Traders, eggs from the Little Rhody Egg Farm in Foster, chicken potpies from Newport's Upper Crust, frozen entrees from Angelo's in Providence, and Sweet Ideas, a line of frozen desserts created by Chef Gianfranco Campanella.

Narragansett Indian Pudding

Indian pudding—named in honor of the Native Americans who taught early settlers how to make this dish—is still often served at church suppers and family get-togethers in the fall and winter. Some Rhode Island families put sliced apples, dried currants, or raisins into the batter, while others add a cup of real maple syrup (never the less expensive imitation pancake syrup). A few restaurants, such as Aunt Carrie's in the southern part of Narragansett known as Point Judith, have Indian pudding on their menus all summer long—served warm with a scoop of vanilla ice cream. Indian pudding is traditionally baked in the oven, but it also can be made on top of the stove with almost the same taste results. Here are both recipes, which are well over a hundred years old.

BAKED INDIAN PUDDING

$1/2$ cup yellow cornmeal

2 tablespoons sugar

$1/8$ teaspoon salt

$1/8$ teaspoon baking soda

3 cups milk, divided

2 tablespoons butter, melted

1 egg, beaten

$1/4$ cup molasses

$1/4$ teaspoon ground cinnamon

$1/8$ teaspoon ground ginger

Whipped cream or vanilla ice cream

In a 2-quart saucepan, combine the cornmeal, sugar, salt, and baking soda. Stir in $1^{1}/2$ cups of milk and the melted butter. Cook over medium-high heat until thick and bubbly. Remove from heat. Set aside.

Preheat oven to 300 degrees.

In a bowl, combine the beaten egg, molasses, cinnamon, ginger, and the remaining $1^{1}/2$ cups of milk. Stir into the cornmeal mixture. Mix well. Pour into a 1-quart casserole.

Bake, uncovered, for about 1 hour, or until a knife inserted into the pudding comes out clean. Serve warm with whipped cream or vanilla ice cream.

MAKES 6 SERVINGS.

STOVE-TOP INDIAN PUDDING

3 cups milk

1/2 cup cornmeal

1/2 cup molasses

1 egg, beaten

1 tablespoon butter

1/2 teaspoon cinnamon

1/2 teaspoon nutmeg

1/4 teaspoon ground cloves

1/4 teaspoon ground ginger

1 teaspoon salt

1/2 cup milk

Whipped cream or vanilla ice cream

Scald the 3 cups of milk over hot water in a double boiler. Gradually add the cornmeal. Stir and cook for 25 minutes or until thickened.

In a bowl, combine the molasses, beaten egg, butter, spices, salt, and 1/2 cup milk. Add the molasses mixture to the hot cornmeal. Cook for 30 minutes, stirring occasionally. Serve warm with whipped cream or vanilla ice cream.

MAKES 6 SERVINGS.

Panettone Bread Pudding

Panettone is a tall, cylinder-shaped, egg-rich cake from Milan, Italy, traditionally served at Christmas and Easter and often given as a gift when visiting family and friends. It's sold at Venda Ravioli and other Italian markets on Federal Hill in Providence. Chef Gianfranco Campanella from Mediterraneo Caffe created this recipe to make good use of panettone left over from the holidays. He says this bread pudding can also be made with *pandoro*, a tall Christmas cake like panettone, imported from Verona. If this looks like too much work, Chef Campanella's line of Italian desserts is available in Stop & Shop supermarkets in the Northeast or through Munroe Dairy, a home delivery service in Rhode Island.

Unsalted butter, at room temperature, as needed to coat baking pan

Sugar, as needed for sprinkling

1 large panettone, cubed or sliced

1/2 teaspoon cinnamon

1/4 teaspoon ground nutmeg

10 eggs

1 cup sugar

1/4 teaspoon salt

1 teaspoon vanilla extract

1/4 cup dried chopped fruit (optional)

1/2 cup chocolate pieces (optional)

1 quart milk

1 cup heavy cream

Butter the inside of a large (9x13-inch) glass baking dish. Lightly sprinkle the buttered area with sugar. Place the cubed or sliced panettone in the dish. Sprinkle the cinnamon and nutmeg over the panettone.

In a large bowl, whisk together the eggs, 1 cup sugar, salt, and vanilla extract. If desired, chopped fruit and/or chocolate pieces can be added to the egg mixture.

In a saucepan, scald the milk and heavy cream. Temper the egg mixture with the scalded milk and cream. That is, gradually add a little of the scalded milk-and-cream mixture to the egg mixture to prevent the eggs from cooking. When the two mixtures are combined, mix well and pour over the panettone.

Preheat oven to 350 degrees.

Cover the glass baking dish tightly with plastic wrap and then with aluminum foil. Create a water bath by placing the baking dish in a larger, deeper baking pan filled with about 1 inch of hot water. Place the water bath in the oven to bake for 1 hour, or until set.

Portuguese Rice Pudding

Roz doce, or rice pudding, is a part of every festival, wedding, and celebration in Portuguese families in Rhode Island, especially in the East Providence area. There are variations—some use port wine as a key ingredient, some are made with many egg yolks. Rice pudding can be made like a risotto on top of the stove or baked in the oven. Often the crowning touch is an ornate decoration achieved by sifting ground cinnamon through a paper doily onto the top of the pudding.

1 cup plus 2 tablespoons rice
   (not instant)

½ cup port wine

1 (14-ounce) can sweetened
   condensed milk

½ teaspoon cinnamon

2 tablespoons sugar

½ cup cream, whipped

Cook the rice according to package directions. Drain well. In a large bowl, combine the cooked rice with the port wine and condensed milk. Mix well.

Preheat oven to 350 degrees.

Pour the rice mixture into a buttered 1½-quart casserole. Cover and bake for 25 minutes.

In a small bowl, combine the cinnamon and sugar. Sprinkle over the top of the cooked pudding. Refrigerate. Serve cold with a dollop of whipped cream.

MAKES 6 SERVINGS.

Tiramisu

Just about every Italian restaurant in Rhode Island offers tiramisu, a rich dessert made of layers of ladyfingers, sweet mascarpone cheese, espresso, brandy, and wine. Tiramisu (pronounced "tee-RAH-mee-soo") is Italian for "pick-me-up" because this sweet dish along with a cup of coffee gives you quite the energy boost. The dish was created in Treviso, Italy, in the 1960s and is now considered a classic Italian dessert. This recipe is how Chef Gianfranco Campanella makes it at Mediterraneo Caffe on Federal Hill in Providence.

4 egg yolks

4 tablespoons sugar

1 pound mascarpone cheese

1 cup whipped cream

1 teaspoon vanilla extract

1 cup espresso coffee, cold

¼ cup brandy

⅓ cup Marsala wine

20 ladyfingers

Unsweetened cocoa powder, for dusting

Beat the egg yolks and sugar until fluffy. Fold in the mascarpone cheese, whipped cream, and vanilla extract.

Combine the cold espresso coffee, brandy, and Marsala wine. Dip 10 of the ladyfingers into the combined liquids. Line the bottom of a 6x9-inch baking dish with the ladyfingers. Cover the bottom layer of ladyfingers with about half of the filling mixture.

Dip the remaining ladyfingers and place them on top of the filling mixture in the baking dish. Cover with the remaining filling mixture.

Cover with plastic wrap and refrigerate for at least 5 hours or overnight. Just before serving, dust each slice with unsweetened cocoa powder.

MAKES 8 SERVINGS.

Chocolate Torte with Strawberry Balsamic and Red Wine Compote

Chocolate and wine are two of my favorite things on earth. Bernadette Ciccione, who owns Ocean State Chocolates in Providence, has come up with a fabulous yet easy-to-make chocolate dessert that's flavored with the Rhode Island Red wine made at Sakonnet Vineyards in Little Compton. The results? A totally Rhode Island dessert experience. Be sure to start a day ahead of time when you make this recipe.

CRUST

1$\frac{1}{2}$ cups finely crushed chocolate cookie crumbs

5 tablespoons butter, melted

FILLING

$\frac{1}{2}$ cup heavy cream

4 tablespoons butter, chopped

20 ounces semisweet chocolate, finely chopped

$\frac{1}{4}$ cup Sakonnet Vineyards Rhode Island Red wine

STRAWBERRY BALSAMIC AND RED WINE COMPOTE

$\frac{1}{4}$ cup balsamic vinegar

$\frac{1}{2}$ cup Sakonnet Vineyards Rhode Island Red wine

$\frac{1}{4}$ cup brown sugar

1 quart fresh strawberries, cleaned, hulled and quartered

First make the crust. Preheat oven to 350 degrees.

In a large bowl, combine the chocolate cookie crumbs and 5 tablespoons of melted butter, stirring to mix together well. Press the crust mixture into the bottom and up the sides of a 9-inch pie pan. Bake for 15 minutes. Remove from the oven and allow to cool completely.

Next make the torte filling. Pour the heavy cream into a large saucepan. Scald to 130 degrees over high heat. Remove the pan from the heat, and immediately add the chopped butter and chocolate. Whisk together until all the chocolate is melted. Add the $\frac{1}{4}$ cup red wine and whisk until the mixture is shiny and smooth. Pour it into the cooled crust. Refrigerate overnight.

To make the compote, combine the vinegar, wine, and brown sugar in a medium saucepan. Stir to mix well, and bring to a boil over medium heat. Boil 1 minute. Reduce heat to low and add the strawberries. Let the mixture steep for 5 minutes, then remove it from heat. Allow the mixture to cool to room temperature.

To slice the torte, dip a sharp knife into a glass of warm water, then cut the torte. Repeat for each slice. Place a slice of torte on a dessert plate and top with a large spoonful of the strawberry compote. Allow some of the juice to drizzle down the slice and pool onto the plate.

SERVES 12 TO 16.

Zeppoles

These baked St. Joseph's Day fritters—also known as St. Joseph's Cream Puffs—are an old tradition from Naples in southern Italy. The baked kind, which are filled with ricotta cream, custard cream or whipped cream, are more popular, hold up better, and are lower in fat. The same sweet is made by Sicilians, but they dip them in honey and call them *sfince*.

---

1 cup water

1 cup (2 sticks) butter

¼ teaspoon salt

1 cup all-purpose flour

4 eggs

1 tablespoon sugar

1 tablespoon grated lemon rind

1 teaspoon grated orange rind

Ricotta Cream Filling (recipe
    follows) or custard cream
    or whipped crea

18 maraschino cherries

½ cup glazed orange peel slices

In a large saucepan, combine the water and butter, and bring to a boil. Add the salt and flour, stirring constantly until the mixture leaves the sides of the pan to form a ball in the center. Remove from heat and allow to cool.

Add the eggs, one at a time, beating them in completely. Add the sugar, lemon rind, and orange rind. Mix well.

Preheat oven to 400 degrees.

Drop by the tablespoon onto a baking sheet, placing the puffs 3 inches apart, or use muffin cups. Bake for 10 minutes, then reduce heat to 350 degrees and bake for 30 minutes or until light brown. Remove the puffs from the oven. Open the puffs immediately to allow steam to escape. Cool.

Fill the puffs with Ricotta Cream Filling, custard cream, or whipped cream. Top with a cherry and 2 thin slices of glazed orange peel.

RICOTTA CREAM FILLING

1 pound ricotta cheese

2 tablespoons grated chocolate

1 tablespoon grated orange rind

Sugar, to taste

2 teaspoons almond extract

3 tablespoons milk

In a bowl combine all ingredients, adding only enough of the milk to make a smooth custardlike mixture. Refrigerate until needed. Any leftover filling will keep in the refrigerator for 2 or 3 days, or it can be used as a filling when making crepes, pancakes, or French toast.

MAKES 18 CREAM PUFFS.

Wandi

Rhode Island seems to be the only place where these deep-fried delicacies are called *wandi*. According to Nancy Verde Barr, a native Rhode Islander who is an expert on Italian food, these delicious pastries—sold from stands at carnivals in Italy—were called *wandi* because, as they wiggled in the hot oil, they looked like the empty fingers of a glove, or *guanti,* which in a Neapolitan accent sounds like *wandi*. Nancy learned how to make *wandi* from her aunt Irma who lived in Warwick. They are available in many Italian bakeries.

3 cups all-purpose flour

1 tablespoon sugar

Pinch of salt

4 large eggs, beaten

Vegetable oil, as needed for
   deep-frying

Confectioners' sugar, as needed

In the bowl of an electric mixer, sift together the flour, sugar, and salt. Make a well in the center of the sifted mixture and add the beaten eggs. Mix together until a dough forms. Knead in the mixer or by hand on the counter, adding more flour if necessary, until a soft dough that does not stick is formed. Divide into 3 balls and set aside under an overturned bowl to rest 30 minutes.

Working with 1 ball at a time, roll the dough into a very thin sheet, no more than 1/16-inch thick. The dough also may be rolled in a pasta machine. Using a fluted ravioli wheel, cut the dough at an angle into strips 1 inch wide by 8 inches long. Gently pull and stretch the strips as you tie each one into a loose knot.

Heat 2 inches of vegetable oil to 370 degrees in a deep saucepan. Drop 2 to 3 strips of dough at a time into the hot oil. Turn immediately and remove with a slotted spoon onto paper towels to drain as soon as they are lightly golden. The *wandi* cook very quickly and should go in and out of the oil rapidly.

Layer the *wandi* with paper towels until all are cooked. After they have cooled, sprinkle both sides of the *wandi* generously with confectioners' sugar. Serve piled high on a platter. They will keep, loosely covered, for many days.

MAKES ABOUT 54 PIECES.

Fried Doughboys with Honey Butter

These doughboys are pan fried rather than deep-fried and are much like pancakes. In many Rhode Island homes of Italian heritage, they are served for holiday breakfasts.

HONEY BUTTER

$1/2$ cup (1 stick) butter, at room temperature

$1/2$ cup honey

$1/2$ teaspoon cinnamon, optional

DOUGHBOYS

1 teaspoon dry yeast

1 cup warm water

1 teaspoon honey

$1^3/4$ cups whole-wheat flour

$1^1/2$ cups white flour

$1/4$ teaspoon white pepper

2 teaspoons butter, melted and cooled slightly

Vegetable oil, as needed

Make the honey butter. In a bowl, blend the $1/2$ cup butter and $1/2$ cup honey (and cinnamon, if desired) together until fluffy. Set aside.

Next make the doughboys. In a small bowl, sprinkle the yeast over the warm water. Stir in 1 teaspoon of honey and let the mixture stand 5 to 10 minutes until it bubbles up.

In a large bowl, combine the whole-wheat flour, white flour, and white pepper, stirring to blend together. Pour in the yeast mixture and the 2 teaspoons melted butter. Mix until a dough forms.

Turn the dough out onto a floured surface. Knead for 10 minutes, until the dough is firm, elastic, and no longer sticky. Add 2 or 3 more tablespoons of flour, if needed.

Place 1 tablespoon of vegetable oil in a large bowl, coating it well. Add the dough, turning to coat the dough and bowl with the oil. Cover with plastic wrap and let rise in a warm area until doubled in bulk, approximately $1^1/2$ to 2 hours. Turn the dough out onto a lightly floured surface. Form it into a log 2 inches in diameter. Cut off pieces 1 inch thick. Press each slice with your palm to flatten. Let the slices rest 10 minutes.

Roll the slices out with a rolling pin until they are ovals about 6x3 inches in size. Lay the ovals on waxed paper and let them rise about 30 minutes until doubled in size.

Cover the bottom of a frying pan with a thin coat of vegetable oil. Heat the oil over medium heat. Fry the doughboys gently until golden brown on both sides. Add more oil to the pan as needed. Serve the doughboys warm with the honey butter.

MAKES 18 DOUGHBOYS.

Doughboys: The Ultimate Rhode Island Dessert

If you are eating a doughboy, more than likely you are down by the shore or on the grounds of a carnival. Also known as fried dough, it is simply a square hunk of pizza dough, about the size of your hand, deep-fried until it is golden brown on all sides, and then sprinkled with granulated sugar and eaten while still warm. The first bite always makes me think I am biting into a cloud with just a hint of a crunch, and then I just can't help but smile as I taste the sweet, chewy dough. It is the ultimate Rhode Island dessert.

Doughboys are forever linked to Oakland Beach in Warwick, where Iggy's has been serving summer food to sunburned families since 1924, making it the oldest beach stand in the state. For years it was known as Gus's, but it's been Iggy's ever since the Gravino family took over in 1989. Nowadays, with a spectacular view of Narragansett Bay and its bridges, the newly expanded Iggy's is open year-round.

Fans claim it's almost impossible to eat just one doughboy. Most people buy them by the dozen. At Iggy's,

IGGY'S, WARWICK

doughboys come in a paper bag, with six as the minimum order. Fried dough can be found in other parts of the country, but Rhode Islanders tend to think of doughboys as a local delicacy.

Orange Walnut Biscotti with Black Pepper

Cindy Salvato is well-known in Rhode Island as a baking and pastry chef extraordinaire, and as an expert on Federal Hill in Providence. She frequently gives walking tours of the old Italian neighborhood with stops in all the best shops for tastings. This is one of her many original recipes. Biscotti are great for dipping into a hot cup of coffee or a glass of *vin santo*, the sweet Italian dessert wine.

---

1 cup granulated sugar

1/2 cup (1 stick) unsalted butter

1 large egg, slightly beaten

1 tablespoon grated orange peel

1/2 teaspoon vanilla extract

1/2 teaspoon almond extract

1 3/4 cups all-purpose flour

1 teaspoon baking powder

1 teaspoon black pepper

1/8 teaspoon salt

1 1/2 cups roughly chopped walnuts

In a large bowl, cream together the sugar and butter until there are no lumps. Add the egg, orange peel, and vanilla and almond extracts. Blend well. Scrape down the sides and bottom of the bowl and then blend again to incorporate the ingredients.

In another bowl, blend together the flour, baking powder, pepper and salt. Add the flour mixture to the butter mixture and mix on low speed, using an electric mixer. Scrape down the sides and bottom of the bowl and then blend again to incorporate the ingredients. Stir in the walnuts with a rubber spatula.

Divide the dough in half. Wrap each half in plastic and chill for at least 2 hours. The dough should be firm enough to roll.

Preheat oven to 350 degrees.

On a lightly floured surface, roll the dough into 2 logs, each approximately 12 inches long. Place the logs on a prepared cookie sheet and bake for 35 to 40 minutes. When the logs are ready, they will be firm to the touch and a rich golden brown.

Remove the logs from the oven and cool for 3 minutes. Carefully transfer the logs onto a clean cutting board and cut the logs into 1-inch slices with a serrated knife. Lay the biscotti on their sides and return the pan to the oven. Bake for 10 minutes. Cool completely before storing in an airtight container.

MAKES 24 BISCOTTI.

Wright's Farm Hermits

Wright's Dairy Farm and Bakery in North Smithfield in the northern part of the state is a working dairy farm where visitors can see 120 Holsteins milked daily between 3:00 and 5:00 P.M. The bakery is famous for its "hermits," made fresh every Tuesday. These old-fashioned molasses-spiced cookies, along with freshly made ice cream and whipped cream desserts, can be purchased at the retail store. The recipe is a family secret, but this old-time recipe comes pretty close to the real thing. Hermits have good shelf life and freeze very well.

1 cup sugar

$\frac{1}{2}$ cup butter and lard, combined

3 cups sifted flour

1 teaspoon ground cloves

1 teaspoon cinnamon

$\frac{1}{2}$ teaspoon nutmeg

$\frac{1}{2}$ teaspoon salt

1 teaspoon baking soda

$\frac{1}{2}$ cup molasses

$\frac{1}{2}$ cup buttermilk or sour milk

1 egg, beaten

1 cup chopped raisins

In a large bowl, cream together the sugar and butter-lard combination. In another large bowl, sift together the flour, cloves, cinnamon, nutmeg, salt, and baking soda.

Combine the wet and dry ingredients alternately with the molasses and sour milk. Add the beaten egg and raisins. Mix well.

Preheat oven to 350 degrees.

Spread the mixture on a greased baking sheet so that it is about $\frac{1}{2}$ inch thick. Bake for 10 to 12 minutes. Be careful not to overbake the cookies. When they are firm to the touch, they are done. Cut into oblong cookie shapes. If desired, you can sprinkle confectioners' sugar over the tops of the cookies while they are still warm.

Note: You can substitute Crisco or another vegetable shortening for the lard. Also, you can use $\frac{1}{2}$ cup brown sugar and $\frac{1}{2}$ cup granulated sugar in place of the 1 cup granulated sugar, and you can add 1 teaspoon ginger and 1 cup chopped walnuts, if desired.

MAKES 24 HERMITS.

Nana's Moon Cookies

This particular Nana is Ruth Peskin, grandmother of David Cicilline, mayor of Providence. One of the mayor's fondest childhood memories involves these cookies flavored with poppy seeds.

4 cups flour

1 cup sugar

4 eggs

4 teaspoons baking powder

1 cup vegetable oil

¼ cup poppy seeds

In a large bowl, combine all the ingredients except for the poppy seeds. Wash the poppy seeds in hot water and strain through a very fine sieve. Then stir the poppy seeds into the cookie dough.

Chill the dough in the refrigerator for 2 hours or overnight. The dough can be kept refrigerated for up to 2 months.

Preheat oven to 350 degrees.

Using a tablespoon, place the dough onto a greased baking sheet. Bake for 15 to 20 minutes, or until golden brown.

MAKES 50 TO 60 COOKIES.

Sweenor's Chocolates

Stopping in at Sweenor's Chocolates is a family tradition for many Rhode Islanders. Since 1946 four generations of the Sweenor family have been making hard candy in twenty-five flavors, along with creamy fudge, almond brittle, hand-dipped chocolates, and confections. Especially popular are the chocolates that look like clams and sea shells. The original Sweenor's is located in Cranston. Other outlets are in Charlestown and Wakefield.

Memere's Lemon Squares

French-Canadian heritage festivals are celebrated regularly in the cities of Woonsocket and West Warwick. Many a French-Canadian grandmother (affectionately known as *memere*) spoiled young and old alike in the family with flaky lemon squares like these.

CRUST

2 cups all-purpose flour

1 cup (2 sticks) butter, at room temperature

1/2 cup confectioners' sugar, plus more for sprinkling

FILLING

4 eggs, beaten

2 cups sugar

1/3 cup lemon juice

1/4 cup flour

1/2 teaspoon baking powder

Preheat oven to 350 degrees.

In a large bowl, combine the crust ingredients. Mix well. Press the mixture into a 9x11-inch baking pan. Bake for 10 minutes. Remove from the oven Set aside to cool.

In another large bowl, combine the filling ingredients. Mix well. Pour the mixture on top of the baked crust. Return the pan to the 350-degree oven and bake for 25 minutes.

Before serving, allow to cool. Dust with additional confectioners' sugar, if desired.

MAKES 12 SERVINGS.

Grandpères

French-Canadian families in Rhode Island say this much-loved recipe has been handed down for generations. (*Grandpère* is French for "grandfather.") It's hard to categorize—is it a dumpling? Pure maple syrup is the key flavor ingredient.

2 cups cake flour

1 tablespoon baking powder

1/2 teaspoon salt

3 tablespoons butter

3/4 cup milk

2 cups maple syrup

2 cups water

In a large bowl, sift together the flour, baking powder, and salt. With a pastry blender, cut in the butter. Add the milk and mix well.

In a saucepan, combine the maple syrup and water. Bring to a boil. Drop the dough by the tablespoon into the hot maple syrup–water mixture. Cover the pan and cook over medium heat for 25 minutes.

Serve very hot and topped with the syrup in which it was cooked.

MAKES 6 SERVINGS.

Pizzelles

Christmas would not be complete without the aroma of pizzelles baking in our kitchen. A pizzelle maker—sort of an Italian cookie press—is needed to make these thin, crisp cookies that are about 4 inches wide. The pizzelle maker leaves an ornate design on each perfectly round cookie. If you like the licorice-flavored liqueur called anisette, you will love pizzelles. They are also available in Italian gourmet shops on Federal Hill in Providence.

1 cup (2 sticks) butter

1$\frac{1}{2}$ cups sugar

6 large eggs

1 tablespoon anise extract

3$\frac{1}{2}$ cups flour, unsifted

$\frac{1}{2}$ teaspoon cinnamon

Pinch of salt

Confectioners' sugar (optional)

In a large bowl, combine the butter, sugar, eggs, and anise extract until light and creamy. Slowly add the flour, cinnamon, and salt. Mix well.

Drop by the heaping tablespoon onto a hot pizzelle iron. Close the cover, and press the handles together tightly for 15 to 20 seconds, or according to the directions that came with your particular machine. Remove the pizzelle from the hot iron. Allow them to cool on a wire rack.

Store the cooled pizzelles in a container with a tight-fitting lid. If desired, sprinkle with powdered confectioners' sugar through a fine strainer.

Note: If you make them just a bit thicker than normal by using extra batter on the iron, they can be used to make excellent ice cream sandwiches.

MAKES 24 PIZZELLE.

Drinks

Coffee Milk

Stirring a tablespoon or two of coffee syrup into a tall glass of ice-cold milk turns a boring drink into something more grown-up, almost exotic. The milk turns from white to brown, and the coffee taste can be intense, depending on how much syrup is added to the glass. In 1993, after much lively discussion, legislators voted to make coffee milk the state's official beverage, beating out the also much-loved Del's frozen lemonade.

---

2 tablespoons coffee syrup

1 (6-ounce) glass of cold milk

Add the coffee syrup to the glass of cold milk. Stir well with a spoon, and serve immediately.

MAKES 1 SERVING.

Coffee Cabinet

The coffee cabinet, called a frappe or a milk shake in other parts of the country, is made by beating together coffee syrup, ice cream, and ice-cold milk until the ice cream dissolves. Most people believe the name *cabinet* comes from the wooden cabinets behind the counter that held the old-time mixers.

---

2 tablespoons coffee syrup

1 scoop coffee ice cream

6 ounces milk

In an electric blender, beat the coffee syrup, scoop of ice cream, and milk for 1 minute, or until ice cream is dissolved. Pour and serve immediately.

MAKES 1 SERVING.

Coffee Ice Cream Soda

There was a time when Rhode Island was the only place you could buy coffee ice cream. Even Howard Johnson's with its twenty-eight flavors didn't always carry it. These days it's a whole diffcrent story. In Rhode Island three of the best places to purchase coffee ice cream are the Ice Cream Machine up north in Cumberland, Gray's Ice Cream in Tiverton over in the East Bay section of the state, and down South County way at Brickley's in the seaside town of Narragansett. In each location the ice cream is made on the premises, so the lines can be long, especially on warm summer nights. Gray's is the oldest of the bunch, dishing up ice cream since 1923. Gray's robust coffee ice cream is very creamy and not overly sweet, exactly how this coffee lover likes it.

2 tablespoons coffee syrup

3 ounces cold milk

A spritz of seltzer

1 scoop coffee ice cream

Add the coffee syrup to the cold milk. Add the seltzer and ice cream. Stir and serve immediately.

MAKES 1 SERVING.

Rhode Island–Style Iced Coffee

Usually iced coffee is made with real, leftover coffee that's been chilled in the refrigerator. This recipe simply combines ice-cold water and coffee syrup.

2 tablespoons coffee syrup

2 ice cubes

8 ounces cold water

Cream and sugar, to taste

In a 10-ounce glass, combine the coffee syrup and ice cubes with the cold water. Add cream and sugar to taste. Stir and serve immediately.

MAKES 1 SERVING.

Rhode Island's Love Affair with All Things Coffee

Rhode Islanders love anything with the flavor of coffee. There's a coffee shop on almost every street corner. We eat more coffee ice cream than any other state in the Union—even in the dead of winter. Rhode Island children drink coffee milk and grow up to be adults who still like an occasional glass of coffee milk, especially when having lunch at a diner.

The official state drink, coffee milk is simply a glass of milk to which sweetened coffee syrup has been added. It dates back to the 1930s, when drugstores with soda fountains used leftover coffee grounds to make an extract that became popular with children. While the rest of America was sipping on chocolate milk, Rhode Island tots were getting a caffeine buzz.

When it comes to coffee syrup, this is perhaps the only coffee-flavored item that has Rhode Islanders divided. You see, some of us were brought up on the darker, thicker, more coffee taste of Eclipse coffee syrup, while others grew up sipping on Autocrat, often described as thin and sweet. Eclipse—the first coffee syrup available for retail sale—was made by a company famous for its marshmallows back in 1914. The Autocrat Coffee Company, a fourth-generation family business now based in Lincoln, acquired the Eclipse label in 1991 and continues to produce both kinds of syrup, which are sold in all Rhode Island supermarkets. Autocrat sells enough coffee syrup in Rhode Island, with a population of about 1 million, to make 20 million servings of coffee milk each year.

Iced Cappuccino

This sweet and frosty drink is a bit expensive at the local coffee shop. Here's how you can make it at home for a fraction of the cost.

2 cups cold coffee

6 teaspoons sugar

1/2 cup milk or half-and-half

6 ice cubes

1/4 cup coffee syrup

In a blender, combine the coffee, sugar, and milk, adding more or less to taste. Blend. Then add the ice and crush it until no large chunks are present. Add the coffee syrup. Mix well. Pour into glasses. Serve immediately.

MAKES 2 SERVINGS.

The Awful Awful

One of Rhode Island's most famous beverages is the Awful Awful, an enormous 32-ounce, rich, creamy milkshake sold at the Newport Creamery stores, a soda fountain and casual restaurant chain. This ultrathick cabinet is awful big and awful good, thus the name. If you can drink three, you get one free—a shrewd offer considering the fact that downing just one of these mammoth beverages is something to brag about. The basic Awful Awful comes in strawberry, vanilla, chocolate, mocha, chocolate mint, and coffee flavors, plus trendy new flavors. No matter which one you choose, you will need a very big straw.

The story of the Newport Creamery begins in 1928. The Newport-based company survived the Great Depression and emerged as a retail operation owned by Samuel Rector. The legend of the Awful Awful started with Bond's Ice Cream in New Jersey in 1948. Rector worked out an agreement with Bond's, so Newport Creamery could use the Awful Awful name. When Bond's went bankrupt in the early 1970s, Newport Creamery officially bought the name for only $1,000.

Del's Frozen Lemonade

Rhode Island's love affair with coffee was contested in 1993 when the state legislature debated what should be the official state drink. Del's Frozen Lemonade, another Rhode Island tradition, nearly won the title, and fans of this slushy drink still argue the case on its behalf.

Rhode Islanders are positively giddy about that first day in spring when Del's opens up for business—a sign that summer is on its way. Del's is a Cranston-based chain of colorful roadside stands and trucks (much like quaint ice cream trucks that roam suburban neighborhoods) hawking paper cups filled to the brim with a refreshingly tart frozen lemonade.

Frozen Lemonade

To approach the nirvana of a Del's Frozen Lemonade, try this similar recipe at home.

1½ cups sugar

1 cup water

1 envelope plain gelatin

2 tablespoons cold water

2 egg whites

2 tablespoons sugar

1½ cups fresh lemon juice

1 tablespoon finely chopped lemon
    rind

In a saucepan, boil the 1½ cups sugar and 1 cup water together for 5 minutes to make a simple syrup. Turn off the heat.

Soften the gelatin in the 2 tablespoons of cold water. Add the softened gelatin to the saucepan. Stir until dissolved. Set aside to cool.

Beat the egg whites until light, adding the 2 tablespoons of sugar. Continue beating until stiff peaks form. Combine the beaten egg whites with the simple syrup mixture. Add the lemon juice and rind. Pour into an ice cube tray and freeze until set.

Turn the frozen lemonade cubes into a blender or ice crusher. Process the cubes until they turn to slush. Pour the slushy mixture into a container with a tight-fitting lid. Store the container in the freezer.

About 10 minutes before serving, remove the container from the freezer and allow the slush to soften. Then pour the lemonade into serving glasses.

MAKES 6 SERVINGS.

Limoncello

Long before it became fashionable nationally, the people of Rhode Island were sipping on small glasses of frosty limoncello after dinner; Mediterraneo on Federal Hill in Providence was the first restaurant in the state to offer this zesty liqueur to its guests as a complimentary after-dinner drink. Nowadays you can buy limoncello in almost any liquor store, or you can make your own as long as you plan ahead. It's an absolute must that you store limoncello in the freezer.

6 lemons

1 (750-ml) bottle 100-proof vodka or pure grain alcohol

3 cups water

1½ cups sugar

Remove the zest from the lemons, avoiding any of the white pith. Place the zest in a half-gallon glass jar. Add the vodka. Cover tightly. Allow the jar to stand at room temperature for at least 10 days, or until the vodka has a deep yellow color.

Strain the liquid into a large, glass heatproof bowl. Set aside the zest in the strainer.

In a saucepan, bring the water and the sugar to a boil. Stir until the sugar is dissolved. Boil for 3 minutes. Pour this hot sugar syrup over the zest in the strainer into the liquid in the glass bowl. Allow the mixture to cool. Discard the zest.

Using a ladle and funnel, pour the mixture, now a liqueur, into bottles. Cover tightly. Allow to stand at room temperature for 5 days. Then store in freezer before serving.

MAKES 2 QUARTS.

Tavern Punch

The Stagecoach Tavern in Chepachet Village in the northwestern corner of Rhode Island has a colorful history that dates back to the famous Dorr Rebellion in 1842. The tavern is known for this punch that's always served at its Heritage Christmas banquets. It packs a serious punch and is sure to keep you warm during the holidays.

2 gallons unprocessed cider
(available at local farm stands)

1 quart vodka

1 quart rum

1 cup peach brandy

1 cup cherry brandy

2 cups fresh beer

1/4 cup fresh lemon juice

1 quart club soda, chilled

In a large container with a tight-fitting lid, combine all the ingredients except the club soda. Refrigerate the mixture for at least 8 hours, preferably overnight.

Just before serving, add the club soda and mix well. Pour the mixture into a large punch bowl.

Note: If hard cider is used, decrease the amount of vodka by 2 cups and increase the brandy by 1 cup.

MAKES 3 GALLONS.

A Sip of Nostalgia

They say a bottle of Yacht Club soda holds decades of memories, dating back to 1915 when Harry Sharp began selling fizzy soda and seltzer out of a barn. Sharp got the idea from a similar operation in England. In 1923 the Yacht Club Bottling Works factory was built in North Providence around a 170-foot artesian well that to this day produces the state's best drinking water.

Today it's a mom-and-pop operation, run by the Sgambato family. With machinery that was last updated in 1948, Yacht Club still makes thirty-two flavors of soda the old-fashioned way—with a secret family recipe, hand-mixed flavored syrups, pure cane sugar, and that special water, poured into glass bottles. You can find Yacht Club soda at a number of markets and restaurants throughout the state.

Dark and Stormy

This cocktail may have been created in Bermuda, but it navigated its way up to Rhode Island where it's quite popular with the yachting crowd. It's usually made with Gosling's dark rum, but any dark or spiced rum can be used. The ginger beer is essential.

2 ounces Gosling's dark rum

1 (12-ounce) bottle ginger beer

1 slice lime

Pour the rum into a glass filled with ice, then pour the ginger beer over the rum. Squeeze the slice of lime into the glass, and then drop the slice into the mixture. Stir and serve.

MAKES 1 SERVING.

Rooting for Old-Fashioned Flavors

Bristol is the home of the Empire Bottling Works, where AJ Stephans Company produces sodas in nostalgic glass bottles filled with the old-fashioned flavors of ginger beer, root beer, birch beer, cream soda, black cherry, and grape. They sweeten their sodas with cane sugar only.

Owner Jeff Rose says the old-time sodas such as ginger beer are especially popular with New Englanders who remember drinking it as kids, and with the local sailing community. Rose suggests that the spiciness of the ginger can soothe a queasy stomach on the high seas. The creamy root beer has a licorice flavor and always has a good head of foam, a lot like real beer.

Nathaniel Porter Inn Wassail

The Nathaniel Porter Inn in Warren is more than 250 years old. It is famous for its Yule Log Celebration held every December. An authentic yule log ablaze in the inn's fireplace re-creates the tradition of burning off your troubles of the past year. Yule log dinners include beef Wellington, beef barley soup, chocolate bread pudding, and the traditional wassail, a holiday punch. So turn your troubles into ashes with a sip of this wassail.

---

1 gallon fresh apple cider

2 teaspoons whole allspice

⅔ cup sugar

⅓ cup fine brown sugar

2 or 3 cinnamon sticks

2 teaspoons whole cloves

2 oranges, studded with cloves

In a Dutch oven or large saucepan, combine all the ingredients except the oranges. Heat to the boiling point, then reduce heat. Cover and simmer for 20 minutes. Strain. Pour into a punch bowl or Crock-Pot. Add the oranges. Serve hot.

MAKES 16 SERVINGS.

Dandelion Wine

To this day, my Italian relatives still make this wine on occasion. My cousin Anne Pasquino says the recipe dates back to the 1950s. She remembers going into pastures in the early spring to pick dandelions by the bagful. Today the recipe makes us feel a bit nostalgic as we look back on a time when people had the time to pick all those dandelion blossoms.

---

4 quarts (16 cups) dandelion blossoms

8 quarts (32 cups) boiling water

6 pounds granulated sugar

2 pounds raisins

4 oranges, sliced

4 lemons, sliced

1 package yeast

In a very large stockpot, combine the dandelion blossoms and boiling water. Cover and let stand overnight.

In the morning strain the liquid from the stockpot into another large stockpot. Discard the dandelion blossoms. Add the sugar, raisins, orange slices, lemon slices, and yeast. Cover and set aside for 2 weeks to begin the fermentation process. Make sure to stir the mixture every morning during those 2 weeks.

Transfer the liquid into clean, glass quart-size jars. Cover and set aside for 4 weeks.

Strain the liquid into clean glass beer bottles. Seal the bottles tightly and set aside for 3 weeks.

After this final period of fermentation, the wine is ready for drinking.

MAKES 8 QUARTS.

Rhode Island Wineries

The small state of Rhode Island is blessed with four successful wineries, each with a unique story. Three are connected to the state's beautiful coastline with the vast Rhode Island Sound to the south. Newport, Middletown, and Portsmouth are the towns that make up Aquidneck Island. To the east are the broad Sakonnet River and the coastal towns of Tiverton and Little Compton. This area is one of the most desirable farming areas in the country. An extraordinary microclimate here results from a combination of the warm waters of the Gulf Stream to the south and the moderating effects of Narragansett Bay. These conditions provide a long, cool growing season ideal for developing the complex flavors in wine.

The oldest and largest winery in the state, **Sakonnet Vineyards,** established in 1975, produces a variety of award-winning wines, from estate-grown to distinctive regional offerings. The 2002 Gewürztraminer won Best of Show at the Monterey International Wine Festival in California. The Vidal Blanc, Chardonnay, Cabernet Franc, and port have also won gold medals in national events. The winery is open daily year-round for tours and tastings.

Located along the Sakonnet River in Portsmouth, **Greenvale Vineyards** is a family-run winery that produces small quantities of estate-bottled wines. The nineteenth-century Victorian farm became a vineyard in 1982 and released its first wine in 1993. The fourth generation of the Parker family continues to oversee the small but beautiful Greenvale Vineyards, dedicated to fine wines, historic preservation, and open space.

The family-run **Newport Vineyards,** one of the most modern in the East, is located just 10 minutes from downtown Newport. The vineyards were originally planted in 1977 on a hill overlooking Rhode Island Sound as a way of preserving agricultural land from rapid development. Open year-round for tours and tastings, Newport Vineyards features a restaurant, gift shop, and exhibitions by local artists.

Since 1976 Claire and Peter Berntson have been making wine at **Diamond Hill Vineyards** in Cumberland in the northern part of Rhode Island. Their 200-year-old home is located in the heart of 33 acres of vineyards and orchards. The couple specializes in producing native fruit wines and an estate-bottled Pinot Noir. The winery is open for group tours, and wine and cheese tastings take place in the gift shop.

Metric Conversion Tables

APPROXIMATE U.S. – METRIC EQUIVALENTS

LIQUID INGREDIENTS

U.S. MEASURES	METRIC	U.S. MEASURES	METRIC
¼ TSP.	1.23 ML	2 TBSP.	29.57 ML
½ TSP.	2.36 ML	3 TBSP.	44.36 ML
¾ TSP.	3.70 ML	¼ CUP	59.15 ML
1 TSP.	4.93 ML	½ CUP	118.30 ML
1¼ TSP.	6.16 ML	1 CUP	236.59 ML
1½ TSP.	7.39 ML	2 CUPS OR 1 PT.	473.18 ML
1¾ TSP.	8.63 ML	3 CUPS	709.77 ML
2 TSP.	9.86 ML	4 CUPS OR 1 QT.	946.36 ML
1 TBSP.	14.79 ML	4 QTS. OR 1 GAL.	3.79 LT

DRY INGREDIENTS

U.S. MEASURES		METRIC	U.S. MEASURES	METRIC
17⅗ OZ.	1 LIVRE	500 G	2 OZ.	60 (56.6) G
16 OZ.	1 LB.	454 G	1¾ OZ.	50 G
8⅞ OZ.		250 G	1 OZ.	30 (28.3) G
5¼ OZ.		150 G	⅞ OZ.	25 G
4½ OZ.		125 G	¾ OZ.	21 (21.3) G
4 OZ.		115 (113.2) G	½ OZ.	15 (14.2) G
3½ OZ.		100 G	¼ OZ.	7 (7.1) G
3 OZ.		85 (84.9) G	⅛ OZ.	3½ (3.5) G
2⅘ OZ.		80 G	1⁄16 OZ.	2 (1.8) G

Index

About the Author

Linda Beaulieu is the author of two best-selling books, *Divine Providence: An Insider's Guide to the City's Best Restaurants* and *The Grapevine Guide to Rhode Island's Best Restaurants*. An award-winning writer for numerous publications, Linda received the prestigious James Beard Award for her magazine article on Native American food.

Linda worked for ten years as a publicist at Johnson & Wales University, where she also taught a course on food writing. She produced the popular *Cooking with Class* TV show, and she was the editor of the PBS companion cookbook, *Master Class at Johnson & Wales*. She now owns and operates Beyond Words, a small public relations firm that specializes in restaurants and chefs. She is a graduate of Northeastern University, Boston, where she majored in journalism.

A native Rhode Islander, Linda lives in Lincoln and has a summer home in Narragansett. Her husband, Brian, is a copy editor at the *Providence Journal*.

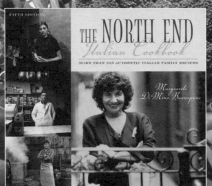

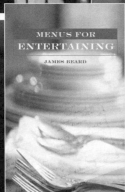